CW00376358

Hello iPhone

The iPhone is the most remarkable mobile on sale today. It's more a portable computer than a cellphone, with its own operating system, built-in applications and a whole world of developers writing exciting, useful, fun and innovative tools for you to install.

It also looks great. Its sleek lines have been refined over three revisions to the point where now we find ourselves with a sleek, dark slab of metal and glass that looks great and feels fantastic in your hand.

The only thing that's missing is a comprehensive instruction manual, and that's where *The Independent Guide to the iPhone 4* comes in. Split into two sections, we cover both the iPhone itself (and its operating system and built-in applications) and the third-party apps you can download from the iTunes App Store. This half of the book deals with the iPhone. Turn over and open from the other end for 200 exclusive application reviews.

As the iPhone has developed, it has learnt new tricks and incorporated new hardware. The latest edition can send multimedia picture messages and shoot high definition video. It has built-in satellite navigation, a compass and, in the iPhone 4, a gyroscope.

There are now four models of iPhone in circulation but in this book we'll concentrate on the two most recent editions, which remain on sale: iPhone 3GS and iPhone 4. Where anything works on only the very latest model, we have made this clear by talking specifically about the iPhone 4.

If you have just bought your first iPhone, then *The Independent Guide to the iPhone 4* is your introduction to a wonderful world of handheld computing. If you're still considering taking the plunge, read on and see what you're missing.

Nik Rawlinson

SQUARE

Fallen for your iPhone 4?
Meet the Mac.
The ultimate PC upgrade.

If you're thinking about getting a new PC, now is the time to take a look at a Mac.
Our Apple experts can show you all the reasons a Mac is great at the things you
do every day. They can also help transfer all your PC files to a new Mac.
Come into Square and see why a Mac is the ultimate PC upgrade.

THE INDEPENDENT GUIDE TO THE

iPhone 4

Words
Author/Editor Nik Rawlinson
Deputy Editor Kenny Hemphill
iPhone App Reviewers Maggie Holland, Claire Hopping,
Jon Lysons, Alan Stonebridge

Art
Art Editor Camille Neilson
Cover Photography Danny Bird
Cover Retouching Jan Cihak
iPhone stock photos courtesy of Apple

Production
Production Editor Jon Lysons
Sub-editor Kirsty Fortune

Advertising
Account Manager Alexandra Skinner +44 (0)20 7907 6623
Account Director Nicky Crawford +44 (0)20 7907 6624
MagBooks Account Manager Katie Wood +44 (0)20 7907 6689
Senior Production Executive Michael Hills +44 (0)20 7907 6129
Digital Production Manager Nicky Baker
US Advertising Manager Matthew Sullivan-Pond +1 646 717 9555 matthew_sullivan@dennis.co.uk

Publishing & Marketing
+44 (0)20 7907 6000, fax +44 (0)20 7636 6122
Managing Director Ian Westwood +44 (0)20 7907 6355
Publisher Paul Rayner +44 (0)20 7907 6663
Bookazine Manager Dharmesh Mistry +44 (0)20 7907 6100
List Rental Inserts Executive John Perry +44 (0)20 7907 6151 john_perry@dennis.co.uk
Marketing Manager Claire Scrase +44 (0)20 7907 6113

MAGBOOK

DENNIS PUBLISHING LTD
PRODUCTION DIRECTOR Robin Ryan
DIRECTOR OF ADVERTISING Julian Lloyd-Evans
NEWSTRADE DIRECTOR Martin Belson
CHIEF OPERATING OFFICER Brett Reynolds
GROUP FINANCE DIRECTOR Ian Leggett
CHIEF EXECUTIVE James Tye
CHAIRMAN Felix Dennis

HOW TO CONTACT US
MAIL 30 Cleveland Street, London, W1T 4JD
EMAIL mailbox@macuser.co.uk WEB www.macuser.co.uk
PHONE +44 (0)20 7907 6000

LICENSING AND REPRINTS
Material in The Independent Guide To The iPhone may not
be reproduced in any form without the publisher's written
permission. It is available for licensing overseas.
For details about international licensing
contact Winnie Liesenfeld, +44 (0)20 7907 6134,
winnie_liesenfeld@dennis.co.uk.

LIABILITY
While every care was taken during the production of this
MagBook, the publishers cannot be held responsible for the
accuracy of the information or any consequences arising
from it. Dennis Publishing takes no responsibility for the
companies advertising in this MagBook.

THE INDEPENDENT GUIDE TO THE
iPhone 4

Chapter 1 009

Chapter 3 103

Chapter 2 031

Chapter 4 125

+200 APPS REVIEWED

FLIP-SIDE COVER

Chapter 1
Welcome to the iPhone

Welcome to the iPhone

It is time to say hello to the iPhone, the most remarkable communications device ever produced. This sleek metal-and-glass creation is a landmark event in a journey that began with Alexander Graham Bell's invention of the telephone in 1876. Who could ever have believed back then, when there were only two heavy handsets in existence, that one day we would be walking around with so much power in our pockets?

For the iPhone is not simply a telephone. It is the best of everything rolled up in one tiny shell: the perfect portable address book, a peerless hand-held browser, and the handiest mobile music player all rolled into one. In fact, despite the various attempts of Nokia, Sony, Creative and Samsung, it seems to be the only gadget produced so far that has any chance of knocking the iPod off the music-playing top spot. Now that is irony.

It is no wonder, then, that Apple kept it under such tight wraps in the years it took to develop.

In this chapter, we will look at the key features of the iPhone and what makes them so great, before walking you through the activation process necessary to get an iPhone working. So come with us as we explore a phone from the future that leaves all others in its wake.

Web browser

The iPhone's web browser (*right*) is a true 'oh wow' application. If you have ever used the Internet on a portable device before, your expectations are probably quite low. No one has really got it right in the past, and so it took some serious rethinking of the whole way the web is presented for Apple to come up with the iPhone's web browser.

In the past, the web had been presented on phones and mobile devices in three ways: Wap, RSS or its native format. The latter of these three choices, native format, in which pages were shown as they were designed yet rendered on the smaller screen, was rarely successful. Few designers ever produced pages with phones and PDAs in mind, because they always assumed they would be viewed on a full-sized screen. Besides, if they did design for mobile displays, they would have looked terrible on our desktop computers. There was a workaround that would allow them to produce separate style files and have the browser pick the most appropriate one depending on whether it was a full-sized computer screen or a pokey portable display, but few did. The result was that pages would drift off the right-hand and lower edges of the mobile's screen, and you would end up reading them piecemeal, scrolling around with a stylus or keypad until you had seen the whole page. Hardly a satisfying experience.

Wap was little better. It used a subtly different language to regular web pages, and for a while it looked as though it may become the predominant method for building mobile sites. Pages were organised into 'decks', like cards, that could be navigated by scrolling down each one using a rocker switch or joystick on your phone and then clicking when you had highlighted a link. Again, it was far from perfect, as it was really designed for a time when it was expensive to pass data over mobile networks, and few phones could connect to wifi. This meant pages were light on both text and graphics and so were, ultimately, unsatisfying. Of course, it also meant developers had to produce each page twice: once for computers using HTML, and once for phones and PDAs using Wap.

Then there was RSS (Rich Site Summary or Really Simple Syndication, depending on who you talk to), which remains popular to this day and is used extensively on regular computers. However, reading RSS is not like browsing the web, as it is simply the content of the page stripped out from the design. That makes it very efficient, and it allows you to combine several streams of information from various sites in a single location. However, as many sites only provide you with a summary of each page

rather than all the information it contains, you often end up having to visit the site itself to get the rest. That would lead you back to the problem of how you present a full-sized web page on a one-eighth-sized screen. Plus, of course, page summaries are no good for showing you things like bus timetables, railway maps or presentation slides.

So it must have been clear to Apple from the very first day its engineers sat down to plan the iPhone's development that if it was to include a web browser people would actually want to use, then it would have to make something more efficient, more impressive and far more usable than anything that had gone before it.

In short, it would have to display full-sized web pages on a tiny screen in their original format in such a way that it would seem they had been designed for just that format.

Apple achieved this in two ways. First, it gave the iPhone a truly massive resolution, so that even when shrunk down you would still be able to read headings and body text on most web pages. That resolution has been increased yet further in the iPhone 4. Second, it let you tap to selectively zoom in and out on the sections of a page that you want to read in more detail. It effectively wrote a browser that was the best of both worlds, taking the tried and tested piecemeal approach of its predecessors, and mixing it with the far superior overview mode of a desktop computer that fits the whole width of a page in the window at once.

 See **page 113** for more on **Browsing the web**

Email client

If you have ever seen anyone use a BlackBerry, or used one yourself, you will know how useful it can be to have access to your email on the move. What makes the BlackBerry great, though, is the fact that you don't have to manually check your email every half hour to find out whether you have any new messages waiting for collection.

That is because the BlackBerry uses a technology known as 'push' email, where the server sends the email to your device whether you have requested it or not. It is a formula that has proved so successful that many users are finding themselves getting addicted to a device that, in some quarters, has been nicknamed the CrackBerry.

Apple has developed MobileMe to offer a similar service to iPhone users, with email received at a designated *me.com* email address pushed straight to the screen of the phone.

So what does all of this mean for you? Simply simplicity, at its most basic level. It takes all of the hassle out of mobile email, because the messages come to you and can be dealt with as soon and as often as you like. And because the email is stored on Apple's servers it enables you to access it from any device in any location. This

means that any email you mark as read on your Mac, PC or iPad will also be marked as read on your iPhone, and any email you send while you are out and about will also appear in the sent items folder on your computer.

MobileMe is not the only emailing service open to you, though; the iPhone can also connect to a host of other services including Ymail, Gmail and regular Pop3 services. However, while connecting to your own Pop3 server means you can use your regular email address on your iPhone, you won't be able to synchronise the read and unread status of your messages, or have a record of those messages sent from your iPhone on your regular computer, unless you cc the same messages back to yourself.

See **page 108** for more on **Emailing from the iPhone**

Maps

Online mapping is nothing new. We have had countless online street maps to choose from since the turn of the millennium, but one service has trumped them all: Google Maps. By mixing street-level mapping with high-quality satellite imagery, Google came up with a winning combination

that has since been copied by half a dozen pretenders to its crown.

Not surprisingly, Apple chose to implement what most consider to be the original and best service into the iPhone, and Google Maps earned itself a dedicated button on the iPhone Home screen. It integrates almost every Google Maps feature, including the invaluable business database.

This allows you to look up local businesses and services (*left*), such as car repair shops and pizza restaurants, and call them directly using the iPhone's telephony features. Indeed, this was one of the most impressive features of Apple CEO Steve Jobs' unveiling of the first iPhone in San Francisco in January 2007. In front of an audience of press and industry leaders, he looked up the nearest Starbucks coffee shop to the Moscone Center, where he was making his presentation, and ordered 4,000 lattes to go. Whether it was a setup or he really did wind up an innocent barista remains to be seen, but it was an effective and impressive demonstration of the usefulness of the Google Maps feature when combined with the iPhone's telephony tools.

The first major addition to the Maps application was the ability for the iPhone to triangulate your position by comparing the strength of signals received from the mobile phone network and to plot the point on the map. This works with every iPhone from the original 2.5G model, although accuracy varied greatly depending on network coverage in your area.

Since the iPhone 3G, this has been enhanced with the addition of a fully-fledged Global Positioning System (GPS) receiver. This accepts incoming positional data from a US satellite network to provide more precise information, plotting your location to within a metre or so. Like the network triangulation performed by the original iPhone, its accuracy does vary depending on a range of factors, such as cloud cover and your ability to see an open sky (so it won't work inside buildings unless you are next to a window), but the information it returns to the phone can be genuinely useful. Already developers are finding ways to build it into their applications, with Loopt (*loopt.com*) using it to run a geographically-aware social networking service.

  See **page 94** for more on **Maps**

Camera

No phone worth its salts ships without a camera. How different that is to the turn of the century when the networks were just starting to push the exciting idea of paying extortionate rates to send pictures to your friends. Now it is almost impossible to buy a new phone that doesn't have a camera, and even those of us who do not use them to send photos over the mobile network find them invaluable as digital notebooks when out shopping or spending time with family and friends.

The iPhone's camera was one of the biggest surprises when Steve Jobs revealed the gadget's initial specifications. Not because it was so advanced, like everything else inside its sleek glass and metal shell, but because in the first models it was comparably conservative. With a resolution of just two megapixels, the camera was easily outclassed by many cheaper competitors and looked like it was decided on well in advance of the iPhone actually going into production, at a time when such a pokey pixel count would have been the norm.

The iPhone 3GS's camera was upgraded to three megapixels and introduced the ability to shoot video. The higher resolution gives you the option of enlarging your images for bigger prints or, should you choose, cropping in on

specific details. This would not be so easy with the lower-resolution sensor as you would have less image to crop while retaining a usable portion. The story is even better on the iPhone 4 where the resolution of the primary back-mounted camera has been increased yet again – this time to five megapixels, which rivals some pocket cameras that were market-leading models just a few years ago. It can also shoot higher resolution videos than the 3GS, which is capped at just 640 x 480 pixels. Videos shot on the iPhone 4 are full 720p high definition (HD) movies at up to 30 frames per second (FPS) with sound.

You will notice that we made specific reference to a 'primary back-mounted camera' there. This is because the iPhone 4 is the first model to also feature a front-mounted camera that faces you as you tap on the screen. The resolution of this camera is lower than the camera on the rear of the device, but still sufficient to enable video conferencing using the bundled FaceTime application.

The focus on all current iPhone cameras is controlled by tapping the screen at the most important part of your image. This gives you far greater creative freedom when using the phone as a photographic device.

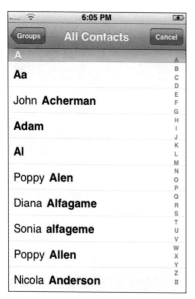

You can also employ a digital zoom to get close to the action. Photos can be geotagged by using the iPhone's built-in GPS receiver to mark them with the coordinates at which they were taken. These can then be used for filing, or for presenting your images on a map. They are also understood by services like sharing site Flickr.

Despite all of these upgrades, in most cases, the resolution of a sensor has less to do with the sharpness of an image than the quality of the lens in front of it. Fortunately this is an area in which the iPhone has traditionally done well.

Address book

From the very earliest days of mass mobile adoption, mobile phones have integrated a built-in phone book (*left*). Its capacity is often seen as a key decision-making factor by many users when looking for their next handset, as few would want to carry both their mobile and a paper or electronic address book in their jacket pockets.

As manufacturers cottoned on to this and tried to build in more and more features, many started to integrate fully-fledged address books that could take street details, email addresses and website URLs, alongside regular numbers. Many live and die by this feature, with some models being criticised by some users for having inflexible address books that can attach only one number to each name.

The iPhone blows even the best mobile address book out of the water, with a fully fledged contact management system that can handle names, numbers, addresses and even photos. It synchronises with your PC or Mac, so that the numbers on your phone match the ones on your computer. In addition, the management tools, such as easy entry and deletion, mean you will not have to navigate a dozen menus just to update a business associate's record when they change jobs.The address book can easily be searched using the built-in search tool, accessed by swiping to the iPhone's left-most Home Screen.

 See **page 058** for more on **Contacts**

Music and movie player

The iPhone is Apple's next logical step from the iPod, so it is only to be expected that it includes a first-class music player. In fact, so confident is Apple that this is a worthy successor that on launch it described the iPhone as a 'widescreen iPod with touch controls'. That was before the iPod touch appeared, of course.

Its key benefit over the regular iPod classic, nano or shuffle is obviously the size of the screen, which allows you to view movies in a more accurate aspect ratio and control playback with a more natural and logical set of controls than the limited scroll-wheel found on most iPods.

Now that the iTunes Store also features movie and TV show downloads and rentals, you can also use your iPhone to catch up on programmes you have missed. Prices vary depending on what you choose to download, but because the system is so well integrated with iTunes on the Mac and PC, and Apple TV – if you have one – in your lounge, it doesn't matter how you buy your media as you can watch it anywhere you choose. For rentals, you must commence viewing within 30 days of downloading the rental, and you must finish it within two days of starting (think of it as best before date). The prices are roughly similar to what you might expect to find in a high street DVD rental store.

👉 See **page 036** for more on **iPod**

👉 See **page 090** for more on **YouTube**

Wifi networking

The iPhone is no dumb telephone – it has a variety of communications tools built in, with Bluetooth (*see below*) and wireless, or 'wifi', networking supplementing its range of mobile features. Wifi is the same networking protocol as that used by wireless computers, laptops, home routers and modems. It is also commonly found in workplaces and coffee shops, so iPhone owners can browse the web without paying high network fees to the mobile networks. The wifi tools built into the iPhone are key to many of its most important features, such as Google Maps and handling email,

but many industry observers had expected Apple to have made more of them, perhaps by including VoIP in its feature set.

With the introduction of iPhone 4 it looks like that may have happened – to an extent – FaceTime which lets you video conference with another iPhone 4 owner using the front-packing camera and only works when connected to a wifi network.

Other VoIP tools are sold as add-ons through the iTunes Store, and the most popular among them, Skype, is available on the iPhone, allowing you to cut costs when calling from abroad by connecting to an open or paid-for wireless network.

Bluetooth

The iPhone's third means of wireless connectivity is Bluetooth 2.1+EDR. This second-generation radio protocol is three times faster than its predecessor and consumes less power, so shouldn't hammer the iPhone's battery so hard when in regular use. The EDR in its specification stands for Enhanced Data Rate, which means it can shuttle the equivalent of three megabits of information backwards and forwards every second. What does this mean in the real world? Well, three megabits is about 360 written characters, so you should be able to transfer one or two address book entries between the iPhone and another device every second or so.

Bluetooth is slower than wireless networking and has a shorter range, with most devices incapable of transmitting further than about 10 metres. So while technically feasible, this radio technology would never be a truly practical means of efficiently transferring large blocks of data or surfing the web. For most iPhone owners, its use will, therefore, largely be confined to transferring small chunks of data, or connecting to a wireless Bluetooth headset.

So why still use such a short-range, slow technology? Simply that it has one major benefit: widespread compatibility. Bluetooth devices are able to see each other when in range and, because they have built-in 'profiles' that describe their features and abilities, they are able to inform each other of how they can interact. This allows for easy set-up, with little or no input from users.

Satellite navigation

GPS features were long-rumoured for inclusion in the iPhone, but until the 3G variant was introduced, nobody could be quite sure whether Apple's engineers would have been able to integrate an upgraded communications chip (3G hardware draws more power than the 2.5G chips used in the original iPhone) with a GPS receiver. But Apple not only worked out how to do this without increasing the size and weight of the battery, it also managed to slim down the physical size of the handset itself. GPS persists in iPhone 4 so you will always know exactly where you are at any time and, as a bonus, can geotag your photos. This allows you to attach position-defining data to your images

so that they can then be positioned on maps. Geotagging is a fledgling technology, but its popularity is growing.

On-screen keyboard

Have you ever suffered from texter's thumb? You know – that dull ache you get from sending too many predictive notes to your friends? Now imagine you had all the power of an iPhone in your hand, but all the letters of the alphabet were still crammed onto just eight number keys, with another one reserved for spaces and punctuation, all arranged in the familiar regimented mobile phone grid.

It wouldn't work.

Fortunately the iPhone has gone the other way and done away with physical buttons altogether. Apart from the power button, ringer switch, volume control and central button on the bottom of the iPhone's fascia, there are no external moving parts on the iPhone, as all of the other buttons have been moved into the software realm and are rendered as graphics on the touchscreen.

Fortunately, it is quite intelligent, and while the keys are small (how else would you fit them all onto the screen in portrait mode?), the iPhone's touch-sensitive membrane is accurate enough to sense where your fingers are falling and magnify each button as you press it, greatly increasing most users' accuracy.

Don't believe us? Well, think back to the first time you started to use T9 predictive messaging. If you were anything like us, you probably spent a lot of time looking at the screen and trying to work out how you could create each word as you typed, so great was the required mind-shift in the move from picking out characters individually. Soon, though, you learned not to think about how it worked, but to just get on with things and – you know what – by the power of technology it did what you wanted, and eight times out of 10, it got the word you wanted.

Treat your iPhone's on-screen keyboard in a similar way and you will not go far wrong as the error correction intelligence built in is highly accurate. As an added bonus, because the iPhone does not have a hard-wired keyboard like a BlackBerry or a traditional non-stylus PDA, it means that Apple can quickly integrate new features, such as a wider range of languages in updated editions. This was first evident with the arrival of the iPhone 3G, which introduced image-based languages in the Far East.

Home screen

The Home screen is where you will find the icons and buttons that link you to every other application on your iPhone. It includes a range of information elements, such as network coverage and strength, wifi availability and remaining battery power as well as the current time. You can return to the Home screen at any time by pressing the physical circular button at the bottom of the iPhone's front surface. You can also rearrange the application icons by holding down on an icon on the dock bar at the bottom of the screen until they all start to shiver. At this point they can be dragged into their new positions.

You can add shortcuts to frequently visited web pages or online applications to the Home screen. This saves you from having to first launch the browser and then navigate to them in the conventional manner. Open the page you want using Safari, press the + button at the bottom of the Safari screen and choose the Add to Home screen option from the menu that pops up.

Display

The screen is more or less your only interface with the phone, and is the surface through which you will interact with your handset whatever you are doing – emailing friends, calling a contact, flicking through your collection of albums or plating a game. In the iPhone 3GS its resolution tops out at 480 x 320 pixels, which is the same as the initial iPhone. However iPhone 4 is the first model to feature an increased resolution of 960 x 640 pixels which, on a 3.5in display, has a density of 326 pixels per inch. This is important, as Apple refers to that resolution as a Retina Display, claiming that the human eye cannot detect a density higher than 300 pixels per inch.

The result is a smoother, crisper display so that when you're reading ebooks on the move your experience is as close as it is possible to get to traditional paper and ink.

Phone

With so many other features, the iPhone's actual phone component becomes something of an 'also-ran' tool (*right*), as it is almost crowded out by more exciting offerings such as the music player, web browser, mapping applications and the fully automated email client.

Yet there it is, sitting square and centre, and well integrated with a whole raft of other tools, including the Address Book and Google Maps.

It features call holding and conference calling, which while they are also found on other mobile phones, is better built and easier to use on the iPhone than on most of its rivals.

iPhone 4 should also deliver clearer calls than its predecessors and many rivals. Not only is the metal band surrounding its casing a large aerial to boost reception, but dedicated sensors allow it to filter out background noise so that your audio stream will be crisp, clear and free of the kind of distortion that could have your contacts continually saying 'pardon'.

Importantly, Apple has introduced a new feature in iPhone 4 to supplement this called FaceTime. This is a video calling tool that allows you to use either of the cameras on the iPhone to place video calls to other iPhone 4 users. At the present time, such calls can only be made when you are connected to a wifi network to maintain a high quality video stream, but it is a feature that has been long wished for on the iPhone and is only now possible with the addition of a front-facing camera.

Before you can use it, though, you need to choose the best iPhone for you, and that's where we're heading next…

Choosing an iPhone

There are several iPhones to choose from – just as there are with iPods, iPads and most products in Apple's line-up. It may not be clear which is the best choice for you, but when you boil down the specifications to their most basic level it becomes clear that the choice is determined more by capacity than anything else.

iPhone 4

iPhone 4 is Apple's latest, greatest phone. It comes in two capacities – 16GB and 32GB – and with either black or white casing, depending on your preference. Unlike previous models this case colour also features on the front, so if you have chosen white then that's the colour you get front and back. Previous editions were always black on the front. You can no longer buy 8GB models, and it isn't possible to get your hands on a capacity of 64GB, perhaps to stop it from competing too closely with the iPod.

Externally, all models have the same features and buttons, they sport the same screens, speakers and wireless features and processors, so that memory distinction is the only basis on which you can make an informed hardware choice.

Your biggest dilemma, therefore, will be the kind of contract to which you should sign up – or indeed whether you should agree to a contract at all.

Since the launch of the iPhone 3GS it has been possible to secure a handset on a pay-as-you-go basis whereby you are not locked into an ongoing monthly contract but pay piecemeal by topping up your account as you use the credit over time. This will cost you more initially as your chosen handset will not attract a subsidy from the network operator, but in the long term will probably work out cheaper, so long as your usage is not too heavy. This is because regardless of how much you use (or don't use) your handset on a monthly tariff you are always paying the same price. With pay-as-you-go, the less you use it, the less you pay. It's not so easy for budgeting as you can't accurately predict your ongoing costs, but if you need to save money it gives you the option of reining in your daily use.

Look for deals that do not require a minimum monthly top-up and ensure that there is plenty of data access included. This will be measured in terms of gigabytes transmitted and received rather than minutes spent browsing the web or checking your email.

iPhone 3GS

If you cannot afford an iPhone 4 but lust after an Apple handset then there is one other option: the iPhone 3GS. Apple has traditionally kept the best of its previous models on sale alongside its latest, greatest iPhone so that it can compete at the lower end of the price range against other manufacturers.

With the release of the iPhone 4, the iPhone 3GS now fulfils that role. It may not have a front-facing camera or FaceTime for video conferencing, but it can run the iOS 4 operating system found in the iPhone 4 and has the satellite navigation and compass features that were missing from the original iPhone so it remains a capable, worthwhile handset.

The one area in which the iPhone 3GS won't save you money, of course, is the ongoing network charges as you will still have to pay for connectivity for both voice and data use.

Key concepts

Where have all my buttons gone?

The most immediate difference between the iPhone and a regular mobile is the lack of a keypad. This is both a blessing and a curse, the latter being that there is no tactile feedback for sight-impaired users. This also means you can easily slip and press more than one virtual button at once and that when you are holding the phone at arm's length to take your own picture with the higher resolution back-mounted camera, you have no idea where the shutter button is, because it is drawn on the screen, which is facing away from you.

However, for the vast majority of users, and those less egotistic than the serial self-portrait takers, it is an excellent implementation, and a few minutes spent getting used to the way it works will repay very real and long-term dividends.

The first thing to realise is that the keyboard is intelligent in two very subtle ways. First, it briefly enlarges each key as you tap it, so you can see its

key cap pop up above your finger to make sure you have pressed the right one (and almost every time you will, because it is clever enough to sense the most likely key you were aiming for). Second, it offers to auto-complete words for you by dropping a suggested completion for partially entered words immediately below the cursor. The built-in default dictionary adapts to your needs quickly, and after entering a unique word just once or twice – your surname, for example – it will be offering to complete that for you, too. To accept its suggestion, just press whatever key would come immediately after the word – a space, the enter key and so on.

Finger gestures

You can frequently do away with the keyboard altogether, because the iPhone uses your fingers in much the same way as a regular computer uses a mouse. On-screen buttons can be tapped to navigate through menus, while double-tapping some elements, such as columns on a web page,

Pinch or stretch your fingers to zoom in and out on the iPhone's display.

will expand them to fill the screen, without you even defining the edges of the text.

Other elements can be swiped, such as album covers in the iPod and pictures in the photos application, which can be slid onto and off the screen just like real-life picture prints on a table.

The cleverest of all the finger gestures, though, is the pinch and reverse-pinch (*right*), which will zoom in and out on various on-screen elements. Test this out by starting Maps, typing in your postcode and then putting your thumb and forefinger in the centre of the screen, both pressed together. Slowly open them up and see how the map expands with them as you zoom in. Doing the same in reverse will zoom out again. This same trick works in several other applications, including photos and websites.

Magnified selections

The iPhone 4 screen sports a very high resolution, and it is certainly much higher than those found on most other mobile phones. However, it is still only 3.5in across the diagonal, which is a fairly limited space in which to fit a whole touch-sensitive operating system, with input boxes, graphics and a keyboard.

Apple's software engineers have, fortunately, acknowledged this and integrated a magnifier (*see page 27*), which pops up automatically whenever the iPhone judges it may be required on the basis of the way you are touching the screen.

Test it by firing up the web browser (the Safari icon on the bar at the bottom of the Home screen), entering a web address and, once the page has loaded, holding down your finger over that address on the input bar. A magnifier will pop up and follow your finger as you move to the left and right through the text. You can use the same technique when entering text in a note or email to position the cursor at one specific location within your document.

Copy, cut and paste

The absence of copy, cut and paste on the original iPhone was a bugbear for many early adopters, but Apple finally added it through a software update.

Using it is easy: hold down your finger on a word you want to copy and, when you lift off, a selection box appears. Pick Select or Select all, and then drag the sliders to refine your selection. When you are happy with the selection, pick Copy or Cut from the menu. Now, if you want to paste, hold down for a second or two on the screen at the point where you want to paste and pick Paste from the pop-up menu that appears.

If you selected copy, then your chosen text will be saved on the iPhone's clipboard and can be pasted into other documents by using the Paste option that will appear beside the Cut and Copy buttons the next time you use this function.

The swivelling screen

Even in its portrait orientation, the iPhone's screen resolution is so high that it is fairly easy to read the text on many regular, plain websites, such as the BBC News site. Not only does this more closely emulate a regular computer screen, but it also gives web sites room to breathe.

However, several applications also work in landscape mode, literally spinning around on the screen as you turn the iPhone on its side, thanks to the integrated orientation sensor.

Not all applications are appropriate to landscape use, but those that are really benefit. The calculator, for example, has two distinct modes, and you choose between them by turning the handset. In portrait mode it is a regular adding machine; in landscape mode it is a fully-featured scientific calculator (*below*).

Some applications only work in one mode or the other – YouTube's bookmarks screen is solo portrait, while its playback mode is only ever landscape, for example – while others change their mode altogether, the most notable example being iPod, which displays menus in portrait mode, and album art when tipped on one side.

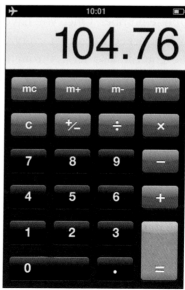

Turning your iPhone through 90° changes the screen display in many apps. When using the calculator it switches between regular and scientific views, giving you two calculators in one handy device.

Security

Before we go any further, a word about
security. The iPhone has a voracious
appetite for information. Contacts,
addresses, bookmarks, notes… you name
it, it will store it, and that's an awful lot of
information to fall into an identity thief's
hands if you happen to lose your handset.

Add an extra layer of security by
applying the iPhone's built-in locks,
through Settings > General > Passcode
lock (*right*). Tapping this will let you enter a
four-digit code that will be demanded every
time you or anyone else switches on the
phone. With 10,000 combinations to choose from – assuming you count
0000 in your calculations – you should not pick something too obvious
such as your year of birth, your anniversary or the last four digits of your
phone number. Once you have entered the number and confirmed it, you
will be asked to enter it every time you turn on the phone.

You can also set it, through the Require Passcode button, to lock the
iPhone after one, five, 10, 15, 30 or 60 minutes of inactivity and demand
the code before it will work again, preventing anyone from browsing your
data should you have the iPhone stolen.

You have not entirely disabled your phone if you forget your code: you
can recover it by connecting it to iTunes and clicking Restore. This will
return the iPhone to the state in which it left the factory and remove the
lock, but in doing so it will erase all of your data.

However, this measure was still not sufficient reassurance to settle
the minds of many businesses, which Apple is hoping to attract with the
iPhone. For this reason, it has also implemented a remote wipe feature,
making it possible to reset all of the information on an iPhone over the
network in the event of loss or theft.

Chapter 2

iPhone Applications

• •

iPhone applications

When Steve Jobs first demonstrated the iPhone, there was great interest in what it could do and how it could be expanded by third-party developers. However, many coders' hopes and dreams were quickly dashed when Jobs announced that, at that time, the iPhone was to be a closed system that would run only Apple-originated applications.

This is not unusual. Most phones are locked by default, largely to stop users from installing applications that may interfere with the smooth running of the mobile phone network. Even those that do allow applications to be installed – usually as Java applets – restrict what they can do and which parts of the phone they can access. They are therefore rarely network-aware and few ever manage to access the mobile calling or data-transfer features.

However, Apple's assertion that in this respect the iPhone was no different has been proved factually inaccurate as more ambitious developers accessed the file system and installed their own applications, many of which are now available for free download.

It briefly seemed Apple may have relented, as Jobs later announced developers would indeed be able to write software to run on the iPhone. However, they would have to do so using Web 2.0 technologies, would have to host them remotely and would have to restrict users to accessing them through the integrated browser. That fell a long way short of what most developers were hoping for.

So the announcement of an authorised Software Development Kit and, with the advent of the iPhone 3G, an App Store for downloading third-party applications was welcomed by all quarters. It is now possible to download over 225,000 different applications for use on the iPhone and iPod touch, and with the addition of the iPad that number look set to grow yet further, making the iPhone one of the most versatile handsets money can buy.

That still doesn't devalue the iPhone's core applications, though, which we will explore here with a run-down of your home-screen icons.

CALCULATOR This is speedy and attractive calculator, highly reminiscent of the one found in Mac OS X's Dashboard. In the iPhone it has been updated so that rotating the device through a quarter turn not only flips the display but also switches between the regular portrait view of the calculator and a massively expanded scientific version, which is more reminiscent of those powerful calculators that come with the Mac OS X and Windows operating systems.

 CALENDAR This, as the name suggests, is a simple time-management application that allows you to store diary items on your iPhone. It can be synchronised with calendars that are stored on the computer, so that your iPhone diary is always up to date. It also works with MobileMe, Apple's online data management suite, allowing you to add appointments to your global calendar on the move.

 CAMERA A small application for controlling the iPhone's built-in camera, the output from which is stored in the Photos application. Something of a one-trick pony in the first iPhone, but since upgraded to shoot video, too.

 CLOCK A world clock, doing what it says on the tin and not much else. Add and rearrange the cities of your choice and use it as a simple way to make sure you will not be calling your most valued international contacts when it is the middle of the night.

 iPOD Who would have believed that the ultimate iPod killer would come from the company that reinvented mobile music in the first place? It may be called 'iPod', but this application is streets ahead of the nano, classic and shuffle iPods. Only the iPod touch comes close to rivalling what it can do with direct downloads from the iTunes Store and, on its glorious 3.5in screen, the ability to show films and TV shows in a format you might actually want to watch.

MAIL Fully-featured email application with pre-programmed settings for Gmail, Yahoo! Mail, MobileMe mail and AOL, and the ability to add your own Pop3, Imap and Exchange server settings for use with corporate email servers. With the simultaneous launch of MobileMe with the iPhone 3G, Apple massively expanded the feature-set of the old .Mac service, which was by then starting to show its age. Now subscribers have a desirable @me.com email address with all messages stored safely on Apple's servers, so that when you read or send one on the iPhone, that fact is reflected on your home or office computer (or both).

 MAPS Portable implementation of the Google Maps website, complete with satellite imagery, route planning and – in some regions – traffic conditions. The best possible demonstration of the power of gesture-based computing used for panning and zooming the image. In the iPhone it is integrated with the gadget's built-in GPS receiver, allowing you to use satellite navigation to accurately plot your position on the on-screen map.

 NOTES Lightweight memo tool that integrates well with the iPhone's email features allowing you to send yourself notes to be actioned at a later point. Pages flip backwards to turn over and, when you are done with them, drop neatly into a rubbish bin for deletion.

 PHONE The iPhone's core feature, appearing by default in the most prominent space on the Dock running across the bottom of the home screen. This, and the email client, also gives you access to the integrated address book. More advanced than the average phone, it lets you put callers on hold or merge them for conference calling.

 PHOTOS A display-centric album for showing photos uploaded to, or taken using, your iPhone. Manages photos stored in albums, so you do not bore friends and family with your entire collection.

SAFARI Apple's cross-platform web browser makes it onto a third platform, the iPhone, in a stripped-down, but capable edition. Intelligent awareness of frame sizes, combined with the iPhone's high-resolution screen make for the best mobile browsing experience yet developed. Unfortunately there is no support for Flash at the current time as Apple has developed its own rival technologies for performing the same functions, and continued animosity between Apple and Adobe make it unlikely it will appear any time soon.

 MESSAGES This is a strange first entry on the iPhone Home screen, but it does point to the increasing importance of SMS text messaging in modern-day communications. The iPhone expands on most phones' abilities by threading forward-and-backward messages together like an instant messaging conversation.

 STOCKS A ticker application that presents a range of user-defined stock prices and historical data, in a Dashboard Widget-like environment. It covers a wide range of stocks from different markets around the world, and can track their rises and falls in real terms or percentage increments.

 WEATHER Keep an eye on the sky by looking in your pocket. Simplistic weather viewer and five-day forecast application for an impressive range of worldwide destinations. It links to Yahoo!'s city guides so that when you know where it is fair, you can head there directly.

 YOUTUBE Dedicated application for viewing, bookmarking and sharing YouTube videos. When Steve Jobs declared that the iPhone was the best environment through which to browse YouTube, he wasn't joking. YouTube itself has done much to enhance the quality of the videos on the service to make them load quickly and run smoothly – and at high quality – on the iPhone.

iPod

This is not just an iPod; it is a massively advanced update on Apple's best-selling music player that is both easier to use and better to look at than the scroll-wheel-based original. Click on the iPod button at the bottom of the iPhone's Home screen to invoke its media playback features and you will see how much it differs from a traditional iPod. Rather than dial your way through the menus using a scroll-wheel, you can interact directly with the interface. Your main options are found on the toolbar at the bottom of the screen, giving you direct access to playlists, artists, songs and videos, with the More option calling up the familiar iPod divisions of Albums, Audiobooks, Compilations, Composers, Genres and Podcasts (*below*).

Customising the toolbar

If you don't ever watch videos on your iPhone, or you are a total podcast junkie, then your first job should be to customise the toolbar so that it

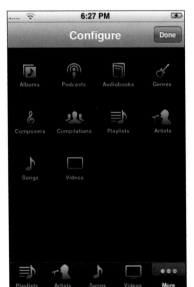

works the way you want it to – not the way some Apple engineer thinks is best.

Make sure you are on the iPod home screen and click on the More button on the toolbar at the bottom of the display, then the Edit button at the very top. This brings up a list of 11 key features, including Albums, Songs and Compilations. Let's add Albums to the toolbar and use it to replace the default Playlists option.

Hold down your finger on top of the Albums icon and drag it down the screen, hovering for a moment over Playlists at the bottom of the display. When the Playlists icon lights up, let go and it will be swapped out for the Albums function.

Now let's reorganise things a little. Hold down the Songs icon, which is already on the toolbar, and drag it to the left. Notice how everything rearranges around it as you move it along the toolbar. When you can't go any further left, let go, and it will fix itself in position as the first entry on the toolbar.

When you are happy with the contents and order of your toolbar, click the Done button to return to the main iPod menu.

Natural searching

Every time you transfer a track from iTunes to your iPhone, you also send across a lot of information about the artist and the album on which it appeared. The iPhone uses this information to file it away on its internal memory and also to allow you to find it at a later date by organising it under the artist or album name, genre and so on.

But when did you last search your music by genre? Most CD owners simply slot their CDs into a rack or dump them in a box, and then leaf through them every time they want something to play.

By borrowing a trick from iTunes called Cover Flow, the iPhone allows you to flick through all the art associated with your albums in exactly the same way.

Turn your iPhone through 90° and the menu will fade away, to be replaced by all of this glorious art, stacked up side by side. Wipe a finger across them and they will ripple through like the pages of a book. When you find what you are looking for, click on the cover to flip it over – as you would with a CD – and it will display a list of that album's tracks (*right*). Click on the one you want and plug in your headphones as it starts to play.

Audiobooks

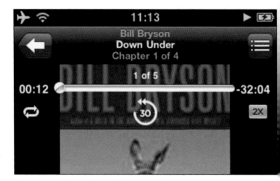

Audiobooks are subtly different to music files. For starters, they are usually just spoken word, rather than tunes, but more importantly the way they are encoded makes them easier to control.

Music is designed to be played back at a defined speed, which is specified by the composer. However, when it comes to books, we all read at different speeds. Apple has recognised this fact, and so the iPod enables you to speed up or slow down audiobooks. The former is great for fiction or cramming revision notes, while the latter really helps in trying to master pronunciation of a foreign language.

When you start playing an audiobook you will notice a button to the right of the progress bar marked 1x. Tapping this lets you switch to double speed (2x) or half speed (1/2x) depending on your preference and what you are listening to.

Podcasts

Podcasts are pre-recorded radio and video programmes designed for downloading at regular intervals and listening to on portable devices such as the iPhone. The name is derived from the iPod, which was the device that popularised them, although their format is universal and they can be listened to on anything from a £10 MP3 player to a £2,000 desktop computer.

They cover a multitude of subjects and by far the easiest way to subscribe is through the iTunes Store. Once you have subscribed to a number of podcasts – almost all provided free of charge – they will be automatically downloaded to your iPhone each time you connect.

Podcasts have their own entry on the iPod section's More screen, and are organised by title. Clicking on each one opens up a list of available episodes, which will start to play when tapped.

Some are presented as 'enhanced' podcasts, in which the audio stream will be accompanied by static graphics and chapter markings that allow you to skip straight to specific parts of the recording. To see whether the podcast to which you are listening has this feature, click on the Playlist button on the top right-hand corner of the screen (three lines beside three dots) and if it is an enhanced podcast the display will rotate to present you with a list of chapter titles. Click on one of these titles and you will jump straight to that section.

Uploading your music

It may share many common features with the iPod, but the iPhone differs in one crucial way: it forces you to be much more organised about the way you manage your music, podcasts and audiobooks.

With an iPod, you can simply select a range of tracks and drag them onto the iPod icon on the sidebar, and they will be copied across. With the iPhone you can't drag anything at all onto it from your music library without changing your default settings. In its default state, to specify which tracks should be downloaded to your iPhone each time you connect, plug it into your PC or Mac and start iTunes. When it appears in the sidebar, click on its icon and use the tabs at the top of the screen to navigate through each of the Music, Podcasts and, if you have any, Video tabs, and click on the Sync checkbox on each one.

By default, iTunes will now synchronise all of your media with the iPhone, downloading new additions each time your connect. However, if you would rather leave your more embarrassing tracks at home, you can tailor just the playlists you want to have downloaded by clicking on the Selected Playlists button and checking off the playlists of your choice.

To manage tracks on a one-by-one basis, click on the first tab (marked Summary) and scroll down to the Options box. Here, tick the check box beside 'Manually manage music and videos' and then click the Apply button at the bottom of the display. You can now drag music from your library directly onto the iPhone's entry in your sidebar to copy single tracks or small groups onto the device.

Sounding good

Let's face it: not all earphones are made
equal, and cheaper, weaker models often
need a little helping hand before they can
do your tunes justice.

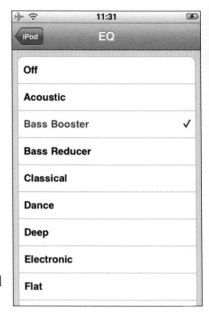

Fortunately, the iPhone has a built-in
equaliser, which is accessed by starting at
the Home screen and clicking on Settings
> iPod > EQ. This features 22 presets to
enhance various music types such jazz,
rock, R&B and spoken word, hardware
such as 'small speakers', or specific parts
of a track such as those that boost vocals
or reduce the bass on particularly heavy
tracks. Use them wisely and they can
make a £20 pair of budget earbuds sound
like a set of £200 studio headphones.

Playing safely

Perhaps in an effort to forestall legal action brought on by irresponsible
users who play their music too loudly, Apple has implemented a Volume
Limit feature in the iPhone's audio system. This will limit the volume at
which the iPod can play tracks to minimise damage to your ears. To activate
it, click on Settings > iPod > Volume Limit from the iPhone Home screen,
and then use the slider to set the maximum volume at which the iPod
application can play tracks. Drag the slider to the left to limit the volume to
a comfortable level.

Now click on the Lock Volume Limit button and enter a four-digit code,
twice, to stop anyone unsetting it. This is useful for parents who want to
protect their children's ears. To unlock the volume, click on Volume Limit
again and then the Unlock button, and re-enter the code. It goes without
saying that you should choose a hard-to-guess number and avoid such
obvious options as 0000, 1234, 9999 or the year of your birth.

The iTunes Store: What is it?

The iPhone is just one step in Apple's move to dominate the music download market. The company kicked off this venture in 2001 when it launched the very first iPod, which had a mere 5GB of hard drive space and room for just 1,000 tracks, and followed up in 2003 with the launch of the iTunes Music Store, since renamed simply the iTunes Store.

On launch, the Store was open to US users only, and its catalogue ran to a fairly conservative 200,000 tracks. Yet it was pretty much guaranteed to succeed. Not only was it tied in to what had by then become the world's most successful and iconic music player, but it was also cheap and ridiculously simple to use, because every track cost $0.99 and every album topped out at $9.99, so whatever you wanted, you knew what it would cost before you even entered the Store.

The Store was built into iTunes, Apple's PC- and Mac-based jukebox software, from version 4 onwards. By version 6, released October 2005, the iTunes Store had started to sell television programmes and music videos to complement the fifth-generation iPod, which had been announced simultaneously and sported video playback features. By then, Apple all but owned the market for music downloads, and it has since become one of the top three music outlets in the US.

So Apple could not afford to throw away all of this hard work by launching an iPhone that had less than perfect integration with its online music store – especially not when the hardware allowed for such an impressive user experience.

For this reason, Apple initially refused to allow users to buy tracks from the iTunes Store over the mobile networks, instead insisting that they buy and download them through its own iTunes software before transferring them to the iPhone. In fact, so key is iTunes to the whole iPhone experience that you will come to know it very well indeed over your years of happy ownership.

Into the iTunes Store

The iTunes Store is nothing more than a web page that can only be accessed through iTunes. It originally sold all tracks at 79p with copy protection measures, and later introduced higher quality, protection-free tracks at 99p. Now all tracks are protection-free and more variably priced.

DRM added small pieces of extra code to each track that inextricably linked it to your copy of iTunes and restricted the ways in which you could use the music, only allowing you to load it onto five different computers and an unlimited number of iPods and iPhones.

This may sound stingy on Apple's part, but in fact it was a measure insisted upon by the music companies before they would allow Apple to sell their catalogues because they were afraid that if the tracks were sold entirely unprotected they would be swapped between users, and the publishers would see a massive drop in record sales.

The iPhone's iTunes application lets you rent or download movies direct from the store, and preview them before making your buying decision.

The iTunes Store is the first place to turn to when you want to download new music to play on your iPhone. Whether you buy it directly over the phone, or via your Mac or PC, most tracks cost 79p, and single-disc albums are £7.99. It goes without saying that you don't get any physical media, but it does give you an instant fix and saves you having to rip your albums yourself.

This angered many users and in early 2007, after Steve Jobs wrote an essay outlining Apple's desire to sell tracks without protection, UK-based EMI announced it would be releasing higher-quality tracks free from DRM through the iTunes Store. iTunes Plus was born, and other companies, including Warner and Universal, were soon experimenting with DRM-free downloads through alternative online stores. iTunes Plus tracks are altogether more portable and offer you a degree of protection, as they can be more easily moved from one machine to another without having to reside in an authorised copy of iTunes. However, that does not mean you have the right

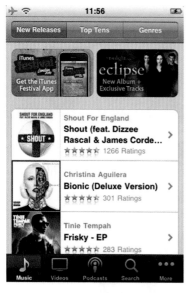

to email them to friends – indeed, you would be extremely unwise to do so, considering each one is tagged to the email address that you used to register with at the Store, allowing publicly available tracks to be traced to whoever bought them in the first place.

Not every track you might want is available, depending on who Apple has struck a deal with and a band's personal preferences. AC/DC is famed for refusing to sell its music through the iTunes Store because it doesn't want customers buying their songs one track at a time, insisting they should be bought only as complete albums, which Apple does not facilitate.

However, there are benefits to buying in this way. Apple frequently sources iTunes exclusives, with tracks available on the Store a week or so before anywhere else. Moreover, each week it gives away a different track for free, which is always promoted on the front page. The best reason of all, though, must be the price. At 79p for a single track and £7.99 for an album, it undercuts most high-street shops by some margin and, with no physical media to ship, it is more environmentally friendly, too.

Buying from iTunes

There are two ways to buy tracks from the iTunes Store: either through your Mac or PC, or directly to the iPhone over a wireless network.

Before you can buy songs, you must first set up an account. This is free, but your details will be used to mark the music you buy, which means if you subsequently pass it on to friends, it can be tracked back to yourself, and you may be held liable for piracy and copyright infringement. You will also need to supply credit card details before you make your first purchase.

Buying music is frighteningly easy. On a Mac or PC, fire up iTunes and click on iTunes Store in the left-hand margin. Search for your favourite artist, album or song name in the box at the top of the application window, and, when you have found what you are after, you can preview the free 30-second clip to make sure it is the version you want.

It is? Great. Click on Buy Now and confirm you would like to add it to your collection by entering your password, and then watch it download.

One word of warning, however: there is a maximum file size that can be downloaded over the mobile network, and anything over 12MB in size will have to be downloaded either using wifi, or by a regular computer running iTunes. Fortunately you'll know if this applies as an error will pop up warning you, so you shouldn't lose your download.

Because you bought the music from the iTunes Store rather than encoding it yourself, it will be accompanied by high-quality album artwork. This will be transferred to the phone when you upload your tracks, and be used when you next flick backwards and forwards through your album covers when choosing what to play.

What is less obvious is all the supplementary data transferred alongside the track relating to the artist, album, genre and year of recording, which will help you later on with searching for specific songs. This is known as metadata, and it is drawn from a large user-contributed database found online at *www.cddb.com*. This is supplied in a standard format compatible with a wide range of music players, meaning that any tracks you buy for your iPhone can also be indexed by an iPod and some regular portable media players.

In general, tracks are supplied in a format known as AAC, or Advanced Audio Codec, although two notable exceptions are the proprietary Audible format used for most audio books and MP3, a widely used audio format popular with podcasts.

Encoding your own music

Of course, you probably already have an extensive CD collection gathering dust on your shelves, and you will not want to buy all of those albums again through the iTunes Store, so the first thing you will want to do is copy them into iTunes. Then you can transfer them to your iPhone for listening on the move.

If you don't have an iPod already, and have not used iTunes before, then you are starting with a clean slate, which gives you the luxury of choice. You can either copy them at the highest possible quality and accept the fact that you are going to have to make some compromises when it comes to filling the iPhone's internal memory, or you can reduce the quality and take more music with you. Most users would be advised to compromise, as few mid-price headphones will be able to do sufficient justice to very high-quality copies and justify the space they consume. This is doubly true of the white earbuds that come bundled with the phone.

Apple's preferred format for copying music is AAC, which is iTunes' default format and the model used for all commercial tracks downloaded from the iTunes Store. However, iTunes, iPods, iPads and the iPhone can also handle AIFF, Apple Lossless, MP3 and Wav file formats at a variety of quality levels. For simplicity, and to get started right now, you could just leave iTunes set to the default format, but if you want to get the best from your music and determine for yourself how it is used away from home. This chapter will walk you through the various options, what they all mean and how they can be put to best use.

How compression works

All of the music we listen to, unless it is played live right there in front of us, is compressed. As it is recorded, the device used to capture it makes some intelligent decisions about which parts of the sound wave to strip out and throw away. This is usually made on the basis of what the human ear can and can't hear, with anything that would be out of our range of hearing immediately stripped out. The resulting sound wave is then chopped up into discrete chunks, a portion of which is also disposed of, with the amount of axed material depending on the bitrate selected. The higher the bitrate, the more of the chunks are kept, the smoother the sound wave, and the higher quality we perceive it to be. The lower the bitrate, the more of the chunks are thrown away, the more stepped is the sound wave, and the lower we perceive the quality to be. It is as simple as that.

Or is it? We will come back to that in a minute.

Naming your tracks and CDs

When you insert a CD into iTunes, it will examine the length of each track and where it sits among the other tracks on the CD. It will then use this information to look up the likely name of the album, artist, year of recording and a range of other information. If you have an account with the iTunes Store, it will also try to find the relevant album cover for use in iTunes and the iPod application.

While it usually gets this right first time, it can sometimes either find two albums that are so similar it needs to ask you to pick the right one, or be unable to find a match at all. If the latter is true, you can enter the necessary details yourself. This can be time consuming and laborious if you do each track individually, but you can dramatically cut the workload by changing common details in a batch.

Select all of the tracks on the album (Command-A on a Mac, Ctrl-A on a PC), right-click and choose Get Info from the contextual menu that pops up. iTunes will ask if you are sure you want to edit the details for several tracks (*below*). We do, so confirm this and use the resulting form to fill in as much common information as you can. By common information, we mean those details that apply to every track, such as album name, year of publication, genre, artist and so on. However, this is not the place to enter individual

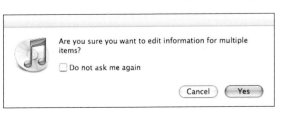

track names unless every track on the CD does indeed have the same name.

Once you have entered these details (*left*), click on OK to apply them to the selected tracks, then right-click on each one and select Get Info from the contextual menu again. You will see that you now have far more options at your disposal, including equaliser presets, sorting options, and the ability to add missing artwork and even tweak the volume for tracks on which it is higher or lower than average. We are interested in the Info tab for the moment, because clicking on it will open up a form identical to the one you had been filling in for the album as a whole. It will be populated with the fields you have entered already, and now that you have only one track selected, you can finally add the track name.

The question of compression

Now that all of the tracks are correctly named, you can start copying them to your computer in readiness for downloading them to the iPhone, which brings us back to the question of compression.

Opening up iTunes Preferences and clicking on Advanced > Importing will let you choose the codec used to encode the tracks and the quality at which they are sampled. The defaults for each of these are AAC and 128 kilobits per second. This will not mean much to most people, but in general it offers a good balance between high quality audio and not taking up too much space on your iPhone's limited storage capacity. The two other options – apart from the custom setting where you can tweak things more precisely – are for 'spoken podcast', which is 64 kilobits per second, and 'higher quality', which is 256 kilobits per second. This is the same as the better-quality tracks available through the iTunes Store and it retains more detail in the audio file for a more faithful copy.

Which one you choose is a matter of personal preference, but we would recommend sticking with 128 kilobits per second because most casual listeners on the move will not be able to tell the difference, they will take up less space on the iPhone, and the encoding process will be completed much quicker, so you can tear through your CD collection in half the time.

If you are only ever likely to use your music in iTunes or on an iPhone or iPod, there is no point switching from AAC. However, for the best possible compatibility, and to ensure that you can play your tracks on other devices should you decide to leave Apple's platform, you should consider MP3, which is by far the most widely accepted format for digital music.

But is it legal?

There is a lot of debate over the legality of copying your music in this way and who you believe depends on which side of the fence you sit on. Some lawyers still insist that ripping your music in this way infringes copyright.

When Sony BMG took alleged file sharer Jammie Thomas to court for copyright infringement of 1,702 tracks in October 2007, the company's head of litigation told the court: 'When an individual makes a copy of a song for himself, I suppose we can say he stole a song.'

If the court agreed this would mean that – in the US at least – copying CDs in this way would be illegal, even for personal use. It would also be illegal to transfer the tracks to your iPhone, since you would then be making a further copy. Things become more complicated if you have bought a track from the iTunes Store, as then you would only be able to listen to it using the copy of iTunes through which it was downloaded, since synchronising iTunes with your iPhone would create an illegal copy.

At the conclusion of the case, Thomas was found guilty of sharing files and fined $222,000. Should the argument about personal copying also one day be accepted by the courts, it would signal a sea change in the way digital music is handled around the world, which would likely do as much harm to the music companies as it would to manufacturers such as Apple. The record companies, then, can't really afford for this kind of encoding and mobile usage to be outlawed.

iPhone TV and movies

Not content with being the content king where music and podcasts are concerned, Apple also wants to be the first place people turn to when they want to download TV shows and films. So, it is not surprising that it has been quietly working behind the scenes to secure deals that expand the range of local video content available on its regional iTunes Stores.

TV on the iPhone

The headline TV shows available on Apple's iTunes Store will vary over time, but the extensive library contains a wide range of styles drawn from every vintage, from puppet-led retro classics like *Thunderbirds* and classic

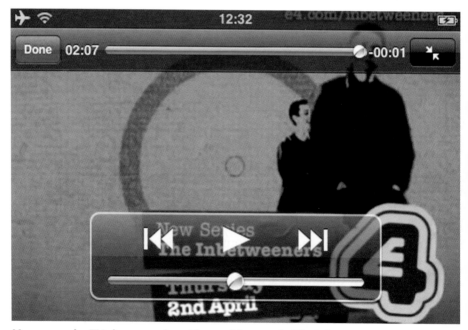

Many popular TV shows, such as Channel 4 comedy *The Inbetweeners*, are available to watch on the iPhone, courtesy of the iTunes Store.

comedies like *Bewitched* to modern hits like Channel 4's *The Inbetweeners* and *Outnumbered* from the BBC. The BBC was the first UK broadcaster to sign up through its commercial arm BBC Worldwide, following deals it had made with YouTube to run its own channels on the Google-owned video service, and the success of BBC iPlayer. Pretty soon, though, other broadcasters followed suit, starting with Channel 4, and later ITV, which started selling classic content from its archive through the Store.

Prices vary according to programme and broadcaster, although most are pegged at £1.89. This will buy you episodes of current and recent programmes, such as *Doctor Who* and *Torchwood*, as well as older modern releases, like *Little Britain* and *Spooks*. BBC programmes available for purchase on the Store appear around one week after their TV debut, allowing for 7 free days of playback on the iPlayer. *Miami Vice*, which is now approaching its silver jubilee, however, is slightly cheaper at £1.49, regardless of whether you are buying a regular 48-minute episode or the hour-and-a-half-pilot. That makes the 14 minutes of *Shaun The Sheep* you can buy for £1.89 look comparatively expensive. Some shows will be offered free as an incentive to encourage you to buy further episodes.

As with music, you can gift TV programmes to other users, so long as they have an iTunes Store account.

Movies on the iPhone

Movies came late to the UK iTunes Store. They had already been available for more than a year in the US when, in June 2008, they finally made the trans-Atlantic hop. When they did, though, it was in no way half-hearted. It launched in the UK with 700 movies to rent or purchase, with new titles added on the same day as their DVD release. That number has since grown exponentially.

Prices vary depending on the age of the movie, with Apple making a distinction between new releases and so-called library titles from a few months or years back. Latest releases cost around £9.99 to purchase outright, and £3.49 to rent. Library titles are generally sold for £6.99, and rented for £2.49. They can be viewed on a Mac or PC, iPod nano, classic or touch, the iPad and any iPhone of any vintage. Where high-definition versions of the movies are also available, these cost an extra £1 each, but because of their extensive hardware requirements and stricter digital rights conditions, can only be downloaded to and played back by Apple TV with an HDMI connection or the iPad.

Some movies can only be bought outright and some can only be rented, but with many you can take your pick and watch them either way. Depending on which you opt for, though, you will be subject to different terms and conditions. Movies you buy outright will be subject to DRM, so that while you can watch them as many times as you want for as long as you want, you can't pass them on to anyone else. Those movies that you rent, though, must be viewed within 30 days of you making the purchase, and will cease to work 48 hours after the point at which you first press play on them.

You can, however, watch them as many times as you choose during those 48 hours, and do so on a computer, an Apple TV, an iPod or an iPhone. The

New movies appear on the iTunes Store at the same time as DVD in most cases. Many can be bought in HD versions, although these cannot be viewed on the iPhone but must instead be played back using Apple TV or an iPad.

conditions for backing up your movie purchases also differ somewhat from those for music. While you can burn music playlists to CD up to seven times, you can't make copies of movies at all, except as backups that will only play within iTunes itself. This is to prevent copyright theft.

You should also be careful when you are deciding how you want to watch your rented movies. If you originally rented a movie using a Mac or PC, watched half of it and then chose to send it to your iPhone so you could finish it on the commute, but somehow got waylaid, you could not then transfer the film back to your Mac or PC to finish watching it in the evening: it is a one-way-only transfer. Unfortunately, high definition movies rented or purchased through Apple TV have to stay there, as neither the iPhone nor the iPod are high definition-capable devices.

Playing back TV and movies

Shows and films are organised and played by the iPod application, which, in the iPhone's default set-up, appears on the dock at the bottom of the Home screen. Open it and then tap the videos entry at the bottom of the screen and pick what you want to watch from the list that appears. Each show will be categorised showing basic details including, in the case of television programmes, the name, episode number and title. You can add and delete shows through iTunes whenever your iPhone is connected to your Mac or PC, but to delete shows on the move, slide your finger from left to right across its entry in the list and tap the Delete button that appears.

When watching shows, you can use the ringer control on the side of the iPhone to change the playback volume, or tap on the screen to bring up controls similar to the ones use by the YouTube application. This gives you a volume slider and transport controls at the bottom of the screen, a progress bar at the top and a Done button to take you back to the menu.

The double-ended arrow button at the top right of the display switches between a programme's recorded aspect ratio, which will usually be 4:3 for older programmes and 16:9 for more recent programmes, and the iPod's native aspect ratio, which sits somewhere in between. You may lose some detail from the edges of the video in the process.

MobileMe

MobileMe appeared at the same time as the iPhone 3G. It replaced Apple's .Mac service, which had gained some bad press in Europe and the UK for being slow. Both are synchronisation, backup, hosting and email services, offering a range of business tools tailored to Mac and now, with MobileMe, PC users.

It works by using a server to store a copy of your contacts, calendar appointments and email, which can then be used to update the same information on a range of computers, iPhones or the iPod touch. The trouble with .Mac is that it could not work across the mobile network, so whenever you wanted to update your iPhone you had to dock it with your Mac or PC. Now MobileMe takes care of the synchronisation and updates for you, and you no longer need to manually initiate each update. Instead, the MobileMe server actively sends the updates in your direction, ensuring that you always have a copy of your most accurate information to hand.

MobileMe requires that you are running software version 3.1 on a first generation iPhone or iPod touch, or have an iPhone 3G or later (iPhone 4 included), and that you are running an up-to-date browser on your computer. On a Mac this means at least Safari 3.1 or Firefox 3 under Mac OS X 10.5.8 or later, while for PC users it means Safari 3.1, Firefox 3 or IE 7.

Calendar and contacts

MobileMe works with iCal on a Mac and with the full and Express versions of Outlook on a PC to synchronise your appointments. They will then show up in the iPhone's own calendar application. Alerts and alarms will also be carried across, so you will be given a reminder of upcoming appointments even when you are away from your computer. Any changes you make to the calendar on the iPhone will then be passed back to your Mac or PC when you next switch them on.

Your PC contacts are also managed through Outlook, Outlook Express or Windows Contacts, while on the Mac they are handled by Mac OS X's

Address Book application, and work in the same way as calendar entries, passing backwards and forwards between the iPhone and any computers registered to your account.

Email

When you sign up to MobileMe, you also get a highly desirable *me.com* email address (previous subscribers to .Mac will find that their old addresses will still work, and be supplemented by a matching .me address, so if you were previously steve@mac.com, you will now also have steve@me.com). This can be used through your regular email software, through the iPhone, and also through a web interface, much like Hotmail or Gmail.

The online version is a fully interactive application, so you will not have to keep refreshing the page to update it. Instead, it works just like a regular email client on your computer, even allowing you to drag and drop messages between folders. Best of all, though, because your email is stored on an Imap server rather than locally, it is available wherever you are, and whichever computer you are using, so long as it has an Internet connection, allowing you to access your email from an Internet café when you are abroad on holiday or business.

Gallery

.Mac always integrated well with Apple's iLife applications – which are sadly not available to PC users – and this continues with MobileMe. The gallery feature has been upgraded with a fresh new feel that now matches that of Apple's high-end photograph management suite, Aperture, and optionally allows visitors to your gallery to add their own photos by email or through the browser. These will then be synchronised with the album on your computer. As a bonus, you can also add photos taken using the camera on your iPhone, allowing you to post updated images for friends and colleagues back home as you travel.

By posting your photos to a MobileMe Gallery, you can control how they are used and who has access to view them. You can also restrict the ability of visitors to download high resolution versions for printing or using in their own creative projects.

Online storage

In the move from .Mac to MobileMe, Apple generously increased the size of the iDisk on each account. This is an area of online storage where you can back up files, or store data that you may need to access when you are away from your computer. Sadly it is only available using a fully-fledged web browser – not the cut-down browsers found on the iPhone and iPod touch – but it now stretches to 20GB for individuals and 40GB for family pack users (up from 10GB and 20GB respectively under .Mac). Paid-for upgrades that previously increased accounts by an additional 10GB and 20GB have also been doubled. This space can be used in conjunction with Backup, the free Mac backup tool for subscribers, and for publishing your own site using iWeb, the online design tool that comes as part of the £71 iLife suite.

iLife comprised iTunes, iMovie, iWeb, iDVD and GarageBand. Of these, iTunes has always been available on the iPhone and, with the advent of the iPhone 4 and its high definition video capture abilities, iMovie has now joined it on the portable platform. Sadly the other applications in the suite are only available for use on the Mac. Apple does not make a PC edition of iLife.

Costs and requirements

MobileMe is a paid-for add-on, and you do not even get discounted membership in return for buying an iPhone. Despite this, we believe the functionality it adds to an iPhone makes its £59 asking price seriously tempting. Equally tempting is the £89 Family Pack, which includes one individual MobileMe subscription plus four Family Member Accounts, each with a unique email address, iDisk folder and 5GB of online storage. It requires Mac OS X 10.5.8 or later, Safari 3.1 or Firefox 3 or later on a Mac. Windows users require Windows 7, Vista or XP Home or Professional, and Internet Explorer 7, Safari 3.1 or Firefox 3 or later. Your iPhone must also be running the version 3.1 software, which comes pre-installed on the iPhone 3G or later.

Apple's MobileMe service lets you synchronise data over a wide range of devices. By using the @me.com email address that comes as part of the package you can send, read and reply to the same messages on a Mac or PC (*top*), iPad (*middle*) and iPhone (*left*), giving you an inbox that is accessible everywhere, whatever your chosen device.

Contacts

Considering the importance of a good address book to most mobile phone users, the Contacts application on the original iPhone was fairly well hidden. It was a sub-section of several other applications, and therefore missed out on a Home screen button of its own. That has now been remedied, and Contacts now has its own entry on the Home screen.

Contacts are organised into groups, but you can only set these using the contacts system on your computer, rather than on the iPhone itself. To view the contents of each one, click on the group's name and scroll through the list of names that appears.

Running down the right-hand side of the screen you will see a small alphabet. Sliding your finger down this will quickly skip through heading letters in your address book, allowing you to scroll much more quickly through your contacts.

Once you have located the particular contact that you are after, you can use their information in a number of ways. Tapping on their name brings up their full contact record (*right*) and gives you one-click access to emailing or phoning them if you have filled in those details already. Or, if your contact has a website and you have included its URL then you can visit that too.

By clicking on the postal address, you will launch the Maps application, which will centre on their home or office address, and tag that spot with their name. In addition to finding their address, this information will also be added to their record in the address book.

Finally, buttons at the bottom of the screen let you message them, while an Edit button at the top lets you make changes.

Bookmarking your buddies

One group that is maintained on the iPhone itself, and has its own button on the bar at the bottom of the phone application's screen, is the Favorites list, where you store your most-used contacts.

Scroll to the bottom of a contact's record and you will see a button marked Add to Favorites. Tap it and when you click on Favorites, you will be given speedy access to their record – and any others you have added – without having to scroll through the whole of your address book.

If you subsequently need to remove a contact from this list, click on Edit at the top of the screen and the red negative symbol appears to the left of their name. You will be asked to confirm by tapping the Remove button that appears to the right. Don't worry – it is not a destructive edit: they are only removed from the Favorites list, not from your address book.

Whether you are using a Mac or PC, it is easy to export your contacts to the iPhone so that you can dial them directly without using the keypad.

Texting from the address book

The Address Book's final feature is integrated text messaging. This is accessed in much the same way as the Favorites list, by clicking on Text Message at the foot of a contact's record. If it contains more than one phone number, you will be asked to choose where the message should be sent and then taken to the messaging application.

Adding contacts

By far the easiest way to manage your contacts is through your PC or Mac. Mac users will do this using Mac OS X's build-in Address Book application, Microsoft Entourage or Yahoo! Address Book. For Windows users, the choices are Windows Address Book (also found in Outlook Express), Microsoft Outlook and Yahoo! Address Book.

On both platforms, you need to synchronise your contacts with the iPhone using iTunes. Set it running and connect your iPhone. When it appears in the sidebar, click on its icon and then on the Contacts tab in the application's main pane. Here you can select whether to copy across every address on your system, or just synchronise a selection of contact groups.

If you need to add contacts when you are on the move, and do so on your iPhone, they will be sent back to your computer when you next connect it. To add one, click on the + icon on the top bar and fill in the form that appears with as much information as you can. When it comes to entering the phone number, you may sometimes need to have the phone pause for a while – for example, if you are automatically logging in to telephone banking. This is easily achieved by tapping the '+*#' button on the bottom left of the keyboard, and then 'pause' from the new keypad that appears. Several pauses can be entered in a row in this way to cope with slower systems.

You can also assign a specific ring tone to new contacts, allowing you to differentiate between different groups of people, so you know whether to dive for your phone on a work day to answer a family call, or let it keep ringing at weekend when the boss-assigned tone starts to play.

Calendar

You would have to go a long way to find a more attractive calendaring application than the one that features on the iPhone. It is bold, smooth and ridiculously simple to use.

Navigating your calendar

By default, the application launches as a monthly overview, with the present day highlighted and any events that take place within the next 24 hours shown below. Days on which events will be taking place are marked with a small dot below the date number.

Clicking on an event calls up any associated details, such as its duration and location, all of which is drawn from the original record, as entered on your computer or on the iPhone itself.

There is a choice of three different views: List, Day and Month. Day will give the most detailed view of the selected 24 hours, with meetings and events shown on a grid as blobs blocking out the hours during which they take place. Any all-day events will be sectioned off at the top of the listing and remain visible at all times, like a frozen row in a spreadsheet.

The final option, List, dispenses with graphics altogether and gives a condensed run-down of forthcoming events, which is by far the most effective way to get an overview of future commitments. You can scroll through it at speed with a flick of the thumb. To skip back to the present day from any of these views, click on the Today button at the top of the screen.

Adding and editing events

You can edit all events in situ by tapping on them and then pressing the Edit button at the top of the screen. This calls up a form with fields for a title and location, start and end times, a repeat frequency (most events will be one time only, so you can ignore this in a lot of cases), whether or not you

The iPhone Calendar is not only good looking: it is also versatile, with a range of views giving you a quick overview of the current day's events, a view of anything on the horizon or a monthly calendar with spots on the days on which you have meetings or tasks to complete..

want to have an alert to remind you of the forthcoming event (if you add one, you will then have the opportunity to add a second one), and a field for general notes.

At the bottom of the form, you will also see a large red button to delete the event. Its function is self-explanatory, but rest assured that should you tap it in error, you will be asked to confirm the deletion, so it will not be lost by shaky fingers.

New events that don't arrive through synchronisation with a computer or MobileMe are entered using exactly the same form as the editing tool. From any of the three calendar views, click on the + button at the top of the screen, and then tap each of the various fields to step through the different data types required.

Note that by default the iPhone will time all new events to start at noon and finish at 1pm on the present day. Change this by tapping the start and end times field to call up the selection tool, which looks very much like the tumblers found in a fruit machine. Each can be individually rotated by dragging them around their axes until they spell out the appropriate time and date.

A slider switch below lets you specify that an event spans a whole day – such as an anniversary – but be wary that as soon as you slide this, the display changes very subtly. The hours and minutes tumblers disappear, quite appropriately, but so does the day of the week, which is much less helpful and leaves you to guess whether 9 September is a Monday, a Wednesday or something else altogether. Our tip is to set your start and end dates using the regular tumblers, and then only activate the whole day event slider when they are correct.

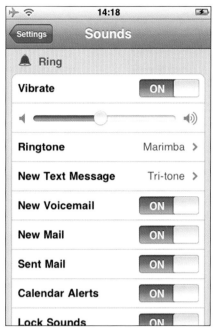

The option to turn on and off audible calendar alerts it found in the iPhone's Settings application.

The alert option lets you specify when you should be reminded of an event that is heading your way before it takes place. You have seven pre-defined options ranging from five minutes to two days in advance of its start, but can't change the tone used to alert you, which is a shame as it is an irritating squeak.

The only option you do have where alerts are concerned is to turn them on or off altogether. This is done through the main system settings tool, accessed from the Home screen through Settings > Sounds, and then the slider beside Calendar alerts. By sliding it to off and back to on, you will be given a demonstration of the sound, and you will see what we mean about the squeak. With audible alerts turned off, reminders will still appear as pop-ups on your iPhone screen.

Note that switching off the alerts option does not disable the option to add alerts to your events, as this would mean they would be missing should you later switch back on the centralised alerts preference. Instead, it simply stops them from sounding when they become due.

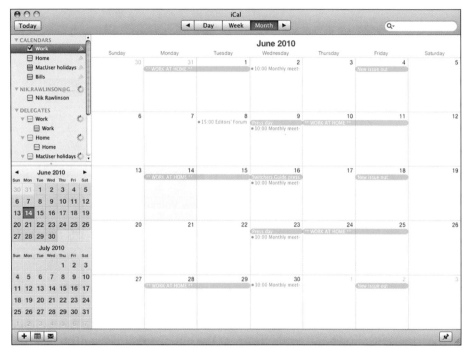

The Calendar application synchronises via MobileMe with iCal on your Mac or alternative calendaring applications on the PC so you are always up to date.

You can manage your calendars directly on your iPhone or through MobileMe if you have signed up for an account, in which case you will use a rendering of the calendar through your browser, which will be available wherever you have an Internet connection. However, the easiest method is to use a calendaring application on your Mac or PC so that you have the freedom to enter and edit entries with a mouse and full-size keyboard rather than a small point and tap interface on the iPhone.

When you have set up your calendars on your desktop machine they can be synchronised wirelessly using MobileMe or by cable whenever you connect your iPhone to your computer by setting up synchronisation through iTunes. Although this will obviously keep your calendar up to date on both devices you must be sure to synchronise the two regularly or entries made by one method will not be reflected on the other device.

Synchronising your iPhone

Most mobile phones are designed to be used on their own. They have very simple internal operating systems that perform a limited range of tasks, and need little or no maintenance. This harks back to the days of the earliest telephones – when they were much larger devices than even the chunkiest modern-day mobile – which did little more than make calls and, if you were lucky, tell you who was calling.

Few even had anything so technological as a built-in phone book, so the idea of music playback, integrated email and route planning with satellite photography did not even enter their designers' minds. That is where the iPhone is different: it is the first phone designed from the ground up to be a fully fledged PC and Mac companion, and work equally as well as an ultra-portable, hand-held computer. For this reason, it integrates closely with iTunes, Apple's free music organisation software, whose ever-expanding functions make its name less accurate by the day.

Whenever you dock your iPhone, it will appear in the list of connected devices in iTunes' sidebar, along with your music and video library, podcast listings and so on. This is much the same as an iPod would do, and clicking on its name will give you a similar range of functions, presenting you with a tabbed interface through which you can control manual or automatic synchronisation of your contacts, music, videos, podcasts and photos.

While the original iPhone shipped with a Dock to facilitate this operation, the iPhone 3G and later's Dock is an optional extra, and not bundled in the box. You may see this as cost cutting, as you do still get a cable for transferring your music, videos and television programmes, and which connects to the bundled power adaptor for charging the battery, but Apple would prefer you to synchronise your data using the MobileMe service and only use iTunes for movies and music. This replaced the ageing .Mac service that had poor PC compatibility, and suffered performance issues in Europe. MobileMe stores all of your contacts, email addresses, appointments, web pages and photo galleries on

Mac users with a copy of iLife can use the suite's iPhoto application to manage photos taken on the iPhone and transferred using the bundled cable.

Apple's own servers, and synchronises them with every device you have registered with the service, including PCs, Macs and the iPhone itself.

The benefit to you is that you always have the most up-to-date set of data at your fingertips, wherever you happen to need it. The benefit to Apple is that it can charge an additional £59 a year for providing the service, which you should factor into your calculations when considering the purchase price of the iPhone and monthly contract fees when deciding whether it is the right phone for you.

MobileMe is by no means a compulsory add-on, though, and you can still synchronise your data manually, in the same way you would with an iPod by using the included cable and iTunes software.

If you are a Mac user, you have by far the simplest choice: you stick with the Apple defaults of iPhoto for photos and Address Book for contacts. Do note, however, that while Address Book is bundled with the operating system, Mac OS X, iPhoto is part of the ever-expanding iLife suite, which costs an additional £71 (£89 for the family edition). The only other way to obtain a legal copy is to buy a new Mac, in which case it will be pre-installed. If you have an old edition of iLife, you may need to upgrade.

PC users have a wider choice of applications. Contacts can be stored in Yahoo! Address Book, Outlook Express, Outlook and Windows Address Book, while photos can be managed through either Photoshop Album 2.0 or later, or Photoshop Elements 3.0 or later, both from Adobe.

However, the iPhone is designed to be more than just a transportation and playback device for your media, with its synchronisation features expanding to encompass browser bookmarks (from Safari on the Mac, and Safari and Internet Explorer on the PC), and your email account settings (from Mail on the Mac, and Outlook or Outlook Express on the PC). Note, though, that if you transfer your email settings you will copy only the information the iPhone needs to know before it can gain access to the server; you will not actually transfer any of your mail messages themselves.

The range of applications compatible with the iPhone shows up some inconsistencies in the way Apple has implemented various features on the device, for while it will happily synchronise with an Entourage address book, it will not draw in Entourage email settings on the Mac. The situation is similar, although not quite the same when it comes to calendars. PC-hosted iPhones will read Outlook calendars, yet on the Mac they will only read calendars administered by iCal – not those overseen by Entourage. There is fortunately a workaround here in that by linking your Entourage and iCal calendars, so that Entourage events appear on Apple's default calendaring application, you will see that entries posted in Entourage are automatically transferred to the iPhone at each sync.

As the term synchronisation suggests, changes are often two-way affairs, with as much information passing from the iPhone to the computer, as from the computer to the iPhone. Fortunately, this interchange has been intelligently implemented, with the iPhone interface software recognising that at times the host computer will need to maintain its existing settings, regardless of what you do remotely to their copies on the iPhone.

Changes made to an email account on the iPhone do not, therefore, affect the status of the account on the host computer, thus allowing you to specify that the iPhone should leave all messages on the server, whether downloaded or not, allowing you to download a permanent second copy at a later point for archiving on your main computer.

By default, all cable-based synchronisation with a Mac or PC will be done automatically, so that every time you connect your iPhone to your computer the two will swap the necessary data to keep them both up to date.

If you would rather not have them automatically synchronise and instead instigate it yourself, open iTunes' Preferences and click on the Devices tab, then check the box beside *Prevent iPods, iPhones and iPads from synching automatically*. Coming out of the Preferences, the option to *Sync only ticked songs and videos*, allows you to tick off the music, podcasts and so on in your library that you want to take with you and leave the boxes beside your B-list tracks cleared to prevent them from transferring. This is particularly important on lower-capacity iPhones where you will want to get the best out of the limited space on offer.

You can prevent iTunes from automatically swapping data between your iPhone and Mac or PC and thus retain greater control yourself by checking the appropriate box in its Preferences pane.

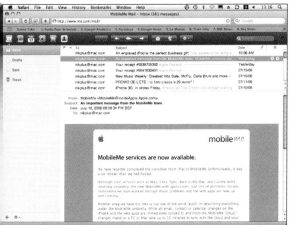

MobileMe makes it easy to sync your data over the mobile phone network or a wifi access point. It also has a web-based front-end so that even when you are away from your computer or iPhone, you can access your calendar, contacts and email. The service, which works with both Macs and PCs, costs £59 per year.

If you frequently connect your iPhone to your computer as a means of charging it, perhaps because you keep the adaptor plug at home but connect by USB with you get to the office, there will more than likely be times when you want to connect it only to charge the battery, and not to swap any data. If you have authorised iTunes to automatically sync your devices, you will therefore want to prevent it from running away with itself. In this instance, pre-empt matters by starting iTunes in advance of plugging in your iPhone, and then hold the Command and Alt (also commonly called Option) keys on the Mac, or the Control and Shift keys on the PC as you connect the iPhone to the computer. iTunes will now ignore the iPhone, and while it will not mount, it will still receive charge.

Apple bundled a Dock with the first edition of the iPhone, which greatly facilitated cable-based charging and syncing. This was not included with the iPhone 4 (or indeed the 3G or 3GS). However, the Universal Dock, which includes a remote, remains an optional extra at £36. This is seen by many as a sensible investment as it allows you to keep an eye on the iPhone's screen while you are working, and keeps it safe from the kind of scratches it could attract if left laying around on the desk.

The phone

A key feature of the iPhone, as its name would suggest, is a highly graphical mobile phone that makes excellent use of the 3.5in high-resolution touchscreen display to give you a great deal of control over your incoming and outgoing calls.

The Phone features sit behind the green Phone icon on the toolbar at the bottom of the Home screen (unless you have moved it to the main screen area), which also gives you access to your contacts and voicemail. Network coverage, meanwhile, is indicated by a signal strength diagram at the top of the screen that shows your service provider name and a ramped graph of five strength bars to indicate the quality of the signal you are receiving. The greater the number of bars you can see, the stronger your phone signal will be. A small badge stating 3G beside this indicates that you have fast mobile Internet coverage. A circle indicates slower coverage that may impact on the performance of browsing and checking email.

Placing a call

The quickest and easiest way to make a call is to tap Contacts or Favorites on the bar at the bottom of the Phone application, and choose a name from your contact list. However, you can also repeat recent calls or return missed incoming numbers by selecting from the list stored behind the Recents icon, or dial a number from scratch using the keypad (*left*). If you decide to opt for the keypad, you can employ a certain amount of automation by inserting pauses in the dialled number, by pressing the # key once for each pause required. Once your call is connected and the iPhone is pressed to your ear, the screen's touch-sensitive surface will be disabled to avoid any accidental button pressing by your cheek or ear. However, removing it from your ear will give you access to a range of call-management features, which you can access through a large semi-transparent interface. This gives you one-click access to muting or placing the call on hold, adding the other party to your contacts list, entering tones using the keypad or simultaneously dialling another number so you can set up a conference call.

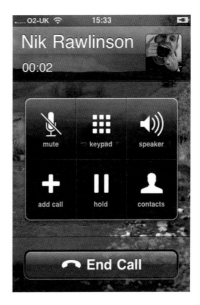

Conference calling

Tapping the Add Call button (*above*) will place any existing callers on hold so you can add a second or third call. Choose your additional correspondent from your contacts list, or dial using the keypad, and you will be able to talk to them before 'merging' the calls so that all parties can conference together. Be aware, however, that even if the original call was incoming, and so would not be billed to you, any additional calls you make to invoke a conference call will incur charges on your own bill.

Visual voicemail

If you miss or decline an incoming call, the iPhone will take a message, like all well-behaved mobile phones. However, where it differs from regular phones is the way it then lets you manage stored messages.

iPhone introduced the idea of visual voicemail, which works in a similar way to text messages, in that you can see details of all received messages and then listen to them in whichever order you choose. This is a network-dependent feature and users of hacked iPhones running on non-authorised networks will not be able to use this feature.

If you have not yet set up your voicemail, you will be asked for a password and prompted to record an outgoing message the first time you tap the Voicemail button. Not everyone likes the sound of their own voice, so there is an option of a default message provided by the network, but some callers do consider network messages rather impersonal. Once you have been through this short setup process, the Phone logo on the iPhone Home screen and the Voicemail logo on the Phone application interface will both show the number of stored messages.

Opening the Voicemail features of the Phone application draws down a list of waiting messages from the network provider's server, tagging each one with the caller's name if they appear in your contacts list.

Tap each message to download it to your iPhone, at which point it will start to play. You can control the message using the play and pause buttons, or by dragging the progress slider to skip forwards and backwards through boring sections to reach important information. Messages are stored on the server for 30 days from the time they are first listened to, at which point they are erased.

Managing your messages

Various control buttons give you further control over the message, with a speaker button at the top that sends it to the iPhone's internal speaker rather than any connected headphones, a red Delete button erasing it from the phone, and a green Call Back button for returning the caller's call.

Deleted messages are not gone for good, however, as they are simply moved to the bottom of the call list, allowing you to listen to them again at a later point.

Sometimes you will receive calls from numbers that are not yet in your contacts list. If you would like to add the caller as a contact, tap the blue circle to the right of each one and select Create New Contact. You will be taken to the contacts application, at which point you can fill in the remaining details. On other occasions an existing contact will call from a number you don't already have in your records, at which point you can tap the same button and instead select Add To Existing Contact.

Weather

The weather application closely mimics the weather widget on the Dashboard found in Mac OS X. It is a simple, graphical representation of the forecast for the next six days, with a large icon at the top showing the current conditions. It is updated by the minute, so you may even notice that this changes for your local area in perfect synchronisation with conditions outside your window.

Like its Dashboard equivalent, the weather widget is a two-sided application. One side is the forecast itself; the other is where you set it up. Tap the 'i' button in the lower right-hand corner to flip it around and then enter the name of the city you want to add to the application. Bear in mind that not all locations will be covered, as not all have a local weather centre, so you may have to try nearby places if yours is missing. Airports are usually covered as accurate weather forecasting is crucial to safe flying, so if you live close to an airfield, try that instead of your home town.

Add as many cities as you need and then flip with widget back around to show the forecasts. If you added more than one you can now scroll through them in the same way you flick through photos in the iPhone camera album, by sliding them across the screen with your finger. The dots at the bottom of the screen show you how many cities have been added to the application, with the brightest showing you the position in the stack of the one you are currently viewing. A final function is integration with Yahoo guides. Tap the Y! icon in the bottom left-hand corner of the screen to check out an events guide for the current active city.

The weather application is one of the many apps on the iPhone that requires an active Internet connection.

Notes

In its default state, the iPhone is missing some key applications, such as a spreadsheet, simple database and word processor. This is not entirely surprising – it is a phone, not a computer, after all – and you can plug the gaps by using online applications, such as Google web-based office suite at *docs.google.com*. This should always be available over the iPhone's wifi or 3G connection, but when you just want to make a quick note it can be overkill.

That is where the iPhone's own Notes application comes in. It is a simple jotter with the appearance of a regular notepad, the only limitation being that you have to enter text using the on-screen keyboard, as there is obviously no way to use the iPhone with a stylus. This also means you can't draw sketches or scribble random thoughts in the margin.

New notes are added by tapping the + icon on the toolbar, and you can flick back and forwards between them using the arrow keys. As you do, you will notice that the buff pages turn over, as they would in a regular notebook. When you delete a note by tapping the dustbin button at the bottom of the page it is sucked down into the icon for disposal.

Like Mail, the Notes application is a good place to draft information you need to send to colleagues, as it connects directly with the iPhone's email client. If you have already set up your iPhone for email usage, clicking on the envelope icon on the toolbar will dispatch the current note using your default account. Rather confusingly, this is set through the Home screen's Settings application, in the Mail subsection.

You can also use the iPhone's copy and paste features to include just small parts of a note in an email if you do not want to send the whole thing.

Calculator

It may seem a waste to buy something so expensive, sleek and technologically advanced as an iPhone and then use it for nothing more challenging than addition and multiplication, but the fact remains that the iPhone's calculator is among the best on any phone. It is clear and has large graphical buttons, really benefiting from the multi-touch display in a way that no conventional phone can ever hope to rival.

In its original incarnation, it was nothing more than a regular upright adding machine with the four key mathematical functions (addition, subtraction, multiplication and division) supplemented by some simple memory functions. Ever since the arrival of the iPhone 3G and the iPhone 2.0 software, both of which have been superceded many times, it has now been massively expanded and is context aware. Using it in portrait orientation presents you with the same regular calculator as was found on the first phone. Rotate it through 90°, though, and it will sense the change of orientation and present you with a range of scientific functions that would rival even the most advanced dedicated calculator. Of course, these features have sustained and appear in iPhone 4 and iOS 4.

There is still no print-out function or virtual paper roll for mobile accountants, but if you want to work out the diameter of a circle, compile log tables or factor the cosine of a variable then you should find it does

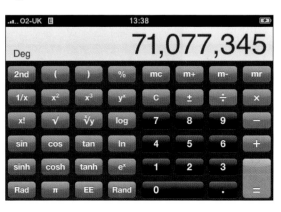

everything you need. The iPhone is never likely to unseat dedicated scientific calculators from the likes of HP – particularly not in the world of academia – but this is a useful add-on that brings features formerly found only in full computer-based operating systems to every iPhone owner's pocket.

Camera

The camera was the only disappointing feature of the original iPhone and the iPhone 3G, as both were limited to 2 megapixels, decided on their own focal point and couldn't do video. The 3GS fixed all of that, upping the resolution to 3 megapixels, introducing tap to focus and recording video, while iPhone 4 features a 5 megapixel camera in the back of the case and an additional personal camera in the front that is of lower resolution and is used for making video calls using the FaceTime application. In this section we shall discuss the primary rear-mounted camera.

In its default mode, the camera is set up for taking still images. You tap on the item in the image on which you want to focus, and take the picture by tapping the shutter button below it (*see below right*). The last picture you took is shown in the thumbnail to the bottom-left of the interface. Tapping this takes you to your camera roll from which you can manipulate and share your images.

Moving pictures

The iPhone 3GS and 4 camera is also a surprisingly competent video camera. The switch in the bottom-right corner of the interface toggles between still and moving images, allowing you to capture smooth motion at 30 frames per second with a maximum resolution of 640 x 480 pixels on the iPhone 3GS and 30 frames per second at 720p resolution on the iPhone 4, which matches one of the standards for high definition (HD) recording. Naturally, they both also record sound. The clever part comes when you have finished recording your video and saved it to your camera roll.

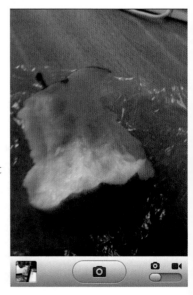

The video interface *(left)* is similar to the one for photos, but with an extra button for playback. Use the yellow sliders around the film strip to trim the movie to just the section you want *(right)*.

Clicking on it in the library calls up the video – just as it calls up a photo –but with a few key differences. For starters, the opening frame is overlaid by a play button. Tapping this starts playback.

More importantly, though, above the image is a film strip showing the frames that make up your video. Tapping on this lets you edit the movie to contain just the portion you want, by dragging in the yellow edges of the film strip towards the centre *(see above)*.

When you have isolated the part that you want to keep, press the yellow trim button to remove the frames that fall outside of the yellow area. Only ever perform this operation after due care and attention, as the removed frames are gone forever: there is no 'undo' feature or recycle bin from which they can be retrieved.

Unfortunately that is the full extent of the iPhone's native video editing tools; it can't splice together separate parts of a movie, or indeed separate movies altogether, but it still represents an advance over most of its competitors that are happy to shoot video but will not take you any further than that.

Once your movie is edited to your requirements, you can email it, post it to a MobileMe gallery, publish it directly on YouTube or send it to a friend's phone by MMS.

Taking things further with iMovie

When he announced the iPhone 4 at 2010's WorldWide Developers' Conference (WWDC), Steve Jobs also announced a forthcoming addition to the iTunes Store: iMovie for iPhone.

This is a spin-off from the company's hugely successful iMovie application for the Mac, which it ships as part of its iLife suite of consumer apps. Apple has a long, strong history of developing video applications, so it will build on the successes it has had at every level, right up to the professional arena where it ships Final Cut Studio, which is used to cut together commercials, TV shows and blockbuster movies.

iMovie is an iPhone 4 exclusive application, so it won't be available for use on earlier models, but if you have upgraded to the latest handset then Apple claims it will allow you to edit true HD movies on the go and publish them to the web from anywhere. It goes without saying, of course, that if you choose to publish to the web when you are connected over the cellphone network then you should make sure you will not be exceeding any data transfer limits on your contract.

Just as Apple re-wrote its iWork applications for use on the iPad where you do not have the benefit of a mouse and may not be using a physical keyboard, so it has retooled iMovie for use with a multitouch sensitive screen. You can drag slips to the required length, zoom the timeline by unpinching and scrub through your movie by dragging your finger across the screen. iMovie ships with five themes – modern, bright, travel, playful and news – each of which comprises video elements and music to brighten up your production. It is even clever enough to dip the volume of backing tracks when your narration kicks in, so you don't need to be an expert editor to get professional-looking (and sounding) results.

Finished projects can be sent as multimedia messages, uploaded to MobileMe or sent straight to YouTube.

Posting photos to a gallery

If you want to share your photos with family of friends, you can post them directly to the web from an iPhone using MobileMe's web gallery features. This can be done through MobileMe's web interface on both the Mac or PC, while Mac users also have the option of posting from iPhoto, which comes with all new Macs and is found in the iLife suite.

If you meet all of these requirements, you will already have a MobileMe email address. Use these details to set up a new email account in the iPhone's Mail application and the Photos application will use the details you supply to link your iPhone to the associated web space.

You now need to put your iPhone to one side and switch to iPhoto 08 or later on your Mac, or MobileMe in a browser. We will deal with iPhoto first. Select a range of images and click on the + icon at the bottom of

The easiest way for Mac users to create galleries is through iPhoto. PC users should create them through the MobileMe web interface.

the screen. This brings up a window through which you can gather the images together in an album, print them in a book or as an individual photo, or publish them online in a web gallery. It is this latter feature that interests us here.

Click on the Web Gallery icon, give the new gallery a name, check the box beside Allow photo uploading by email, and then click on Publish. If you would rather create galleries through the browser, log in to your MobileMe account, click on the photo icon at the top of the screen (a sunflower) and then the + button at the bottom to create a new album. Give it a name, tick the box to allow adding of photos via email or iPhone and then click on create.

Done all that? Good. You have now jumped through all the hoops you need to start publishing from your iPhone.

Return to your phone and open the Photos application. Navigate to the album from which you want to post to your newly created Web Galleries and pick the appropriate images. When they are displayed, tap the Action icon in the bottom left-hand corner and tap Send To MobileMe on the menu that appears. The iPhone will interrogate your MobileMe account and call up a list of available galleries to which you can post. Choose the one you want, give your photo a name and a short description and then tap Publish at the top of the screen.

Your iPhone will quietly send your image to your MobileMe gallery (previously it invoked Mail at this point and sent it as an email) and, once it's done, it pulls up a menu allowing you to view the image on your site or tell a friend (or close the dialogue if you'd rather do neither). The first of these options opens the gallery in a browser, while the second starts a new email with a link to the image that you can send to the contact of your choosing. You must have Mail set up to do this.

Spotlight search

One of the most radical features in Apple's computer operating systems – whatever device you are using – is a search tool called Spotlight. It makes an extensive index of the contents of your internal and connected hard drives and flash storage and produces speedy and comprehensive search results when you type a term into the box that drops down from the menu bar at the top of the screen.

The results include not only files, based on their file name, but also photos, documents and spreadsheets (based on their contents as well as their name), entries in your address book, definitions from the system dictionary and even applications, allowing you to launch an application with a few taps on the keyboard.

Now, with the iPhone's operating system being based on the same code as the full-size Mac OS X, Spotlight has appeared on the iPhone.

It is hidden to the left of the first menu screen, and accessed by sweeping the screen to the right. This reveals a very simple interface: just an input box and the system keyboard.

To use Spotlight, type your query into the box and tap Search. The iPhone will then populate a live list of results that will grow the longer you leave it running. If it doesn't include the results you want right away, just leave it running for longer and they will probably appear, or type some further text into the input box.

The results cover all of the native applications on the phone, and are split up according to application for ease of use. Tapping on any result will take you to its entry in the relevant application, saving you from remembering where you filed any particular piece of information.

Voice memos

You don't need a tape recorder if you have your iPhone with you. That's just as well really, because they're horribly out of date, and nobody wants to be bothering with fiddly cassettes these days.

With the release of the iPhone 3.0 software update, Apple added a brand new application: Voice Memos. At first appearances this looks like a very simple tool, but once you start to explore you'll see that it has several cool features. It remains on the iPhone as part of iOS 4.

When first launched, you're presented with a simple graphic showing an old-fashioned microphone, beneath which is a volume meter and a two buttons: one record button with a red spot, and one menu button sporting three horizontal lines.

To make your first recording, tap on the record button and speak close to the microphone. You'll see the needle on the volume meter at the bottom of the display twitch to indicate how well it is receiving your voice. You should aim to keep this at around the '0' mark, just before the meter

turns red, to make a clean recording with the minimum of background noise or overloaded distortion.

The top of the screen turns red to indicate that you are making a recording, and a stopwatch counts up, timing your recording. You can pause at any time by tapping the record button again – which has now become a pause button – and stop by pressing the menu button, which will have transformed itself into a stop button sporting a classic black square.

As soon as you have stopped the recording, it is saved to your library, and can be accessed by pressing the menu button. You will now be presented with a list of

memo files. If you have made more than one they will be listed in reverse chronological order, with your most recent at the top. Each one is marked by the time and date it was made, with its duration shown to the right. Beside the duration is a button taking you to extra features. Tap this and you can start to customise the information attached to each recording. For example, the time is not a good descriptive device to help you remember what each one is about, so start by tapping the large box at the top of the next screen and, when given a choice of pre-defined tags for your file, click Custom and enter one of your own.

For example, you might want to use the tag 'Shopping List' if the recording is a number of items you know you need to buy next time you go to the supermarket.

Returning to the information screen you'll see that the new tag has been applied as the file's name, and it will also be used in the file listing on the menu page.

However, the customisation screen also lets you share your recording by emailing it to a contact, at which point it is attached to an email in m4a format, with your tag again used as the file name.

There is no way to upload voice memos direct to a web site, unfortunately, even if you change the tag to something appropriate like Podcast. If you want to do this, your best bet is to email it to yourself and then upload it once you have received it on your Mac or PC.

Messages

No mobile worth its salts would get anywhere without a text messaging application. For many users, texting – not phoning – is the very reason for having a mobile in their pocket all day.

Messaging works a little differently on the iPhone to the way it does on a regular cell phone. In the first instance, that's because it uses the iPhone's on-screen keyboard, with intelligent error correction, rather than the poky hardware-based keyboards of most mobile phones.

As such, the iPhone does away with one key feature of modern mobile phones: T9, better known as predictive text. Standing for Text on 9 keys, T9 was invented as a way to speed up texting, allowing mobile phone users to press just 4663 4663 when they wanted to say we have 'gone home' (the letters g-o-n-e and h-o-m-e are found on the keys 4, 6, 6 and 3) and then scroll through all the possible words that combination makes. For those who have got used to it, it is a massive time-saver.

Before T9, though, there was so-called Txt spk, or text speak, where abbreviations like 'm8', 'lol' and 'cu l8r' would be used as substitutes for the more cumbersome 'mate', 'laugh out loud' and 'see you later'.

And now we have the iPhone, which has once again revolutionised the way text messaging works. It does understand some text speak, capitalising lol to LOL as appropriate, but in all other ways it throws out the rulebook. This can be a boon, allowing you to quickly construct coherent, well put together messages without tapping each button several times, or scrolling through suggested options for each key combination. This can be a blessing or a curse, depending on your point of view. If you're the recipient, it's probably a good thing as it means you won't have to decode obscure abbreviations and unnatural capitalisations. If you're the sender, though, you might not be so keen, as it means you have to type your notes in full, and may not be able to get all that you want to say in a single message. Fortunately most iPhone tariffs come with a very generous number of messages included as part of the deal.

However, the most radical difference between texting on a regular phone and an iPhone is the way that the iPhone handles message conversations.

Most mobile phones have a separate inbox and sent messages folder, which means that you can only track one half of a conversation at a time. If you want to follow the thread, you need to skip back and forth between the two. The iPhone overcomes this annoyance by interleaving the two sets of messages (*left*) so that they appear within speech bubbles like exchanges in iChat and some other computer-based instant messaging applications.

As well as making it possible to quickly track back exactly who said what and when, this means that your messaging screens are kept tidy, and you only ever need to visit one thread to see all of the exchanges between yourself and each contact.

Messages are organised through the SMS entry on the Home screen, with a menu showing you a list of all the contacts with whom you have had SMS contact. Tap one and it will bring up a conversation-style record of those contacts over time, with each part time and date stamped. Any messages to or from someone who is not yet in your inbox will be filed under their number, with a button to add them to your contacts.

Sending a text message

New messages are composed by tapping the square button with the pen inside it at the top of the menu screen, which will open a new blank message and position your cursor in the To: box, ready for your contact's number. If you want to send a message to someone already stored in your address book, press the blue + button to the right of this box and select your contact. Alternatively, just start typing your contact's name and, if they are in your address book, the application will attempt to complete the entry for you. You can add several contacts by pressing the + button again for each additional person, and the iPhone will send identical messages to each one in turn. Once your contacts have been added, tap in the oval entry box just above the keyboard and type your message, and tap Send when you are done. Be sure you have checked your spelling before you do this and that the iPhone's built-in spelling checker has not introduced any words you did not expect, as it is sent immediately.

If you only want to send a message to one single contact, you can do so by tapping the Text Message button below their entry in the Address Book. This will drop you into the SMS application and pre-populate their details in the To field.

Your sent messages will be archived under the contact's name or, if they're not in your address book, their number, with replies added below it as they arrive.

Requesting receipts

One feature that is missing from the iPhone's default messaging tools is delivery reception, which informs you when your message has arrived at the recipient's inbox. This is a surprising omission, from both the application itself and its entry in the centralised Settings application.

However, there is a work-around, which is to use your network's reception report short code. In the UK, on O2, this is *0#. To request a receipt, add the short code to the start of your message like this:

*0# What time will you arrive?

When you send this message it may take a few seconds more to arrive on your recipient's phone, but when it does the *0# will be stripped out, and they will only see what follows. The network will then bounce back a report to your iPhone telling you that the message was received. The receipt will appear in your Messaging inbox, as part of the thread of messages you are having with your contact, and take the form:

> Message [message ID] to [recipient phone number] was delivered at 13:56 on 18/08/10. Text: What time will you arrive?

If you are on a different network then obviously O2's receipt code will have to be changed as appropriate.

Picture messaging

Picture messaging – so-called MMS or Multimedia Messaging Service – was introduced with the iPhone 3.0 software update. However, as with GPS functionality and the integrated compass, it is also hardware reliant, so if you

bought an original iPhone and haven't yet upgraded to an iPhone 3G or later (including iPhone 4), you won't be able to either send or receive picture messages – simply upgrading your operating system isn't enough.

If you are still using the first generation iPhone (with the brushed aluminium back), picture messaging is off the cards, in both directions. There will be no option to activate the feature in the Settings, no option to attach a photo to a text message, and no way to receive a picture message on the phone itself. Instead you'll receive a message (*left*) asking you to visit your network provider's site and enter your phone number and a pin code to view the image online. If you have

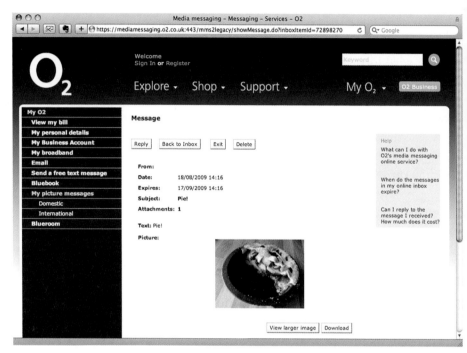

If you don't have an iPhone 3G or later, you will have to log on to your network provider's site with your number and code to access incoming picture messages.

one of the more up to date models, however, incoming images will appear in the conversation exchange as an image within a speech bubble. To send a multimedia message, tap the camera icon on the bottom bar and pick either Take Photo or Video, or Choose Existing, to insert it in the conversation stream. Original iPhone users will not see this button, and neither will anyone with a later iPhone who has disabled MMS through the iPhone Settings dialogue to prevent running up high roaming charges.

Organising your messages

Over time you will want to start culling some of your messages. For one thing, they all take up space, and for another, your texting conversations can start to look quite long. It also makes sense to periodically cull more sensitive exchanges, such as those containing phone numbers that you might not want to become public knowledge for anyone who happens to pick up your phone.

Fortunately organising your messages is just as easy as organising your emails in the Mail application. Start by opening the conversation thread you want to moderate and tap the Edit button at the top of the screen. Each entry will shift slightly to the right to reveal a check button on the left. Select the messages you want to manipulate by tapping on the buttons beside each one, and then select either Forward or Delete, depending on what you want to do.

Forwarding a message will send it on as though it originally came from you. Deleting it will wipe it from the conversation thread. Be wary of doing this without careful thought: as there is no Recycle or Trash bin on the iPhone, you won't get the message back, and there is no confirmation step.

You can also delete whole conversation threads by returning to the message index screen, tapping Edit and then the delete buttons to the left of each thread. This time around there is a confirmation step, as you must press the Delete button that appears to remove the message.

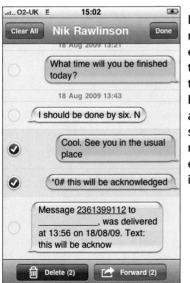

Delete text messages or even whole threads by tapping the Edit button and then selecting the relevant entries in your inbox list.

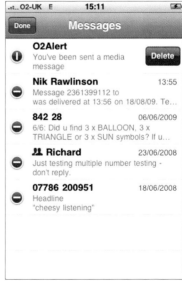

YouTube

Google's online video sharing site is one of the web's most popular, so it was little wonder that as it has been working so closely with Apple on several initiatives over the years, it should also feature on the iPhone.

The application is a custom-written front end to the site, allowing you to watch featured and most viewed movies from the opening screen, or search for new videos. Tapping the 'more' button lets you search for top rated and most recently added videos, trawl your history, watch movies you have uploaded yourself, and manage your subscriptions and playlists.

The presentation is excellent, with a thumbnail of each video, details of when it was uploaded, how it has been rated by other YouTube visitors and how long it lasts. Clicking the blue arrow beside each one will start them playing.

The iPhone YouTube application lets you email and bookmark favourite clips.

Steve Jobs said the iPhone was the best way to view YouTube, and it is easy to see why. Apple has taken an already-excellent website and wrapped it in a first-class interface that simply blows the browser-based version out of the water. If this is what the future of TV-on-the-go is destined to be, it can't help but succeed.

Not only is it largely free from advertising – at least until Google starts a more widespread roll out of ads wholesale across the videos – but it takes full advantage of the iPhone's high-resolution screen, cutting out the surrounding web page, so you can focus entirely on the video content. In addition, now that Google has encoded YouTube's content using H.264, the results are sharper than ever.

For the sake of an easy introduction, click on the most viewed option and pick a video from the list.

Controlling playback

YouTube is a landscape application, so turn your iPhone through 90° with the earpiece to the left to get the best view, and click on play to start the show. After a moment, the controls will fade away, but tapping the screen at any point during playback will call them up, allowing you to change the volume by dragging the slider at the bottom of the screen, pause by clicking on the central button, and skip either forwards in the playlist or back to the beginning of the current clip using the transport buttons to either side.

At the top, you will see the timeline. This shows you how long the clip lasts and how far you are through it. By touching and dragging the little progress indicator, you can move backwards and forwards quickly through a clip to either skip to the action or relive a laugh-out-loud moment.

On the furthest extremes of the lower control panel where you pause and change the volume are two extra buttons. One looks like an open book, and the other an envelope. Clicking on the book icon saves a link to the current movie in your YouTube bookmarks, letting you quickly re-find it in the future. Clicking on the envelope will attach the same reference to a new email, allowing you to share it with a friend.

One final button, showing two arrows in the top-right corner of the interface switches between shrinking the playback window so that it all fits on screen, and maximising it so that it fills the window, but with a little chopped off either top and bottom or left and right.

When the clip comes to an end, the iPhone switches back to the upright display and calls up the best YouTube interface of all. From here, you can share or bookmark the clip, play it again or view other clips on a similar theme. Scroll down the page to pick a new clip or use the Bookmark and Share buttons to save or spread the movie.

Organising your bookmarks

When you are watching videos, it is all too easy to bookmark almost every one you see, which will make your bookmarks list close to useless. From time to time, you are going to have to thin them down, or the true gems will be lost among the general clutter. Click on the Bookmarks button on the bottom bar, then hit Edit at the top. This will shift your video selections to the right to make way for a red delete button beside each one. Tap the button beside the movie you want to delete, then confirm by pressing the Delete button to the right. It will now slide off to the left of the screen and the remaining bookmarks will rearrange to fill the gap.

Solving the YouTube stutter

Don't forget that these videos are streamed live over the net. That means YouTube performance may suffer at busy times of the day, when network traffic is high or there are lots of users watching. If you would rather not watch your video piecemeal, click on the pause button and let the progress bar fill up some way before resuming playback. This should give you enough of a buffer to get all the way through the video without any further stalling. Be wary of watching too many videos over the cellphone network rather than your home or office wifi network as they will quickly use up your data transfer allocation. Only view YouTube videos on the 3G network if your contract allows for unlimited data use.

Taking things further

Once you have finished viewing a video, you are presented with further information about the video, including tags, category, and any comments that have been posted by other viewers (*see right*). Tapping the Rate, Comment or Flag button just below the Tags lets you add your own thoughts to the discussion. You can only do this if you have a YouTube account with password.

In order to sign up, visit *youtube.com* in a regular browser and click the Create Account link at the top of the page. If you are already logged in to Gmail, Google Mail or any other Google service you will probably need to log out first. Accounts are free to set up and use.

Once you have viewed your chosen clip, clicking More Videos will take you to a list of other postings from the same user, assuming they have made any. Clicking the left-facing arrow at the top of the screen that bares the clip's name will take you to a list of related videos from all YouTube users, allowing you to find similar short movies online.

Maps

Google Maps is the best online mapping service you could ever hope to use. It has been heavily invested in so the results are accurate, comprehensive and flexible, allowing you to switch between standard plan-style mapping and intriguing satellite views.

Many of its best features have been carried across to the iPhone and its own slimmed down Maps application. If you haven't used it before, you'll be surprised at just how much information you can fit on (and manipulate on) a 3.5in screen.

At its simplest, the Maps application lets you look up places by name, address or postcode. It understands plain English descriptions like 'The White House' or 'Dartford Crossing' just as easily as standardised address elements such as 'W1T 4JD' and display, the results in three

different ways: as a drawn plan, as a satellite photo or as a hybrid image in which a satellite photo has drawn lines and written text overlaid upon it for easy recognition.

However, it can also be used as a route planning tool like the online alternatives from the likes of the AA. The directions can be presented in four different ways depending on how you want the information rendered and how you intend to travel. From left to right in the images below, we are viewing directions for travelling from central to west London by car (5.2 miles and a 14-minute journey), public transport (a 12-minute journey) and by foot (the most direct route, but the longest journey time at over an hour and a half). With this information it is possible to make a more informed decision with regards to your mode of transport than it would be if you were looking at a regular map.

Tapping the curled up page icon in the bottom right corner of the screen calls up an option to change the view mode, with choices for map,

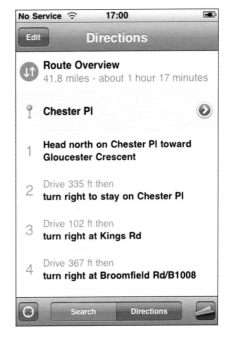

satellite, hybrid and, our fourth view – a list of directions in plain English that we can follow as we use our chosen means of transport.

Finding yourself

As already discussed, you can search the Maps application by entering plain English search terms and postcodes (*above right*), but assuming you are not in Airline Mode in which all wireless networking features are disabled you can also use the iPhone's built-in location services.

Tapping the target icon at the bottom left of the screen uses the iPhone's various communications tools to plot your position on the map. The more of these features you have at your disposal, the more accurate will be the result (*below right*). Clearly the most accurate location service is GPS, which will deliver a pinpoint-accurate rendering of your position on the map. If this is unavailable for any reason (perhaps you are indoors or there is poor reception due to dense cloud cover) your iPhone will fall back on alternative tools at its disposal – namely cell triangulation and wifi identification.

It may be possible for your iPhone to locate itself by looking up the IP address through which it is connected to

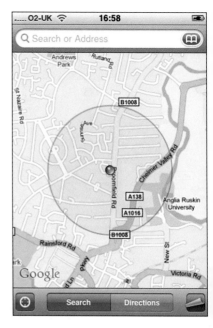

the Internet. This is often highly accurate and can usually identify your position down to the postcode level. It may use this as supplementary information to the positional data it can glean from the mobile phone network by measuring the strength of the signal put out by the various masts within range of where you are standing. By plotting these strengths on the map it can fairly accurately judge where it may be.

Photos and traffic

Maps downloads satellite imagery as and when it is required, so doesn't keep a large store of map tiles in its memory at any time. The closer you zoom by unpinching on the screen, the better and more detailed the results (*above left*).

Another data form that it downloads on the fly is traffic information, which colours roads according to their conditions. This image (*left*) has two carriageways of a major road leading into London coloured red and amber. The red sections were experiencing very heavy traffic at the time the image was captured; the amber sections were busy, but not so busy as the other parts.

Traffic is not available for all roads, but in those areas where it is accessible it can help you to make sensible choices about routes and transport.

FaceTime

Phone calls are so impersonal, aren't they? Well not any more. iPhone 4 introduced FaceTime, an integrated video calling tool that uses a new front-mounted camera to initiate video and voice calls between iPhone 4 users. At the present time it will not work with other mobile phones and obviously won't work on earlier iPhones due to the lack of a front-facing video camera.

FaceTime only works over the iPhone's wifi network connection, so you can't make video calls on the 3G network at this time, most likely on account of the high level of data transfer that would be necessary to maintain a smooth, skip-free signal and the speed it would have to maintain.

Despite this, you can initiate FaceTime calls while in the middle of a regular phone call. The menu screen that is displayed during a call has had a new button added to the bottom row, marked FaceTime. Tapping this pops up a message on your contact's screen asking if they would like to switch to video calling.

You don't need to set up a new account to use FaceTime – it's not like an instant messaging application – and if you are not already on a call you need only tap the FaceTime button beside a contact's entry in your address book and, assuming they also have an iPhone 4, your handset places the call over your network.

During the FaceTime chat, a toolbar at the bottom of the screen lets you mute the conversation, end the call or switch cameras. This lets you show your contact what you can see going on from your point of view, rather than showing them the view from the front-facing camera mounted beside the iPhone's earpiece.

Apple isn't the first company to introduce video calling, but FaceTime looks like one of the easiest to use implementations to date, and one of the best to appear on a mobile handset. Whether it will be enough to encourage your friends to upgrade to iPhones so you can video chat together remains to be seen.

The App Store

For many people, the biggest problem with the original iPhone was that it was a closed, sealed unit. And we're not just talking about the hardware, for just as you couldn't change or upgrade the battery, you also couldn't install your own applications. Well, not legally, anyway.

In truth some enterprising owners found workarounds that allowed them to hack a way into the iPhone's system and add their own applications – or those they had downloaded from the net – to its core system files. It worked, but it was risky, as Apple didn't authorise such modifications. This meant that some users who had hacked their iPhone discovered that it no longer worked after downloading a firmware update.

Then Apple announced a Software Development Kit, and a store through which the results could be downloaded. It is not surprising, then, that when he announced the iPhone 3G, Steve Jobs spent around half of the event highlighting all the new applications that had been written specifically for the iPhone by third-party developers as well as those written by Apple. Now, with iPhone 4, there are over 150,000 applications to choose from. We have highlighted many of the best in the other half of this magbook.

Every application on the App Store, which is accessed through iTunes, must be approved by Apple. This sounds draconian, but it is not surprising: few network operators are happy to have their users installing their own software onto their handsets for fear that they may cause damage to the networks themselves. They can be free or charged for, and all are developed using Apple's free Software Development Kit. Before they can have their applications certified for use on the iPhone, however, developers must pay a $99 registration fee that buys them an electronic certificate to prove to Apple who they are, and that they are a reliable developer.

Large applications must be downloaded through iTunes on your Mac or PC, but applications of 10MB or less can be downloaded wirelessly over the wifi or mobile phone network direct to the handset itself. Each one is registered on the phone, which monitors the App Store for updates and

The App Store resides within iTunes on the Mac or PC and apps purchased from it are transferred to the iPhone when it syncs.

notifies you of any that are available by posting a small red number beside the App Store icon.

For developers, Jobs outlined six key benefits in developing for the iPhone and distributing applications through the App Store. Key among these was the fact that the developer gets to keep 70% of revenues, and that they themselves can pick the price at which they sell their products. Other benefits include access to Apple's payment mechanism, meaning they do not have to deal with credit card payments themselves (which is also a benefit for us end-users as it means we are always dealing with a trusted company), no hosting, no marketing fees and regular payments.

More impressively, from a developer's point of view, is that as the applications are hosted within the iTunes Store, they benefit from Apple's own digital rights management software, FairPlay, so end-users will not be able to buy one copy and then pass them around between one another.

If you would like to try your own hand at developing applications for the iPhone, the software development kit can be downloaded from *developer.apple.com/programs/iphone*.

App Store applications

So what can you expect to find on the App Store? Steve Jobs was keen to point out that it runs the full gamut, all the way from games to business applications. Key among the games that he demonstrated during the original App Store launch was Super Monkey Ball, which uses the integrated accelerometer to roll a moving ball as you tilt the iPhone forwards and backwards, and side to side, through 110 levels of play. An eBay application lets you track and bid on auctions without using the web browser, and the team behind WordPress has ported an edition of its hosted blogging software to run on the iPhone, allowing you to update

Smaller applications can be installed directly over the 3G network or by wifi.

readers on your latest train delay while you are still delayed. Perhaps most excitingly, this latter application will even let you post pictures from the iPhone's camera straight to your blog. If you wanted to post iPhone photos to an online journal before, you first had to download them to your computer. Fans of social networking will welcome the many tools for uploading images direct to Flickr, for updating your Facebook status and for posting tweets to Twitter.

If you would rather not rely on trawling the web yourself or using an online RSS reader application then check out one of the main RSS reader applications, or indeed the dedicated newspaper applications from some of the UK's biggest broadsheet and tabloid publishers. For your fortnightly fix of Mac and iPhone news, be sure to search for *MacUser*'s application, which presents a digital copy of every issue for viewing on an iPhone or iPad screen.

All can be reviewed and rated so you can see what others thought of each one before you spend any money, but do bear in mind that the most common ratings will be given by those who have not enjoyed using an application rather than those who have. This is because every time you remove an application from your iPhone by holding its icon until it shakes and then tapping the 'x' that appears in one corner you will be asked to give it a rating. Although you can refuse, if you are uninstalling because the application didn't deliver what you were after you are likely to mark it down. Those who continue using the application because it does everything they need will be unlikely to rate it at all as it requires a visit to the App Store, which takes more effort. Ratings are useful, but should be read with this caveat in mind.

Signing up for downloads

Before you can download anything from the iTunes Store, of which the App Store is a part, you need to sign up for an Apple ID. If you have downloaded music from the Store for use on an iPod then you already have an ID – just as you have if you are a MobileMe subscriber. The easiest way to get yourself an Apple ID is through the link in the right-hand margin, online at *service.info.apple.com*.

Chapter 3

iPhone Online

• •

Online

With so many great applications pre-installed on the iPhone, and so many opportunities to waste hours playing with them, it is easy to forget that it is, at heart, a communications device. Its name would suggest that it's a phone, but it should more accurately be described as a fully fledged, Internet-enabled mobile communicator, with integrated email, web browsing, video-streaming and route-planning tools. Not bad for something thinner than a pack of playing cards.

Many of these applications rely on an Internet connection to work, which is why Apple has integrated 802.11b/g/n wireless networking into the device. Often referred to as wifi, this is a globally-accepted standard that allows you to get online at home, at work, and in coffee shops, railway stations and airports around the world.

However, because wifi is an inherently insecure medium, network administrators often put in place several safety measures, with which your iPhone setup will need to comply before you can gain access. Each will be set up in a different way, and you will have to talk to the administrator of each network to find the exact details, but these are the most common security measures in use and the best way you can make your iPhone compliant.

MAC address filtering

Every wireless networking device, including Bluetooth modules, is identified by a string of eight alpha-numeric digit pairs. For example,

Available	6.1 GB
Version	3.1.3 (7E18)
Carrier	O2 5.0
Serial Number	7U743Y2WWH8
Model	MB213B
Wi-Fi Address	00:1C:B3:54:82:9A
Bluetooth	00:1C:B3:54:82:99
IMEI	01 130100 983179 2
ICCID	8944 1100 6423 1032 289

00:b3:c7:d8:0a:2f. The code pairs are in hexadecimal, with numbers running from 0 to 9, and the letters from a to f. No two devices will ever carry the same identifying string, which means these combinations can be used as a highly effective security tool.

By interrogating each wireless device that attempts to connect to it, such as an iPhone or mobile computer, a wireless access point can individually authorise and deny network access to each one, and no matter how many passwords you have at your disposal, it is almost impossible to circumvent this measure in any conventional way.

If your network administrator has used MAC address filtering, you will need to ask them to add your iPhone to the list of authorised machines by giving them its unique MAC address. To find this, click on Settings > General > About from the Home screen (*facing page, left*) and read off the number beside 'Wi-Fi Address'. You can safely ignore the MAC address beside the Bluetooth entry at this time as that interface is not used for accessing the Internet directly, but instead for connecting with external devices such as keyboards, headsets and mobile phones.

Hidden network names

Sometimes networks are not only filtered in this way but hidden altogether. All networks are given a name, which is not necessarily unique, and they broadcast these along with their regular data signals so that users can easily identify them and connect. However, almost every wireless access point can optionally hide this name to make it more difficult for casual passers-by to connect without authorisation. This is a good security measure, as while it would be possible to detect that a network is present, an unauthorised user would have to guess not only the password to each one, but also what it is called, and the chances of doing both are slim indeed.

If you know that you are in range of such a network and would like to connect manually, tap Settings > Wi-Fi > Other and enter the network name exactly as given by the network administrator. You may be asked for a password here and can supply it if you know what it is by tapping the Security bar and choosing the necessary security protocol. However, if

Your iPhone will search for available wireless networks (*left*) but if the network you need is obscuring its name you will need to enter it manually (*right*).

you do not know what security measures are in place then simply tapping Join will throw up a dialogue asking you to enter the appropriate password, leaving the iPhone to negotiate the security settings on your behalf.

What is encryption?

On gaining access to a network, your data would by default be sent backwards and forwards over the wireless connection totally unencrypted. This would allow nefarious users to intercept your communications and read all manner of sensitive data, including emails, banking details and website passwords.

Fortunately, all networking devices are capable of encrypting this data so that it is much more difficult to read (although still not entirely impossible) using WEP or WPA encryption. Your iPhone is fully compatible with

these protocols, so assuming you are
connecting to a secure network you
can browse the Internet with few
worries. Look for a padlock symbol
beside the name of your network in
the Wi-Fi Network section of the
Settings app as this indicates that the
network is appropriately encrypted.

The mobile Internet

By default, the iPhone will use a
wireless Internet connection whenever
it can, but it is also possible to connect
over the mobile phone network. Bear
in mind that if you do this while away
from a regular wifi network, you will
pay usage fees based on the amount of
data you pass over the connection.

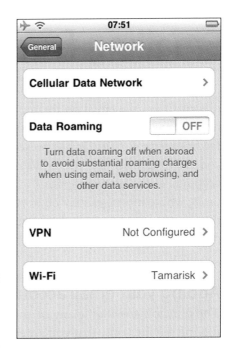

Therefore, try to limit your non-wifi browsing to low-bandwidth
content wherever possible unless you are on a truly unlimited contract,
and certainly avoid videos and streaming audio, as this will quickly rack up
expensive charges if you exceed the transfer limits stipulated as part of
your chosen contract.

If you are roaming onto other networks when using your iPhone
overseas these charges will be even higher and are unlikely to be included in
your bundled data quota. To avoid being charges high fees for use overseas
(and particularly for email collection, which may happen automatically at
set intervals depending on your settings), you can disable data roaming and
still be able to make phone calls and connect to wireless networks in hotels,
coffee shops and so on. To turn off data roaming tap Settings > General
> Network and move the Data Roaming slider to the Off position (*above*).
From this same screen you can also manually select your preferred cellular
network if several are on offer while overseas.

Emailing from the iPhone

Apple learnt a lesson from the BlackBerry when it was developing the iPhone: users like email on the move. And like the best students, it went out into the world and did better than its teacher. Email on the iPhone is far from a weak point. It has presets for Gmail, Yahoo! Mail, MobileMe and AOL, and also lets you add a regular Pop3, Imap or Exchange email account. These last two options will be of particular interest to business users, where messages may be hosted on a central server rather than downloaded on an ad-hoc basis and deleted. MobileMe, which replaced the old .Mac, works in much the same way.

Adding your email account

The principle for adding any of the preset account types is the same, as the iPhone requires only that you enter four pieces of information: your name, your email address, your password and a description used to identify the account if you are setting up more than one. If you have one of these accounts, set it up by tapping its icon and when you click on Save, the iPhone will check that the information you have provided is valid.

Sometimes you may see an error message stating that the iPhone is unable to connect and asking if it can try connecting without SSL. Say yes to this, but bear in mind that it is a less secure way of connecting and will not solve all problems. If you are trying to connect through a corporate network, it may be worth talking to your network administrator, and asking them to open up any necessary ports on their firewall.

If you have a regular Pop3 email account supplied by your Internet service provider (ISP), then things are a little more complicated. Tap the Other line below the icons for the default services and select the appropriate protocol from the three options at the top of the screen. For most accounts, this will be Pop. Type in your name, email address and a description for the account. You will need to ask your ISP for the details to complete the Incoming and Outgoing Mail Server sections, and once you have entered them, click on Save to store the settings. Assuming all was correct, you should then be taken to your inbox.

If you don't already have an email account that you would like to use with your iPhone, you can set up a free account with three of the four pre-set services in the iPhone's mail application by visiting the following sites using a regular web browser (not an email client):

Yahoo! Mail   *www.ymail.com*
AOL Mail   *www.aol.com*
Google Mail   *www.google.com/mail*

However, by far the most useful for any iPhone user is MobileMe (*www.me.com*), which provides you with a push email account. This transfers messages to the iPhone as soon as they are received, mimicking the BlackBerry's way of working, and saving you from having to manually invoke a collection.

Picking up messages

At the moment, your email will be set to only pick up when you tell it to. This is great for making sure you rule your messages, rather than allowing them to rule you, but it is not entirely convenient.

To set your iPhone to poll the server and download new messages automatically, return to the iPhone Home screen, tap Settings > Mail, Contacts, Calendars > Fetch New Data and choose from every 15, 30 or 60 minutes, depending on how much of an email junkie you are (*see top image, p110*). Of course, if you are waiting for an urgent message you can still check manually from the Mail application by clicking on the circular arrow symbol at the bottom of the Mail window. Once you have picked up your messages, you will naturally sort through them, reading them, replying to the ones that need immediate action, and postponing others. A lot of messages can be deleted right away, which you can do by tapping the Bin icon at the bottom of the screen. Obviously, you will have to then tap again to confirm, at which point the message will sweep down from the screen and into the bin.

Others will need some thought, and so naturally you will want to mark them as unread. To do this, and with the email open on your iPhone screen, tap the Details button beside the sender name and an Unread button will appear (*below right*). This resets the message's read status, so that it appears as a new message in your inbox listing.

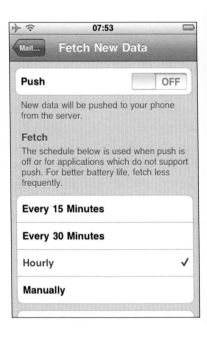

Sending messages

You can send a message from anywhere in the Mail application (*top image, facing page*), without having to return to the main mailbox screen, by clicking the small square and pencil icon in the bottom right-hand corner. If you already know the address of the person you want to message you can type it straight

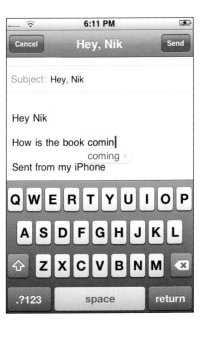

in, but it is easier to tap the blue + icon to the right of the To field and select the person from your contacts list where you will be given the chance to pick the appropriate address if they have more than one in their record.

The procedure for replying to messages that you are reading is the same as above, except that instead of tapping the square and pencil icon, you tap on the backwards-pointing arrow, which would give you the option of either forwarding or replying to the presently-displayed message.

You will probably want to set a signature line to appear at the bottom of every email you send, containing information such as your name, web address and phone number (but think carefully when deciding what to include, bearing in mind that this information may be passed on to others should the recipients forward your email). To do this, return to the iPhone home screen and tap Settings > Mail, Contacts, Calendars > Signature (*left*) and type in the message of your choice. It is good practice to precede your signature with two dashes and a space ('-- ') and then start the footer on the next line down. In this way, most email clients will trim it off when your message is quoted back to you in a subsequent email and save on bandwidth use.

Managing messaging defaults

Several iPhone features, such as emailing video links from YouTube or jottings from the Notes tool, will always use your default email address to dispatch messages. The default address is whichever one you set up first, which might not be the one you prefer.

If you have set up several accounts and would like one of your later additions to work as the default, and so handle email from other iPhone applications, change it through Settings > Mail, Contacts, Calendars > Default Account.

Pop3 messages not syncing?

Although you can synchronise the Pop3 email accounts on both your iPhone and your desktop or laptop computer, this only transfers across the account settings, not the messages themselves. If you therefore set your regular computer to download messages and delete them from the server, they will not appear on your iPhone unless it accesses them first.

Get around this obstacle by setting your regular computer to only delete messages a week after they have been collected, which will give you time to connect using your iPhone and pick up a second copy. Alternatively, use an Imap or Exchange service, or Apple's own MobileMe to store your messages on the server at all times so that what you see on your iPhone will always match what appears on a regular computer.

If your emails are not appearing in your iPhone inbox, check that they are not being removed from the server by your Mac or PC before your iPhone can see them.

Browsing the web

The iPhone's name may suggest it is primarily for making calls, but all of the most compelling features involve retrieving information from, or sending data across, the Internet. Sometimes this is done using a plain email client, and at other times using highly customised applications that access just a single website and wrap it up in an intuitive interface such as the Maps and YouTube applications.

It is only right, then, that the iPhone should also include a first-class browser that works just as well as a desktop or laptop equivalent. And there is good reason for this. The iPhone uses Safari, Apple's default browser, which is bundled with its operating system, Mac OS X. This is the full-blown edition of the portable operating system that underpins the iPhone.

Safari is the default browser on the Mac and is now making inroads on the PC.

If you are a PC user, there is a possibility you will not have come across Safari before, although it has been available as a Windows application since mid-summer 2007. Many saw this as an important move in the development of the iPhone as it meant that website developers no longer had to buy a Mac to test their creations using the iPhone's default browser. Why is this important? Because when Apple explained how developers could write their own applications for the handset, it initially restricted them to writing online applications optimised for use in a browser running on a 3.5in screen.

However, Safari's history is long and colourful. Although it is best known for its appearance on the Mac, its core engine, which decodes the pages and assembles the words, images and styling on your screen, is based on the open-source Konqueror browser, which is one of the most popular options for Linux users. It is therefore well supported and although there was some hesitation from online banks, many of which took a long time to get around to recoding their sites so that they would not reject the browser out of hand, there are now very few websites that it doesn't render as well as, say, Internet Explorer or Mozilla Firefox, whether on Windows, the Mac or an iPhone.

Basic concepts

Safari works just the same as any other browser. Fire it up (it is found by default on the toolbar at the bottom of the iPhone's screen) and you will find that it comprises two main parts: the page area, in which the sites you visit will be rendered, and an address bar, into which you will type the URLs of the websites you visit. Because your iPhone comes

preconfigured for a mobile network, all of the necessary access details for using the Internet on the move will have been entered already, so you don't need to worry about setup. However, if you also want to access the Internet when in your home or office by using your wireless network, then you will need to set up the iPhone for wifi access. In a business environment, this may involve talking to your system administrator to ensure that Internet access is not blocked by a corporate firewall, to obtain any passwords necessary for gaining access to the wireless access point, and to have your iPhone unblocked if the network uses MAC address filtering.

Bear in mind that while the only noticeable difference may be that your localised, wifi-based Internet browsing may be faster than browsing over the mobile phone network when you are out and about, you will incur service charges for any data downloaded online that exceeds the amount bundled with your service contract.

Visiting pages

Now that you understand the difference between wifi and mobile phone-based browsing, it is time to start using the browser. Tap in the address bar at the top of the screen and you will see that the iPhone keyboard pops up, ready for you to enter an address. The numbers and some punctuation marks are hidden on a second keyboard, which sits behind the main character-based keyboard and is accessed using the special key at the bottom.

If you already have an address entered and you want to type a new one, tap inside the box and tap the X button to the right of the existing address, which wipes it out and lets you start afresh. If you only need to amend what is already in place, hold down your finger in the box and you will see that a magnifier appears above it. As you move your finger to the left and right inside the box, you will see that this shows you precisely where you are positioning the cursor, allowing you to target a specific point in the address without having to clumsily use a finger that is several times larger than the letters beneath it.

Once you have reached the point you need, lift your finger off the screen and the cursor will be left in place, ready for you to amend the address using the keyboard.

Navigating pages

How quickly pages load will depend on several factors. These include the speed of your network, the wireless connection between your iPhone and the access point (802.11b networks are older and slower than 802.11g and n networks and will make a big difference to the speed at which websites appear), the size of the page, including its number of graphics, as well as how many other people are accessing the website and your connection at the same time as you.

However, performance should be roughly comparable to a desktop browser as the networking hardware is, to all intents and purposes, the same. The actual speed of the Internet connection will therefore be determined more by the amount of data being downloaded, the number of people with whom you are sharing the network connection and the load on the remote server hosting the site.

You may be surprised at how legible pages are at the default zoom level, regardless of whether you are holding the iPhone in either portrait or widescreen orientation. However, reading long tracts of text at this size is not ideal, and with many designers now expecting us all to use larger and larger screens, you will probably want to zoom in.

You could use the regular spreading-finger gesture to zoom in the same way that you would with a photo or map in other applications, but because Apple has made the iPhone browser aware of the way in which pages have been styled and where the text boundaries lie, you can simply double-tap a text column and it will zoom in so just that column exactly fills the screen

iPhone 4's display makes web pages easy to read even when zoomed out (left) but tapping columns zooms text to their full screen, making them even clearer (*right*).

from left to right. The same is true for photos which, when double-tapped, are zoomed in to fill the whole of the browser window.

Although you sometimes can't help it, try not to do your double-tap on top of a link, as you may find yourself navigating to a new page, which usually only requires a single tap. However, if you do, then use the left-pointing arrow at the bottom of the screen to skip backwards and, at a later point, the right-facing arrow to move forwards again through the chain of previously visited pages.

Should a link open a page in a new browser window, you will see that the page you are viewing shrinks slightly and moves to the left to make way for a new window, which will then assume full screen. An indicator in the bottom-right corner will then show you how many windows are open. Tapping this will make the windows shrink once more so that you can scroll through the various pages by sliding them to left and right using your finger, finally tapping on the centre of your chosen page when you want to use it.

As you do this, you will notice that each page has a red button with an X at its centre, on its upper-left corner. This is the close tab, and tapping it will close the page. If you had only two pages loaded before doing this, the one remaining page will be loaded full screen. If you had more than two pages open, you will be left in the scrolling mode to carry out further page selection tasks. This sounds radically different to a desktop browser, but if you liken the individual pages in the single Safari application to several pages opened in tabs inside a single instance of Internet Explorer or Firefox (or even Safari) on your desktop machine, then you will see that the two are broadly comparable.

Bookmarks

If you have found a page that you like, you will want to save it, which is done by tapping the '+' icon at the bottom of the Safari window and selecting Add Bookmark. To return to it later, tap the open book icon on the same bar and select it from the list that appears, navigating through your Bookmarks folders as necessary.

Bookmarks can be organised into folders (*above*) to make them easier to find, but you do need to set up your folders before you try to use them. Do this by tapping the open book icon on Safari's bottom bar, followed by the

Edit button at the bottom of the screen. You will now see a New Folder button, whose function is fairly self-explanatory. Once you have created and saved a new folder, tap Done twice to return to your web page, then tap the '+' button to bookmark that page. You can now navigate to the

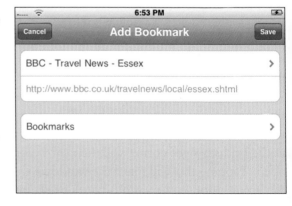

folder you have just created to find your bookmark. You will also have the chance to give it a more descriptive name and to edit the specific link used. Tap Return to switch between each one, and then tap the Bookmarks bar and select the new folder you just created. This will return you to the Add Bookmark dialog, where you tap Save to complete the operation.

RSS

Of course, web pages are only half the story, as the web is about content as much as it is design, and the best way of presenting standard text- and image-based content is RSS. Standing for either Rich Site Summary or Really Simple Syndication, depending on who you choose to believe, this is a method of stripping out the raw data in a page and presenting it in a single, unified interface, along with content from other sites. It is a great way of keeping up with the news and monitoring changes on several websites at once without having to visit each one individually.

RSS feeds can be syndicated and incorporated within other websites, but by far the easiest way to access them is using a so-called aggregator. Unfortunately, the iPhone does not have a built-in RSS aggregator, but Apple has implemented one as part of its MobileMe service (*below*). Don't bother visiting it using a regular browser, as the only thing you will see is an error message telling you it was designed for use on an iPhone.

However, the implementation is very simplistic. It presents you with a stripped-down list of headlines and summaries, which you click on to view the complete article, but it does not keep track of the stories you have read, which would be done by a software-based aggregator.

Our top tip would be to use the RSS reader as an access point for commonly

scanned news sites, and to add RSS-parsed pages to your bookmarks so you can skip straight to them, but all the time bear in mind that, even on an iPhone, visiting the web page itself will always deliver a far superior experience. Alternatively, if you prefer a software-based solution, search for RSS on the App Store as there are many excellent options available for downloading.

Browsing safely

The iPhone browser is a fully featured window on the web, and so it suffers from many of the same problems as regular full-sized browsers. One of the most annoying, although least dangerous, is pop-up windows opened by the pages you visit. These can sometimes be useful, but are usually simply a means of delivering advertising that you would really rather not see.

Fortunately, these pop-up windows are easy to block, along with a whole range of live media that use plug-ins and scripts. This is accessed through the Home screen by tapping Settings > Safari (*below*). Here, you will see sliders for switching on and off pop-up windows, JavaScript rendering and plug-ins. Use these settings with care, and be aware that by disabling

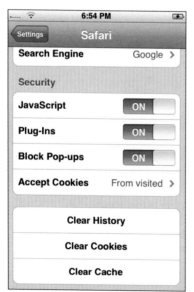

plug-ins you will be unable to access some online audio and video (although this will not affect the YouTube application).

Turning off JavaScript could be more problematic, as it is key to many features on Web 2.0 sites. Web 2.0 is a catch-all term coined to describe the kind of information-sharing, application-driven websites of which we are now seeing more and more. Prime examples include Gmail, Google Docs, Facebook and Wikipedia. While the last of those websites will not suffer from an absence of JavaScript, the others may, and some of the best, most intuitive features may disappear.

More importantly, JavaScript makes possible a wide range of applications written specifically for the iPhone as it was initially the only way to develop for the device. Fortunately, with the advent of the App Store, this is no longer true, but by disabling JavaScript you will still be denying yourself access to an extensive library of iPhone-specific online applications. The most pressing concern online today, however, is privacy, and despite the efforts of legislators around the world, there remains a whole range of perfectly legal ways in which various companies and individuals can keep tabs on your online activities. The most common of these is the use of cookies.

Cookies are small data files that help to uniquely identify your browser. Mostly they are harmless and on the whole they are very helpful. For example, you would not be able to use an online bank without cookies as the site would be unable to verify that you are authorised and logged in to its system. Cookies also handle the contents of online shopping baskets and can remember passwords. On the whole, they are a very good thing indeed.

However, cookies can also be used for less-noble purposes. Because they stay resident in your browser and can be read by all websites, they can inform site owners where you have come from, where you are going, and where you have been in the past. Advertisers often set cookies on your system so that they can more accurately tailor the ads they are showing you. Through their use, advertisers can build up an accurate representation of the websites you visit by using them to track on which sites you saw their advert over the life of the cookie. If this bothers you – and for some it is a real concern – then you should periodically remove cookies from your system by tapping Clear Cookies within the Safari settings application.

The truly paranoid can disable cookies altogether from here, too. Although in the same way that we would urge you to think carefully before disabling JavaScript, we would recommend that you continue allowing Safari to accept them at least by using the setting, From Visited, meaning that only the websites you load in your browser can set cookies, but the advertisers shown on them can't.

Finally, consider regularly clearing out the cache. This is where Safari saves snippets of useful information, such as images that it thinks it may have to render again, or the addresses of websites you have visited in the past. Why? Two reasons. First, it will free up valuable memory. Second, you may not want your more embarrassing online hotspots popping up when someone else uses your phone.

Apple has so much faith in the iPhone's mobile edition of Safari that it does not create a mobile edition of its website, proving that a rich media online presence really does work when you're out and about.

Stocks

There are plenty of ways to check the performance of your stock market over the course of the say: radio, dedicated TV channels like CNBC and Bloomberg, newspapers, websites... but what happens when you are away from your desk, the radio or your TV? If you are serious about making money from the world of shares then you can't afford to be out of touch with market movements for any longer than is absolutely necessary because this is one instance when time really can equal money.

Fortunately the iPhone ships with its own Stocks application. It isn't very advanced, and it doesn't let you track the specific value of your own portfolio by allowing you to enter how many shares you have in each company, but it does let you specify the stocks that you would like to track and then track their moves as either percentage changes or real terms financial differences.

Stocks draws its data from Yahoo, so you need to be online in order to use it, either by wifi or over your 3G connection.

Your first job on starting it up is to enter your own stocks and remove the defaults. Tap the 'i' button in the bottom right-hand corner of the display and it will flip around. Now tap the '-' bar beside any stocks you don't hold to remove them and use the buttons at the bottom to choose between using percentage change, financial change or market capitalisation indicators. Now add your own stocks to the application by tapping the '+' button at the top of the screen and entering their ticker symbols. If more than one stock market around the world has a company listed using that

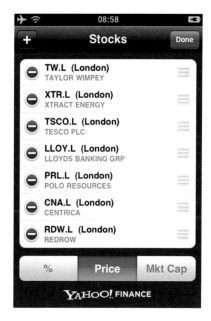

symbol you will be presented with a list of options from which you can choose the right one. Tap Done when you have finished to return to the application's front facing.

Your stocks' prices and changes will be now be shown on two panels. The top panel shows their prices and can be scrolled vertically. The bottom panel can be scrolled horizontally, as shown in the three images above, to display a price change graph (use the 1d, 1w, 1m and so on buttons to change the timeframe shown), general company data, and market news related to that company. For more detailed charts, turn your iPhone to landscape orientation for full screen renderings (*right*) and swipe the screen left and right to scroll through the graphs for each of the companies that you are tracking. Stocks won't make you a millionaire, but it could help you judge when to buy or sell.

Chapter 4

Everything iPhone

iPhone evolution

The iPhone did not just appear fully formed from thin air. Quite apart from the development work that went into its creation, it comes at the end of a long line of related consumer products from both Apple and other hardware manufacturers.

The most obvious relative is the iPod, which first appeared as a chunky hard drive-based music player in 2001 (*below*). Contrary to popular belief, it was not an immediate success. Initially only available for the Mac, its bulk and weight were not fully compensated by the underwhelming storage capacity, and it was bundled with iTunes 1, which was fairly primitive. It could not even say how many times that you had played a certain track. Nonetheless, things should be put into context. These were early days for MP3 players; the market was young, with competitor products boasting equally meagre specifications.

The iPod only really took off when it was spotted in the hands of

celebrities in the gossip press. People suddenly started taking note of those distinctive white earphones and the iPod's fortunes – and those of its parent company – were changed forever.

There have now been seven generations of full-sized iPod, incorporating first colour displays then video playback features. These have been accompanied by four generations of iPod nano, the latest of which now also play and shoot video, and three different iPod shuffle designs, the latest of which is barely any larger than a stick of gum and comes in a range of colours. The full-sized iPod is now called the classic, and it has lost its spot at the top of the range to the iPod touch, which appeared shortly after the

iPhone's first US appearance. The touch is much slimmer than the iPhone and is missing some of its features (*above left*).

That the iPod was an important predecessor of the iPhone is obvious from the importance of similar features in the iPhone itself, not to mention the fact that Steve Jobs calls it the best iPod Apple has ever made.

Likewise, the fact that it interfaces with your computer through iTunes is a mark of its heritage. iTunes, like the iPod, was initially a Mac-only product and the first four versions were little more than music ripping, organising and streaming applications. When Apple finally launched the iTunes Music Store, as it was then called (it has since dropped the Music part), it sold only a couple of hundred thousand tracks and no videos at all. Podcasts were as yet uninvented, and most of us continued to buy our music in the traditional way – on CD.

iTunes remains an important part of the iPhone system, largely because it runs on both the PC and Mac, and it is through this that you synchronise not only your music, but also all of your data, such as contacts, web browser bookmarks and photos.

However, the iPhone is more than just a mobile with music playing features: it's a fully fledged computer. Apple has gone down this road before, with the Newton MessagePad. These was bulky by modern standards, but nonetheless a breakthrough product, among the first on the market to understand hand-written input and sporting enough ports and add-ons for them to work as standalone computers, rather than organisers that must regularly check in with a desktop partner.

They were championed by Jobs' predecessor, Gil Amelio, but when Jobs returned to Apple after several years developing computers at NeXT, he canned the whole line, along with several other initiatives on which the company was working, including licensing the rights for other manufacturers to make Mac-compatible computers. Many saw this as a bad move, but Jobs' determined management turned around the struggling company as it launched one successful product after another, starting with the semi-transparent iMac and ending up today with the iPhone 4.

However, when Apple bought NeXT, it didn't just buy Jobs; it also bought the company's assets, intellectual property and existing projects, many of which were kept in development. The most important of these was the NeXT operating system, NeXT Step, which eventually became Mac OS X, the operating system that runs the Mac.

Why is this important for the iPhone? Because a cut-down edition of the very same operating system is what holds it all together. Key features such as Cover Flow – the ability to flick back and forth through your album covers in the iPod application – also feature in Mac OS X.

Psion's Series 5 popularised the idea of computers that let you type on the move.

While it may have been the most advanced pocketable computer of its day, the Newton MessagePad was not the first personal digital assistant. If we discount the earliest calculators with built-in address books and calendars, a lot of the credit for popularising palm-top computing really has to go to UK-based company Psion.

In 1984, it launched the first Psion Organiser. It had a single-line screen and was followed two years later by the Organiser II. These were bulky devices with alphabetically arranged keyboards and text-based screens sporting one, two or four lines, depending on the model. They did not look much like an iPhone, but the two devices share many key features, including an address book and calendaring application. Psion followed these with the Series 3 and Series 5 machines, which sported full Qwerty keyboards and ran the Epoc operating system, which evolved into Symbian and is now used on many modern iPhone competitors.

However, Psion wasn't the only company investigating mobile computing. While it soldiered on with a button-based physical keyboard, US Robotics' Palm Computing launched the PalmPilot, a stylus-based organiser with much the same form factor as the iPhone. In many ways, these devices were similar to the Newton MessagePad line-up in that they employed a fairly sophisticated form of handwriting recognition called Graffiti. This sometimes required the user to use specific shapes rather than natural letters, such as squared-off 7 for a T, and an upside-down V for A, but it was quick and easy to learn.

Microsoft adopted a similar system for its early pen-driven Windows CE devices. These were designed to look like the regular computer-based versions of Windows available at the time, and thus required fairly hefty hardware. Microsoft did not make any devices itself. Instead, it licensed the operating system to other hardware manufacturers, starting in late 1996. It has been through various updates since then and now, as Windows Phone, drives many of the iPhone's most serious competitors.

So, while Apple's mobile phone gadget may be the most advanced phone/music player hybrid yet created, it is certainly neither a first-to-market device nor anything other than a natural evolution of at least five product lines that came before it. However, in packaging it in such a desirable form, and ensuring the hardware and underlying software work perfectly together, Apple has delivered a device that it claims is years ahead of any competitor. From the looks of the various so-called 'iPhone killers', none of which should cause it too much concern, that claim may not be entirely wide of the mark.

iPhone expert

As with many Apple products, the iPhone seemed to appear from nowhere and quickly mop up the market. The massive and unprecedented media interest and the speed at which it grew may have had you believing that this remarkable device appeared fully formed from Steve Jobs' pocket after just a few days' development. Of course, that is not the case. It takes years of development and research to produce something like the iPhone and, as with all of Apple's products, this one was shrouded in the utmost secrecy until the day it was unveiled to the world. That did not stop rumours circulating, though, some of which were surprisingly accurate. Come with us as we investigate the behind-the-scenes story of the iPhone, where it came from, and how it came to be.

The build-up

The iPhone was a will-they-won't-they story for three years before its first appearance. What started out as a logical supposition on the back of the iPod's phenomenal success turned into semi-believable rumour and, eventually, credible reportage as time rolled on. Finally, in January 2007, in front of an audience of 4,000 at the Moscone Centre in San Francisco, Steve Jobs whipped the sleek device from his pocket and even the wildest of rumours and expectations were proved to be hugely conservative.

But let's rewind and start our story with the registration of an unremarkable, and easily missed domain: *www.iphone.org*. This was snapped up on 16 December 1999 – before even the iPod came to market – and from that date started linking to *www.apple.com*. By November 2006, it was pulling in about 550,000 hits. Not bad for a site with no specific content, and in fact a far better performance than the *www.ipod.com* domain, also owned by Apple.

But then Apple's domains are both extensive and varied, so few were eager to read too much into this virtual property. It also owns the highly specific *www.itunes.com*, the radically generic (and valuable) *www.airport.com* and entirely bizarre *www.mammals.org*. Go figure. We asked the Apple contact listed on the domain's record whether the company had been the original registrar or bought it from someone else. The two-word reply was a curt 'No comment'. Just how big a secret was the iPhone project?

Such a response is not uncommon from Apple. The company is famously tight-lipped when it comes to new products, and traditionally it has had a policy of refusing to comment on anything which has not been officially announced. Even within the company there is a culture of secrecy and silence, with individual teams unaware of what others in the same building are working on. Indeed, it is said that software and hardware teams working on two halves of the same product often have little contact with one another, yet somehow they manage to put out products so perfectly paired and crafted as the iPhone, where the hardware's touchscreen is so integral to the operation of the internal software.

Yet the iPhone was not Apple's first foray into the mobile phone market. Previous tie-ups with Motorola were little more than a branding exercise, with a cut-down iTunes player built into a range of compatible handsets, but hobbled so it could access no more than 100 tracks at a time. That is less than 10 albums, and at the time it left many convinced that Apple was doing no more than piggybacking a respected brand to see whether the music and phone combination really was viable.

With 20/20 hindsight, we can see that this was indeed probably the case. The Motorola experiment was not a complete flop, but its success was muted and much of the criticism aimed at the venture focused on the Motorola hardware rather than the Apple software. If ever Apple needed convincing that it had to take the hardware development in house, this was probably the

Apple's first foray into mobile phones with Motorola had limited success.

turning point. It had the right software; it just needed the vehicle through which to deliver it.

Traditional mobile phones are poorly-suited to delivering the kind of luxuriant interfaces and bright, high-resolution graphics we have come to expect from Apple. While their reliance on physical buttons for dialling, texting and inputting data are too inflexible to perform the iPhone's most impressive tasks. What Apple needed was more akin to a mobile computer, but with Steve Jobs having already discounted a tablet PC running Mac OS X, and the company having burnt its fingers with Newton-line of MessagePad products, it needed to come up with something radically different, yet still familiar and unintimidating for the buying public.

Dow Jones, cited in an October 2006 issue of the *New York Sun*, reported a patent filing for a 'multi-functional hand-held device', which could act as both a mobile phone and a portable music player. Its invention was not attributed to Apple, but instead one Steven Hotelling. Who is he? A frequent patent filer based in San Jose, California, often named as inventor on Apple patents.

Other patents were more specifically Apple property. In late October 2006, CNN reported that Apple had been granted the patent for a speech-recognition technology that would enable a portable device to interpret spoken commands, such as 'call home' or 'pick up voicemail'. A couple of weeks later, it was granted a patent for an 'actuating user interface for media player'. This described a successor to the scroll-wheel, which had been deemed unwieldy and fiddly on anything more complex than a simple music player. 'This is especially true when you consider that the functionality of hand-held devices have begun to merge into a single hand-held device (for example, smart phones),' the filing stated.

The Newton MessagePad was Apple's first hand-held computer and was one of the first product lines that Steve Jobs axed when he rejoined the company with its buy out of NeXT.

And, of course, now that we have seen how it works, we know just how different the iPhone's implementation of its music playback features is. Gone is the scroll-wheel, and in its place we have Cover Flow, which lets you flick back and forth through your album cover art. And can you do this with a single hand? Of course: hold it in one hand with your thumb around the front, and flick, flick, flick away. Cover Flow now appears on the scroll-wheel-based iPods with screens – the nano and classic – but the implementation is neither so appealing nor so effective and you do not get the same feeling of flicking through your CD collection as you do with the iPhone or the iPod touch.

On the exact same day as the patent for the new navigation device, Apple was granted a third patent, this time for a universal docking station for hand-held electronic devices. Such devices explicitly mentioned in the filing included 'a portable music player, a mobile telephone or a personal digital assistant'.

More and more often, the magical 't' word – telephone – was cropping up undisguised in Apple filings. No wonder the rumour mill was starting to churn out stories of a black ops department inside Apple working on a mobile phone to beat all others.

Then, in mid-November, the *China Times* reported that an iPhone product had been finalised and sent out for production at Foxconn's Fushikang plant, which by February 2007, it said, would be turning out between 500,000 and 600,000 units a month. Reporting the story, Apple Insider listed a raft of suppliers that had been signed up to the project, including AlusTech, which would manufacture its reported two-megapixel digital camera (which did indeed turn out to be a two-megapixel device) using lenses from Largan and Cmos sensors from Micron. Intel, Sharp, Tripod Technology, Broadcom and Sunrex were supplying the remaining components, while Catcher Technology, the company behind the iPod's external look and feel, would produce the iPhone casing.

So by late 2006, there was plenty of chatter in the market and lots of speculation, but not enough to save the Wikipedia administrators from deleting the iPhone entry on the grounds that it was based on speculation and rumour. 'This article is about a "future product", the "iPhone". However, there is no evidence that Apple intends to release a telephone, or that such a telephone is even in development. Unlike products such as Microsoft's Zune, which the company has stated it intends to release, Apple has never made any statements regarding the production of a phone. This page is not at all encyclopaedic, citing sources that are nothing more than rumours and speculation. Until there is something more than guesswork to back up the existence of such a product, this page should not exist,' wrote Paulus89, a Wikipedia contributor whose personal page carried a prominent anti-censorship badge.

Well, no. Apple had not officially commented on the presence or absence of an iPhone in its labs. But, then, until Jobs previewed the Apple TV, the only forthcoming products it had ever talked about before their actual launch were updates to the operating system, so it was not entirely surprising. In fairness to those Wikipedia contributors who made a good stab at putting together a forward-looking iPhone page, the closest anyone inside had come to giving official sanction to the project was an obscure comment from Apple chief financial officer Peter Oppenheimer. As reported by *Forbes*, he 'whet appetites for a phone by telling analysts the company isn't "sitting around doing nothing" about the wireless market'.

Where Apple is concerned, that is as close to confirmation anyone was likely to get. With reports coming in from so many different sources, though, it was starting to look more likely than ever that the iPhone would have been on sale in the US by early spring 2007, and in Europe perhaps six months later. Neither of these proved wildly wrong.

The unveiling, and a battle over the iPhone name

The iPhone was finally released on 18 December 2006. Hang on, you're thinking, that can't be right. But it is. The iPhone – the very first iPhone ever – hit the market on 18 December 2006 and immediately sent Apple into a spin. Why? Because this iPhone was nothing like the sleek glass-and-metal gadget we now associate with the name. Instead it was an Internet telephony device produced by network giant Cisco, which had owned the right to the iPhone name since it acquired the name's original owner, Infogear, in 2001.

Apple was its usual over-confident self and went ahead with the launch of its own iPhone on Tuesday 9 January 2007. 'iPhone it is,' *MacUser* magazine reported. 'In Apple's words not a single device, but three revolutionary products in one: a mobile phone, a widescreen iPod with touch controls and a "breakthrough" Internet communications device. It is also a camera and, at a push, a PDA.'

Steve Jobs was typically ebullient. 'The iPhone is a revolutionary and magical product that is literally five years ahead of any other mobile phone,' he said, ignoring the impracticalities of 'literal' time travel. 'We are all born with the ultimate pointing device – our fingers – and [the] iPhone uses them to create the most revolutionary user interface since the mouse.'

Competitors lined up to offer faint praise. Anssi Vanjoki, head of Nokia's multimedia unit, commented two days later that 'it is quite an interesting product, but it is lacking a few essential features such as 3G, which would enable fast data connections.' He further derided Apple's stated aim of capturing 1% of the mobile phone market as being 'not at a very high level', and claimed Apple's entry would boost the market and prove that Nokia's multimedia strategy – which he headed – was right.

The reaction from Motorola was barely any better. 'iPhone, iPhone, iPhone! I'm just bored of this damned question,' said European marketing manager Simon Thompson when asked about Apple's launch two months later. He did concede that it looked 'very pretty and white', according to quotes in *MocoNews*, but pointed out that while 'there will be a billion phones sold next year, on a good year there will be 10 million iPhones'.

Cisco, naturally, was the least impressed with Apple's launch, and that despite what it saw as infringement of its right to exclusive use of the iPhone name, Apple had gone ahead regardless.

Talks ensued, but it soon came to light that German law firm CMS had filed an application for Cisco's rights to use the name to be revoked on the basis that it had not used it in the previous five years. Many suspected Apple had put CMS up to the job, but nonetheless European law stated Cisco's dormant ownership of the name could still have cost it the right to use it on the Internet telephony product it launched mere days before Apple unveiled its own iPhone.

Apple claimed it had the right to use the name itself, as it was the first time it had been applied to a mobile phone, but Cisco fought back by issuing a trademark lawsuit against Apple for infringement.

'We think Cisco's trademark lawsuit is silly,' countered Natalie Kerris, Apple's director of music public relations. 'There are already several companies using the name iPhone for VoIP products and we believe that Cisco's US trademark registration is tenuous at best.'

However, it soon became clear Cisco was not looking for Apple to license the iPhone name from it in return for a healthy cash payment, but to open up the platform to interoperability. 'Fundamentally we wanted an open approach,' wrote Mark Chandler, Cisco's senior vice-president, on the company's blog. 'Our goal was to take that to the next level by facilitating collaboration with Apple. And we wanted to make sure to differentiate the brands in a way that could work for both companies and not confuse people, since our products combine both web access and voice telephony. That is it. Openness and clarity.'

If there is one thing for which Apple is famed – aside from consumer electronics enrobed in smooth white plastic – it is a lack of openness. Over the years, it has refused to license the digital rights management technology it uses to protect downloads from the iTunes Store, or even allow manufacturers to build it into the firmware of their own music players.

Cisco claimed Apple had tried to license the iPhone brand in 2002, five years before the iPhone's eventual shipping date, and that when Cisco had refused Apple had launched a campaign of 'confusion, mistake and deception' in an attempt to muddy things. It had even, Cisco claimed, set up a separate company called Ocean Telecom Services to apply for an iPhone trademark of its own. Apple declined to discuss Ocean Telecom Services, and emails sent to it by *MacUser* magazine went unanswered.

Fortunately, Apple and Cisco continued to discuss the matter in a drive to avert court action, which would have been costly and could have been embarrassing for the party that came off the worse. Negotiations dragged on until late February 2007, with Cisco giving Apple extra time to prepare an adequate response and come to some kind of agreement over use of the name.

Finally, on 22 February, the two sides issued a joint statement. 'Both companies acknowledge the trademark ownership rights that have been granted, and each company will dismiss any pending actions

Queues formed outside Apple Stores right across the US in anticipation of the iPhone's first appearance.

regarding the action,' it said. 'In addition, Cisco and Apple will explore opportunities for interoperability in the areas of security, and consumer and enterprise communications.'

Finally, Apple was free to use the name as it saw fit and could progress with taking the iPhone to market. The next stage in that process was to obtain FCC authorisation to sell the product in the US, without which it would be little more than an expensive hunk of plastic. Approval is a lengthy but important step, and when it finally came through on 18 May, the financial markets took note and Apple's share price immediately leapt 2.2% to $109.70.

Of course, there had been little doubt it would sail through, but Shaw Wu of American Technology Research, who is a regular commentator on business developments affecting Apple, confirmed that the increase could be directly attributed to the iPhone taking another important step towards the shop shelves. 'They are a brand-new player in this space, so it is a big deal,' he said.

The effect that this news had on Apple's share price was a welcome relief for both investors and the company alike, after a faked internal email sent through its own email server and purporting to come from a high-up member of the management team claimed the iPhone was running behind schedule and would not ship on time. This leaked email was widely reported on blog-based news sites, few of which checked the validity of its contents. Investors panicked, with many selling their holdings, leading to a dramatic decrease in the company's value. Whether it was a prank gone wrong or a piece of corporate malice has never been revealed.

The reality of the situation, however, was that Apple was devoting more resources to the iPhone than to just about anything else in production, even taking engineers off its operating system team to work on its firmware.

Nonetheless, Apple continued with its preparations for the launch of the iPhone, building units as quickly as it could, readying points of sale and banning all cameras from the back rooms of its stores. Employees were required to hand over cameras and camera phones as they turned up for work each day, and even Apple's own laptops, which sport cameras built into the tops of their screens, were temporarily outlawed.

As the world entered its last iPhone-free week, analysts started to talk up its prospects like no product Apple had ever launched before, estimating that if all went to plan, it could conceivably sell in excess of half a million units in its first weekend on sale. Apple, clearly in agreement with them, reportedly put in calls to its key suppliers and upped its component orders, with the touchscreen, so important to the device's way of working, at the top of its shopping list.

Now it could only sit back and wait for the storm to make landfall.

The iPhone goes on sale

Finally, at 6pm on Friday 29 June 2007, the iPhone went on sale in the US. Customers had been queuing up outside the company's stores country-wide for days in advance of its release as it generated almost as much consumer excitement as the final Harry Potter novel, released just over a month later. On that day, Apple closed all 164 of its US stores at 2pm to give staff time to prepare for the biggest launch in the company's history. Four hours later, the doors opened to serve customers on a first-come, first-served basis, with a strict limit of just two phones apiece for those lucky enough to get served before stocks ran out. 'Apple retail stores were created for this moment,' said Ron Johnson, Apple's senior vice-president of retail. 'To let customers touch and experience a revolutionary new product.'

The first person to get his hands on one was a guy called Greg, who started queuing outside the New York Apple Store four days early. Apple was not entirely appreciative of his dedication, with one Store employee quoted as saying, 'It is not necessary to camp out. Major Apple retail stores will be well stocked. [Customers] are just wasting their time camping out.'

The Internet was immediately awash with lengthy reviews as the myriad tech news sites did their best to out-do each other in the depth and authority of their coverage. Flickr galleries were quickly populated with pictures both of and taken by the iPhone, and Apple fan-boy blogs spoke of nothing but their owners' new-found loves for mobile communications.

The rest, as they say, is history. The iPhone did, indeed, turn out to be the biggest product launch in Apple's history, and despite what that unnamed Apple Store employee may have claimed, several shops did sell out, with wannabe customers ending up heading home empty handed.

The iPhone returns

Steve Jobs admitted at its UK launch several months later that a second iPhone was already in the works, and that the company was also making plans for the third edition, even before the first generation had proved its worth. That second edition, of course, turned out to be the iPhone 3G, which built in some exciting new features, such as 3G connectivity courtesy of less power-hungry chips, and satellite positioning through the inclusion of a GPS receiver. Since then we have had the 3GS and now the iPhone 4.

When it came to selling the iPhone 3G, Apple formed a completely new business model that more closely matched that operated with the vast majority of mobile phones available. Rather than charging the end-user for the full price of the device and then extracting a share of the subscription fees from the mobile phone network, Apple announced a price reduction in the hardware by allowing the networks to subsidise the device in return for ending the subscription revenue sharing agreement. 'The vast majority of agreements we have reached do not have those follow-on payments,' said Tim Cook, Apple's chief operating officer. 'So you can conclude that the vast majority of carriers do provide subsidies for the phone.'

Apple stuck with its existing network partners in rolling out the iPhone 3G, giving early adopters the chance to upgrade their phones without having to extract themselves from an 18-month contract that still had time to run. As a bonus, O_2 in the UK said that it would not be asking for owners of the original iPhone to return the handsets, allowing them to hang on to them if they chose to upgrade to the iPhone 3G, and run them with a pay-as-you-go Sim in place of the monthly subscription. Over the years new agreements have been signed with other networks, giving owners unprecedented choice.

The iPhone 3G was announced on 9 June 2008 at Apple's annual Worldwide Developers' Conference (WWDC) at the Moscone Centre in San Francisco – the same venue as the announcement of the original iPhone. Showing it off to the assembled developers and journalists, at the same time as the upgraded iPhone 2.0 software for original iPhones, Jobs described it as 'really nice', trumpeted its battery life as offering an 'industry-leading amount of [usage] time' and unveiled its GPS satellite navigation features.

It was all very impressive indeed, but not quite so impressive as the fact that, in line with rumours, Apple was upgrading its .Mac service to offer over-the-air synchronisation with the iPhone (and renaming it MobileMe to increase its appeal to PC users) as well as making it possible to install new applications on the device. All of this was bundled up in a slightly better sculpted body than had housed the first edition of the iPhone. Yet for all its greatness there were a few disappointments: the lack of a higher resolution camera was one, and the fact that there wasn't a second camera in the front of the device to allow 3G video conferencing being another. Both of those points have been solved, with the iPhone 4 sporting two cameras, one of which boasts an impressive resolution of 5 megapixels.

Third-party manufacturers immediately swung into action, announcing cases and add-ons for the new device within a matter of days, but

competing mobile phone manufacturers were silent. In the days following the launch of the first iPhone, some competitors had discounted the device, and claimed that Apple, which has no experience of the mobile phone world, would struggle to make its mark. This time, however, those companies, which had now seen how successful the iPhone was in its first incarnation, were not nearly so bullish.

Apple gave the world just over a month's notice of the new device, naming 11 July as the date the gadget would go on sale in 70 countries around the world. 'Next time you are in Malta and you need an iPhone 3G it will be there for you,' said Steve Jobs, perhaps to put to rest the minds of those who were only too aware that Apple rolls out its products in the US first before distributing them around the world once its native demand has been satisfied. It is a model that has served the company well, with it selling 6 million units of the original iPhone before it announced the update, and the company's chief operating officer, Tim Cook, remaining confident that Apple would hit its target of 10 million iPhones shipped by the end of the year.

However, it did not deliver everything that we might have hoped for. The camera remained stubbornly stuck at its original two-megapixel resolution and there was still no way to buy applications from any source other than Apple's own authorised Store. With the iPhone 3GS, Apple upped the resolution of the camera, added a compass and made the device much faster, and while apps must still be downloaded from its own Store, the iPhone is evolving, and it is sure to continue doing so. Now as we welcome iPhone 4, our advice is simple: keep your eyes peeled for the fifth generation…

Where next for the iPhone?

It was no surprise that Apple came up with a second, third or indeed fourth iPhone. The first edition was an enormous success, but it lacked some key features that were commonplace on less ambitious but cheaper rivals. Key among these was 3G connectivity. Less of an issue in the US, this was a serious omission in Europe, where this faster technology is more commonplace than the Edge networks used in the US, and on which the original iPhone was built. But while this may have been the guarantee that a second iPhone would be built, it was by no means the only factor that led to a second edition – or a third, or a fourth.

So where does Apple go from here? It has surely fixed everything on the third attempt, hasn't it? Well no, not quite.

The camera

The original iPhone – and its follow-up – was criticised for having only a two-megapixel camera, while some competing cameras had already reached five megapixels. Steve Jobs explained that the decision was made to stick at two megapixels because at that level the company could be assured of the quality of the pictures it would produce. This was surprising as many Sony Ericsson phones already exceeded this and still managed to produce images that could rival those taken with a low-end digital camera.

Well, the iPhone has now caught up, with a fully-fledged 5 megapixel camera in the back of its case. Indeed, you could say that it now exceeds the abilities of many of its competitors (if not *most* of them) because it can shoot not only stills but also video – and high definition video at that. With the addition of the optional iMovie for iPhone application it puts a fully-fledged video production tool in your pocket.

The trouble is, only one of iPhone's two cameras sports such a high resolution, with the front-facing camera intended for use with FaceTime, Apple's video conferencing application, sporting far more conservative specifications. This front-facing camera is an obvious upgrade target –

particularly as it is perfect for taking self-portrait shots with landmarks behind you thanks to the fact that when you're using it you have the benefit of the iPhone's bright 3.5in screen facing you, so you can see how you're framed.

The battery

Although Apple seems to have overcome the problem of providing decent battery life with more power-hungry 3G chips, it could still work to improve on the active use time for its mobile handset, which changed very little in the move from the iPhone 3GS to the 4 model.

The 3GS could sustain talk time of five hours on 3G and 12 hours on 2G networks; the iPhone 4 manages a respectable seven hours and 14 hours respectively. Both of these are good, but if you find yourself away on business without your charger, they may still be enough to give you pause for thought. Video playback didn't receive any time boost, remaining stuck at 'up to 10 hours' on the iPhone 4 – the same as the 3GS – despite audio playback receiving a very impressive 33% boost, up from 30 hours to 40 hours. Standby time remains stuck at 300 hours (12.5 days, so almost long enough for a fortnight's holiday, particularly if you turn it off at night) and Internet use now tops out at six and 10 hours on 3G and 2G networks respectively. Both of those figures is one hour shorter on the iPhone 3GS.

All of these are impressive in themselves, but Apple has spent a lot of time in recent years trumpeting its eco credentials. It has removed a lot of harmful materials from its products, which has rightly won it plaudits, and continuing to push the life of its batteries will go further still in winning it friends in the green movement.

The screen

The iPhone screen is better than most and, with a density of 326 pixels per inch, it is capable of producing impressive results when viewing photos or watching movies and TV shows. Apple describes this resolution, which it claims is finer than the human eye can detect, as Retina Display. The main benefit is that it produces supremely crisp images, so activities such as reading eBooks are pleasant and enjoyable. This is important as the company is locked in a battle with the likes of Amazon and Sony in the digital books market. It has rolled out the iBooks application that first appeared on the iPad to the iPhone 4 and opened its own online iBookstore.

The chance of an even higher resolution is very slim at the present time, but a switch to a lower power technology such as OLED may be a possibility as it would enable Apple to extend the battery life still further and reduce the iPhone's current body depth (iPhone 4 is 9.3mm thick), while alternatives that do not require a backlight should remain readable in all lighting conditions and optionally remain in view on the screen even when the iPhone is powered down. Do not expect this technology any time soon, though. Although development started in the 1960s, OLEDs remain expensive to produce and problems with the blue diodes mean that they have shorter lives than the red and green ones that go to make up each array.

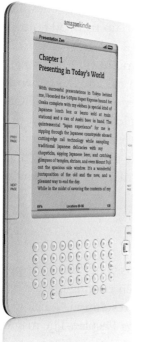

If the iPhone is ever to fully rival dedicated eBook readers (and we hope that one day it will), it will need to adopt a low-power, low-glare screen technology that won't drain the battery just as we reach our novel's climax.

Capacity

One of the best things about the iPhone is its simplicity, provided in part by the sealed box approach mentioned above. The downside here, though, is the fact that the storage capacity you choose when you first buy your iPhone is the one you are stuck with for good. Download a 300MB

With its higher resolution display, the iPhone 4 offers serious competition to established eBook readers, such as Amazon's Kindle device.

half-hour TV show and you have already used up a sizeable chunk. Transfer a movie to watch on a flight and you have eaten up even more. Even if you do not plan on using it as an iPod and so only ever use it to transfer data over MobileMe, it would still be good to know that if you make heavy use of the camera you have the safety net of a removable card to get at your photos should the unthinkable happen. The 32GB capacity of the top-line iPhone 4 will be adequate for most users of today, but over time as our demand for ever greater quantities of portable data increases and we install a wider selection of third party applications we may start to feel the pinch.

FaceTime offline

Right now, the FaceTime video conferencing feature on the iPhone 4 is only available if you are connected to a wifi network. To encourage mass adoption, Apple will need to make it available over cellular networks, too, so that you can use it wherever you are without first finding a wireless hotspot. Moreover, the service will need to see widespread adoption by other mobile manufacturers if it is not to be labelled an iPhone 4 curiosity. Plenty of phones have front-facing cameras like the iPhone 4 – they, too, should get a little face time.

Long-term maintenance

Over time Apple will continue to maintain the growing legion of iPhones already in existence in the form of software updates delivered either through iTunes or, eventually, possibly over wifi and the 3G network. These will have as much of an effect on existing phones as they will on later hardware revisions, but you can almost guarantee that they will do as much to encourage further purchases as they will to shore up security holes in ageing kit. We have already seen this, with iPhone 3's MMS features unavailable to users of the first-generation iPhone and iOS 4's folders invisible to the iPhone 3G. Free upgrades are always welcome, but if they require a hardware purchase, they can sometimes work out expensive.

Glossary

The iPhone may have been designed with ease of use in mind, but it still lives in a world of acronyms and jargon. To really get along with your handset, there are a few words and phrases you really ought to know, starting with these.

3G Third-generation mobile phone network technology offering speeds high enough to enable rudimentary video conferencing and mobile television streaming. It is widely available across much of Europe, but was first introduced for public consumption in Japan in 2001.

802.11A/B/G/N See **wifi**.

AAC Advanced Audio Coding. Audio file format favoured by Apple due to its high quality and ability to incorporate digital rights management features. The default format for tracks downloaded from iTunes Store, or ripped from CD into iTunes.

AIFF Audio Interchange File Format, developed by Apple in 1988 and most commonly used on its Mac computers.

AOL America Online. A popular Internet service provider that, despite its name, has a global presence and is often a good choice for travellers who need access to a single email address across different countries.

BITRATE Means of expressing the number of audio samples processed in a set period of time, usually a second. See also **kilobits per second**.

BLACKBERRY Personal communications device popular with many business users. Although most work as a phone, for many their main use is as a portable email client, through which messages arrive automatically without the user having to instigate retrieval.

BLUETOOTH Short-range radio networking standard, allowing compatible devices to 'see' and interrogate each other to discover their shared abilities and then use these abilities to swap information. It is commonly used to connect mobile phones and headsets for hands-free calling, but is also seen on keyboards and mice used with desktop computers. Beyond headset use, its most common implementation in mobile phones is to swap small data files such as business cards or photos between users. The name was derived from Harald Bluetooth, a Danish and Norwegian king renowned for uniting warring factions in the same way Bluetooth, the technology, unites compatible hardware devices.

COMPRESSION When images on a website or music on an iPhone or iPod are made smaller so that they either download more quickly or take up less space in the device's memory they are said to have been compressed. Compression involves selectively removing parts of the file that are less easily seen or heard by the human eye and ear.

COVER FLOW Technique by which the iPhone and modern iPods allow you to scroll through album covers when choosing a track. This was first introduced on a large scale in iTunes on the Mac and PC.

DOCK Cradle designed for use with an iPhone or iPod that supports the device while it is charging and transfers data to and from a host computer using a bundled 30-pin connector.

DIGITAL RIGHTS MANAGEMENT DRM. Additional encoded data added to a digitised piece of audio or video that controls the way in which it will work, usually preventing it from being shared among several users. See also **FairPlay**.

EDGE Exchange Data rates for GSM Evolution is the network technology used in the first iPhone upon its introduction in the US and Europe. It offers higher speeds than 2.5G networks, but lower speeds than the battery-hungry 3G networks, so has been termed by some 2.75G.

ENCODING The process of capturing an analogue data source, such as a sound or an image, and translating it into a digital format. Although files can be encoded with no loss of quality, the process usually also involves compression to reduce the resulting file sizes.

EXCHANGE Server-based mail handling application developed by Microsoft. It allows for web-based logins in the style of Hotmail or Gmail, and for messages to be either browsed from or downloaded to a remote device such as the iPhone. It is very common in business environments.

FAIRPLAY Digital rights management system developed and used by Apple. It is a closed, proprietary system that Apple has so far refused to license to third-party software and hardware manufacturers, or to music owners on the basis that this could lead to its compromise.

FIREWALL Hardware or software device that controls the flow of data in and out of a machine or network. It can also help to rebuff attacks from hackers. Frequently used by network administrators to ensure that local users do not access external services that could compromise the integrity of the network.

FIREWIRE High-speed computer interface initially developed by Apple and subsequently licensed to other manufacturers. It allows high-speed data transfers and remains popular with video hardware manufacturers, as it also allows a host computer to control a connected, compatible video camera. It was the only interface with which the earliest iPods would work, although later models have dropped it in favour of USB, as used by the iPhone.

FIRMWARE Software built into a device such as the iPhone that controls all of its core functions. The closest equivalent in a regular computer is the operating system that hosts the various applications it runs. Windows and Mac OS X are two examples. Most phones use the same firmware for their whole working lives, but the iPhone is more closely allied to a hand-held portable computer, so will receive periodic firmware updates through iTunes. These will be used to plug security holes, fix problems and introduce new features such as the wireless iTunes Store.

GB Gigabyte. One billion bytes, and a means of measuring the capacity of a device. A byte is made up of eight bits, and a bit is equivalent to a single character, such as a, b, c, 4, 5, 6 and so on. As digital files are encoded using the characters 0 and 1, each digit that makes up part of its encoding will represent one bit, every eight characters will make one byte, every 1,024 bytes will equal a kilobyte and every billion bytes will equate to a gigabyte. To put this into context, the iPhone has a capacity of up to 32GB. If this was devoted entirely to music, then, by Apple's calculations for the equivalent 32GB iPod touch, it would be able to hold about 7,000 songs at iTunes' default settings, although in practice few iPhones will ever carry this much music as some space will have to be given over to contacts, photos and so on.

HOME SCREEN As used within this book, the term used to describe the screen within the iPhone's interface that displays the icons for the various installed applications

HTML Abbreviation for HyperText Mark-up Language, the code used to program web pages. It is a plain-English language, which uses simple tags such as <b> to denote bold, <i> to instigate italics and <p> to mark the start of a paragraph. Several applications, such as Adobe Dreamweaver, greatly simplify the task of writing web pages by allowing programmers to work in a desktop publishing-style layout mode, rather than having to manipulate raw code. HTML is often supplemented by attached styling information in the form of Cascading Style Sheets (CSS). Browsers, including the one in the iPhone, combine the two to construct a page.

IMAP Internet Message Access Protocol. A server-based means of hosting incoming and outgoing email messages such that they can be accessed using a remote client such as the iPhone. The primary benefit of working in this way is that the messages will always be accessible from any device, anywhere and at any time.

iPAD Portable computer device built and sold by Apple. Uses the same operating system as the iPhone and can run compatible applications, but boasts a 1024 x 768 pixel, 9.7in screen, making it easier to type on. Does not have phone features, but connects to the Internet by means of wifi or a 3G cellphone network connection.

iPHONE All-in-one communications and entertainment device from Apple, produced as a follow-up to its phenomenally successful iPod line of portable music players. The iPhone was developed amid utmost secrecy, and finally revealed to the public in January 2007, following massive blog and media speculation. As well as regular telephony features, it incorporates an address book, music and video player, mapping application and full-blown email client with push-email services.

iPOD Portable music player made by Apple. First introduced in October 2001, there have since been five variations on the full-sized iPod, seeing it first gain a colour screen, and latterly incorporating video features, while its capacity has been increased from 5GB in the earliest models to 160GB in the latest version, now called the classic. Over the years, it has been joined by several other models, including two generations of the screenless iPod shuffle, which selects and plays songs in a random order, and the sleek nano.

iTUNES Music management software produced by Apple, also used to manage the connection between an iPhone and Mac or PC. It gives access to the iTunes Store for purchasing music, audiobooks and video content, and will also handle podcast subscriptions.

KILOBITS PER SECOND. A measurement of the number of audio samples that go to make each second of music in a digitally encoded track. The higher this number, the smoother the sound wave will be, and the truer to the original it will sound.

MAC ADDRESS Machine Access Code address. A unique hexadecimal number organised into six pairs of digits that identifies the wireless hardware inside a device such as a computer or the iPhone. As no two devices can ever have the same MAC address, this string of numbers is often used as an identifier to restrict access to wireless access points and other wifi- or Bluetooth-enabled devices.

MALWARE Catch-all term used to describe software and routines that can cause damage to a system or be used to capture users' data, which can then be used for questionable or illegal means.

MEGAPIXEL One million pixels. A measurement used to quantify the ability of a digital camera to capture information. The higher the megapixel measurement, the more information it will capture, leading to larger file sizes, but allowing for the captured image to be either printed on a larger scale or cropped to highlight smaller details. It is a common misconception that higher megapixel counts lead to sharper images, which is not always the case, as image crispness often depends as much on the quality of the lens in front of the sensor.

MOBILEME Online service run by Apple to provide a range of features of use to Mac owners, including email, online storage, calendar synchronisation across multiple machines and basic backup tools. On a Mac it appears as a connected drive, but it has no real support for Windows users, who therefore miss out on being able to post photos to web galleries from an iPhone. Following criticism of the integrated features and level of service, it was given a significant upgrade in summer 2007 and a new look in 2009.

MP3 Shorthand term used to denote audio tracks encoded using the Motion Picture Expert Group codec 2 (Mpeg-2), level three. Arguably the most common audio format found on the web thanks to its widespread use by portable music players. Capable of being read by the iPhone and iPod, but it is not Apple's preferred format.

OS X Operating system developed by Apple. Used inside the iPhone and later versions of the iPod under the name iOS. It shares a common core with Apple's modern operating system for laptop and desktop computers, Mac OS X, which was developed from code it inherited when it acquired Steve Jobs' NeXT computer company. The X in its name is pronounced 'ten' since it is the tenth major iteration of the operating system.

PAC Porting Authorisation Code. This is the alphanumeric code you need to obtain from your existing mobile phone network to move your number (port it) to a different network, even if you have run past the end of your contract. This will be required if you want to transfer an existing mobile phone number to an iPhone. Transfers using a PAC can usually be completed within 30 minutes if you meet all of the necessary requirements.

PLAYLIST Menu of audio tracks or video files waiting to be played. The iPhone and iPod are both able to share playlists with those created on a computer using iTunes.

PODCAST Pre-recorded audio or video programme distributed over the Internet and optimised for playback on portable devices such as the iPod and iPhone. Initially the province of bedroom broadcasters, podcasts have since been embraced by newspaper publishers such as *The Guardian* and *The Times* in the UK, as well as international broadcasters such as the BBC. Video podcasts are sometimes called vodcasts. Apple's GarageBand application, part of iLife, is well suited to their creation.

POP3 Post Office Protocol 3. This is the predominant technology for email delivery used by most consumer-level Internet service providers. All good email clients, including Mail that is built into the iPhone, can use this protocol to receive email.

PUSH EMAIL The technology by which emails are sent from the central server that holds them to a client device, such as a mobile phone or BlackBerry, without the owner having to manually instigate a retrieval for their messages. This is implemented on the iPhone through Apple's own subscription-based MobileMe service.

RIP A term used to described the act of extracting audio from a CD for digital playback from a computer, or portable device such as the iPhone or iPod. *She ripped the CD to her iPhone.*

RSS Rich Site Summary, or Really Simple Syndication, depending on who you are talking to. RSS is a means of presenting the content of a web page without the layout and design so it can be integrated into other sites or read in dedicated applications called aggregators. Google Reader (*reader.google. com*) is an example of a web-based application. RSS aggregation remains a common, infrequently used feature on many mobile phones.

SIM Subscriber Identity Module. The small half-stamp-sized (or smaller) card found in every digital phone handset that identifies it on the network, containing its number and other data.

SMS Short Message Service. Commonly referred to as text messages, SMS is a means of sending brief notes between mobile handsets, which was initially developed as a means for network operators to send messages to their subscribers. SMS messages are generally restricted to 160 characters or fewer, although many phones can thread together multiple discrete messages to make a single, longer communication. The iPhone handles SMS messages in an innovative way, organising them as though they are exchanges in an instant messaging application, allowing for the progression of a conversation to be tracked.

SMTP Simple Mail Transfer Protocol. This is the most common – almost default – means of sending email from any client that works on the basis of composing messages using a standalone client rather than a web-based system such as Imap, as used by the MobileMe service, or the Exchange system developed by Microsoft and popular in businesses.

SSL Secure Sockets Layer. A method used to encrypt data sent across wireless connections and the Internet so that it is less easy for uninvited third parties to intercept.

SYNC Short for synchronise. The means of swapping data between the iPhone and a desktop or laptop computer so that the information on each – including music, photos, contacts and so on – mirrors the other.

TOOLBAR Any area within a piece of software that houses buttons to perform common functions. On the iPhone, all toolbars run along the bottom of the screen. Navigation buttons appear at the top.

USB Universal Serial Bus. A socket, plug and cable system that allows almost any peripheral to be connected to a Mac or PC, including printers, mice, keyboards and so on. The iPhone and iPod also use USB as a means of exchanging data with a computer and, as the cable can carry power, charging their batteries. Due to faster variants, USB is rapidly taking over from the once more popular FireWire in consumer video cameras.

VBR Variable Bit Rate. A means of varying the effective audio resolution of a sound file based on the complexity of its contents. More complex sections of a track will thus have a higher bitrate, while less complex parts will be more heavily compressed.

VOIP Voice over Internet Protocol. A method of compressing voice signals so they can be sent over the Internet and decoded at the receiving end, and so allowing for cheaper or sometimes free phone calls. With built-in wireless networking, many expected Apple to include a VoIP client in the iPhone, but it never appeared in the final specification, although the iPhone 4's wifi-only FaceTime feature may be considered an equivalent application.

WAP Acronym for Wireless Application Protocol. A once-popular but now largely outdated method for programming Internet pages for use on small portable devices with limited screen space, such as mobile phones. Rather than design pages, as with a regular website, the programmer would put together a 'deck', like cards, that could be navigated using hyperlinks and the rudimentary controls found on most standard mobile phones, including joysticks, rocker switches and scroll-wheels.

WAV Short for Waveform audio format. A format used to store audio of all types developed initially by Microsoft and IBM. It remains more popular on Windows computers than Macs and can be played back by both the iPod and iPhone.

WIFI Once colloquial, but now a generally accepted term for wireless networking. It embodies several standards, of which the four most common are 802.11a, 802.11b, 802.11g and 802.11n. The 'a' and 'g' variants can each achieve a maximum data throughput of 54 megabits per second, while 802.11b runs at 11 megabits per second. 802.11n, the fastest standard at 248 megabits per second, is as yet unratified, although draft standards have allowed it to be built into many wireless devices already, giving it good overall industry support. The iPhone uses 802.11b, g and n.

WIRELESS ACCESS POINT Hardware device that connects to your network or broadband connection and replicates the features of wired networks in a wireless form to provide network and Internet access to wifi devices such as the iPhone.

WMA Acronym for Windows Media Audio. A file format developed by Microsoft, with massive industry support, although conspicuous by its absence from the iPhone and iPod. It is the preferred format for many non-Apple online music stores due to its ability to include strong anti-piracy measures inside the encoded file.

Log in, plug in and play

What makes the iPhone such a great gadget? Is it the hardware? Perhaps. The operating system? Maybe. The applications it can run? Almost certainly.

When Apple launched its first mobile phone – the original iPhone – it was very strict about third-party applications. The rule was simple: they were forbidden. Anyone who wanted to develop for the platform had no choice but to write applications that ran through the browser.

This led to many enterprising coders cracking the phone's operating system, a process known as jailbreaking, which allowed them to run unauthorised applications on their handsets. Apple didn't like this, and neither did its network partners, as it meant that customers could use untried and untested software, which had the potential to bring down the networks and cause disruption for other subscribers. Something, clearly, had to be done.

That 'something' was the birth of the iPhone App Store. Apple released its own software development kit and set up a registration system, allowing developers to write their own applications, which would be tested and authorised by Apple itself, then hosted on the iTunes Store. Apple would take a cut for administration, and the developers would get to keep the rest.

It was successful beyond anybody's wildest dreams and now, two years later, there are more than 150,000 applications to choose from. Apple has served more than a billion downloads, allowing iPhone owners to expand their phones' abilities, so that as well as making calls, taking photos and browsing the web, they can now play games, edit office documents and keep in touch with friends in ways they never imagined possible.

Over the next 100 pages, we'll review 200 of the best iPhone applications, helping you to choose the best add-on for your phone.

Nik Rawlinson

CONTENTS

10,500+ Cool Facts

bit.ly/aMjrrA
By **Webworks and applications**
Price *Free*

On opening the Cool Facts app, you're greeted by a random, but cool, fact straight away. Ours informed us that bananas contain the same natural chemical found in Prozac. We wondered why bananas make us so happy and now we know.

You can shuffle through other such facts – some cool and some a bit odd but still very interesting nonetheless – by swiping your finger across or up the screen, in the same way you'd view a photo album.

Each page looks as though it's actually turning similar to a small notepad, which is a nice touch that adds to the pleasant user experience.

You can also press a button in the bottom left-hand corner that allows you to take the day's IQ quiz. It shows you the high score of the day – a challenge there for the taking.

While the quiz was quite fun, in order to get your score you have to enter your mobile number. It then claimed it had sent us a PIN code (needed to receive your score), but we didn't get the text so our no-doubt fabulous score remains a mystery.

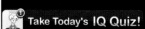

Bananas contain a natural chemical which can make a person happy. This same chemical is also found in Prozac.

Take Today's IQ Quiz!

Good, silly fun that will come in handy down the pub only slightly marred by the need to enter details for the quiz.

8,500+ Drink & Cocktail Recipes Pro

bit.ly/dv1iB5
By **Webworks**
Price *59p*

As the name would suggest, 8,500 Drink and Cocktail Recipes is a recipes app for the iPhone.

It features a huge list of cocktails and drinks with an ingredient list and directions for making each. You can tick off each ingredient if you so wish, although this isn't necessary.

You can find a cocktail by searching down an alphabetical list, browsing through the extensive categories or by selection ingredients to create a cocktail from what you may already have in your larder. If you're feeling risky, the app can randomly pick a cocktail for you to try.

Sometimes you may come across a cocktail that includes ingredients that aren't available in the UK, such as George Dickel and Cheri Beri Pucker, nor are there explanations to what these ingredients are, but they are easy enough to find replacements for if you perform a quick search on the web.

Although the basis behind 8,500 Drink and Cocktail Recipes is simple, it holds a huge amount of information in one app. You're unlikely to drink your way

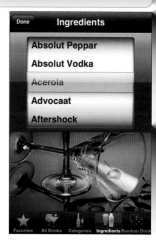

through every cocktail, but the interface is seamless for such an app, especially with all the different search options.

abc PocketPhonics: letter sounds & writing + first words

bit.ly/csaXsD
By **Apps in my Pocket**
Price **59p**

abc PocketPhonics is one of an increasing number of applications available on the App Store aimed at teaching children.

The app is designed to teach children how to say and write letters and simple words in a fully interactive way.

The first time you start up ABC PocketPhonics, you can decide how you want to learn sounds. You can opt between cursive, lowercase or uppercase, although the app recommends cursive or lowercase because this is how children are taught sounds at school. You can also decide between a US or UK voice. You can change these later in the settings menu if you wish.

Fire up abc Pocketphonics and you'll be presented with the sounds screen. Tap on any of the sounds to practice writing them and listening to the sound. The voice will encourage you to repeat the sound to learn it.

There are also other teaching methods, including word games where the voice will say a sound and you have to tap it. When you've chosen letters to make a word, it is then recited and you're encouraged to pronounce it.

abc PocketPhonics is a very basic application in functionality, but it is effective, with a simple, child-friendly interface.

Advanced English Dictionary & Thesaurus

bit.ly/9AK6cE
By **jDictionary Mobile**
Price **59p**

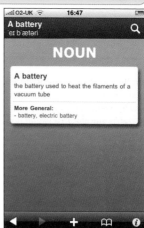

The maker of this app has previously produced English dictionaries for other mobile devices such as Symbian-based handsets and BlackBerrys, and now it's brought one to the iPhone too.

But this is no ordinary digital dictionary. In addition to being a vast resource of words and what they mean, it also educates you as to how words are linked. Indeed, as well as word definitions, synonyms and opposites, hypernyms and meronyms are also served up for you to feast on.

In addition to providing speedy dictionary services at the click of a finger, this type of app goes down well with people keen to expand their mind and knowledge base. There are 250,000 entries featuring more than 1.5 million words in this app so there's plenty to you busy and learning all the time.

It certainly came in handy when we were trying to write an email while on a train and wanted to be sure we were using the correct word. It's a new take on an old, but incredibly useful, concept and one that will no doubt gain many fans who want to remember what *that* word means, as well as for those users who want to brush up on their spelling.

Air Mouse Pro

bit.ly/dnTU37
By **RPA Tech**
Price **£1.19**

Air Mouse Pro is a virtual
mouse and keyboard that you
can use to control your computer.

To use the app, you have
to download the Air Mouse
server for your computer from
the above website, but once it's
installed and opened, the iPhone
app will find the computer and
automatically connect.

Air Mouse Pro is the most
in-depth virtual keyboard and
control tool for the iPhone.
There are four different types
of navigation you can use: a
trackpad, a mouse, music keys
that can control your preferred

music player and a web surfing
interface that includes a home
button, search button, forward
and back keys, function button
layout and a keyboard for typing.

The keyboard can be pulled
up at any time, just in case you
need to type in any one of the
other modes. Whenever you tap
an area on the iPhone's interface,
the action will be highlighted.
For example, if you swipe the
trackpad, an orange glow will
indicate that you've made contact.
If you open an app, the app's
name will appear on the iPhone.
Air Mouse Pro is a highly effective

virtual keyboard app for the
iPhone. With several different
content-specific functions, it's
a real winner in our book.

 ## Air Video

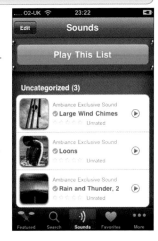

bit.ly/ckODYM
By **InMethod**
Price **£1.79**

Air Video makes content stored
on your PC or Mac available over
a wifi network on your iPhone. It
converts any files that would not
normally play on the iPhone to a
format that it can handle.

It requires you to install
a small application on your
computer. You tell it which folders
and iTunes playlists to keep
an eye on and their contents
become visible in the iPhone app.

You can convert video ahead
of time, but with a powerful
enough computer, Air Video
can do it on the fly, too. On your
iPhone, you can choose the

resolution and bitrate at which
they're streamed, which allows
you to balance your desired
quality against the bandwidth
needed for other family members
to browse the web. Don't bother
trying to stream DRM-protected
video such as TV shows and
movies from the iTunes Store,
as Air Video won't do anything
with them, but it does work with
movies that you've shot yourself,
and other unprotected files.

You'll find the app especially
useful if you've got an 8GB
iPhone 3GS or a 16GB iPhone 4
and want to watch some video

without having to wipe other
things from its memory that
you want to have available all
of the time.

Allrecipes.com Dinner Spinner

bit.ly/cTF6t3
By **All Recipes Inc**
Price *Free*

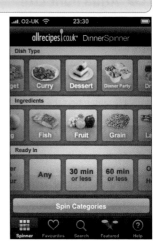

As soon as you launch this app, you're greeted by a fruit machine style plethora of options organised in three strands on a spinner: Dish type, ingredients and how long it takes to make.

Like a fruit machine, you simply set the lines in motion (with a swipe of the finger or by pressing the Spin Categories button) and they move along until they stop. A reassuring 'ding' suggests the app has found a match between the dish type, ingredients and length of time to cook. You then simply click to view the matches.

Our random selection was a dessert, made with fruit that takes 30 minutes or less. We were presented with 21 pages that matched our selection, the first being toffee bananas. To get to the other recipe options you just swipe across, while to access the full recipe and reviews, you click the corresponding buttons.

You can also search the myriad recipes, save your favourites and browse through a selection of 'featured' recipes all at the touch of a button.

Some of the recipes do take a little while to download, but this could be down to speed of connection rather than anything else. All in all, this app guarantees to spice up your dinner time.

Ambiance

bit.ly/c32ZnC
By **Urban Apps**
Price *£1.79*

It's a well-acknowledged fact that there are people who prefer perfect silence in which to sleep and there are those that need some kind of background noise in order to relax. But that background element certainly doesn't extend to building works, planes or motorways – the joys of modern living.

Some claim ambient noise-generating machines can help as they program your mind to filter out the annoying stuff and instead focus on the sounds it projects instead. However, these can be very expensive.

For just short of £2, this iPhone app can give you a little piece of calm wherever you are. If you find yourself traveling a lot and your latest hotel room is next to a lift shaft or you're staying at a friend's house and they live next to a busy road, this app could help you out.

You simply select an ambient sound from the list, sit back and relax. You can also preview a sound before downloading it and create a playlist if you want to mix it up a bit.

There's a vast array of sounds to choose from and if you can't make up your mind you can always look at the most popular and see what everyone else has opted for instead.

Aqua Punt Lite

bit.ly/c2wspU
By **Playtoniq**
Price *Free*

Anyone under the age of 40 probably remembers the water-based, handheld game where you had to push buttons to make air shoot out, pushing balls into through the water and into hoops. Now you can recreate that experience with Aqua Punt Lite.

Okay, so the only sporty aspect is the American football-shaped pieces that you have to propel through the air, but there's nothing wrong with that. You could even start your own tournament with friends to make it more of a competition.

The app is superbly made. When you tap on the touchscreen buttons, you actually feel like you are up against the water pressure to try to get those footballs through the goal posts.

Every time you succeed in getting the ball through a goal post, you get points and free turns. Every time you miss, you lose some turns.

There are three different modes of play crammed into this simple app too – free play, one minute and three minute where you're up against the clock to rack up as many points as possible.

Aqua Punt Lite is a well-made app that will take you back in time to holding one of those plastic games in your little hands.

 Arcade Claw

bit.ly/9OebOb
By **John Moffett**
Price *59p*

Arcade machines can be very addictive, which can often be just as bad for your social life as your bank balance. But this app costs mere pennies and is something you can play under the table while you're with friends, meaning you get the best of both worlds without the scary letter from your bank manager.

Arcade Claw is a classic arcade game brought to the iPhone – a game we love on a device we love. You just use the on-screen 'joy stick' to move the claw around and grab. It's as simple as that. The items up for

grabs range from cuddly toys to footballs and more. Each have certain points and you can play for credits to unlock other parts of the game.

The accelerometer is also put to good use in certain areas of the game to move the items on the screen around. You can even swipe your finger around to get a different view of the game's casing, which is pretty neat.

Once you've played this game, you're hooked and before you know it you've whiled away several hours. Whether you're on your way to work or it's two in

the morning, you're likely to find yourself with a strong craving for this game. But it won't make you gain weight or empty your wallet.

AroundMe

bit.ly/bdPNRj
By **Tweakersoft**
Price *Free*

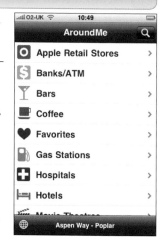

There are few things as dispiriting as arriving in a new area and not knowing where anything is, which is why AroundMe is an excellent app for the iPhone.

It's a point of interest (PoI) search tool that relies on triangulation location techniques together with a GPS signal to find local PoI around you, including banks and ATM machines, bars, coffee houses, petrol stations, hospitals, hotels, parking, pharmacies, restaurants and supermarkets for starters.

The app picks your location up faster than any navigation app will on the iPhone, even loading faster than Google Maps.

If your location isn't accurate, you can enter the postcode, city or even district name, although we found it to be very accurate, even when indoors.

When you select one of the categories, you can view the closest options near where you are, with the distance, a map and phone number, with the option to email the details, add to your favourites and post to Twitter. You can also get directions.

AroundMe is a simple-to-use app, with a vast number of PoIs in its database. Although you will need a GPS connection, it's leaps and bounds better than other similar apps.

 ## ATM Hunter

bit.ly/by0eLT
By **MasterCard**
Price *Free*

There's nothing worse than going into a bar or restaurant, having a really good meal and few drinks then finding out their card machine is broken. It always happens when you only have a few pennies in your pocket.

Worry no more thanks to this handy app from MasterCard. Thanks to GPS, the app can tell you where the nearest cash machine is so you don't have to run around asking people in a bid to get back to the establishment to pay your bill and get them to release the rest of your family that you've left there as 'insurance'.

You can drill down the search if you only want to use your bank's cash machines (to avoid possible charges) as well as typing in an address to see what the cash machine situation is in that location – useful if you're visiting friends or going on holiday. There's also the opportunity to filter for those that offer wheelchair access and deposit services

The app will also go into detail as to whether the ATM in question is attached to a bank or one that has found its way into a shop or pub.

ATM Hunter is the app we all want to have in our pockets for the moment we need it most. Now we can.

Atomic Web Browser

bit.ly/cfrRU4
By **RichTech**
Price **59p**

Browsing the web on Apple's touchscreen devices is so easy because of the gesture-driven navigation of pages. Atomic Web Browser develops that aspect, and it packs in some extra features that Safari lacks.

Its full-screen mode makes great use of the iPhone's limited screen space. It's started with a three-fingered tap. Atomic shows multiple pages as traditional tabs, and horizontal swipes with two fingers jumps between them.

Two-fingers swipes and tapping with three fingers can be assigned new actions.

Configurability is a real strength.

There's also an ad blocker and you can stop images loading altogether to save bandwidth.

Even the search bar is better than Safari's, as you can add any engines that you want to use, not just the ones Apple provides. Sadly, searching within the current page caused us problems when looking for text that was in a collapsed section of a page.

Atomic can import bookmarks exported manually from your computer's browser, and you can keep them under lock and key by setting a Pin code

for the browser. Safari sets the bar high for mobile browsers but Atomic clears it comfortably with its genuinely useful additions.

Audiobooks

bit.ly/91SmOn
By **Cross Forward Consulting**
Price **Free**

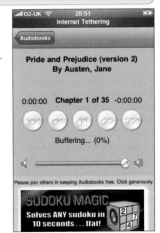

Audiobooks works just like your iPod playlist. Start up the application and you can select an audiobook by Author, Title, Most Popular, or you can pick one at random.

If you opt to browse through the list of available books, they're presented alphabetically in list form and you can scroll through them by swiping your finger down the list. While at the top of the Browse Titles list, there's a search box that allows you to find a title quickly.

There are more than 2,000 books on the Audiobooks

application, all streamed from eBooks site LibriVox. Streaming was pretty fast – the app plays and streams at the same time, so as it plays the first segment, the next part is buffering. This means the quality is clear and you won't have to wait while it buffers the next part of the book.

Unfortunately, you can't stream the content over the 3G network, so you'll have to make sure you have a wifi connection. This also means you won't be able to use it when you're on the move.

Recordings and sound quality is decent for streamed

content, although it's not as good as streamed music you'll find on music services and radio apps such as Last.fm or Capital 95.8.

AutoDesk SketchBook Mobile

bit.ly/cfJHDV
By **Autodesk**
Price **£1.79**

If you're looking for an app to sketch out ideas for visual projects, look no further than SketchBook Mobile.

Open the app and you'll see a blank canvas. The only visible tool is a cog at the bottom of the screen that elegantly conceals the app's power. Tap it and the toolbox appears as a ring of eight items with a loupe in the middle.

The loupe is a representation of the current tool's brush size, which is adjusted by tapping and holding it, then dragging left and right. While you're doing this, a numeric indicator appears on screen to show the brush's diameter. These small touches make SketchBook's interface uncluttered and a joy to use, even on the iPhone's limited screen space.

The toolbox includes a pencil, a pen and a selection of brush styles whose softness, radius, opacity and spacing can be customized. Decisions can be reversed with the eraser and the undo and redo tools. Documents are 1024 by 682 pixels and support six layers on the iPhone 3GS and 4, though these are lower on older models. Creations can be emailed as flat PNG files or layered Photoshop documents that you can develop further on your computer.

AutoStitch Panorama

bit.ly/c7QVRY
By **Cloudburst Research**
Price **£1.79**

Some compact cameras have a panorama feature, but the iPhone's Camera app is short on clever features. The beauty of the App Store is that AutoStitch Panorama plugs the gap.

It's not a bad idea to take your shots with a third-party camera app that offers anti-shake and rule of thirds guidelines to help judge the recommended amount of overlap.

Pick up to 30 photos then tap the Stitch button to set the app to work. It lets you choose the scale at which it processes the selected input images.

The end result can be cropped to a neat rectangular photo. It's saved back to the camera roll. The app can export various sizes up to 20 megapixels, depending on your iPhone model.

On our 3GS, it took less than 40 seconds to make a five-megapixel panorama, and about 150 to render it at 20 megapixels. Some of our panoramas showed ghosting of blended images, but well-lit outdoor shots were much better.

AutoStitch is a great addition to the iPhone's photo capabilities and a must-have app if you want to share an impressive vista with your friends as you stand right in front of it.

Awesome Note

bit.ly/9eaHHN
By **Brid**
Price **£2.39**

Although there's a native note-making app on the iPhone, the interface and functionality doesn't come anywhere near to that of Awesome Note.

If your filing system currently comprises a heap of disorganisation, Awesome Note ensures that all of your virtual notes are kept in order.

When you open the app, you're presented with a number of different coloured folders, set by default as All notes, My idea, Study, Work and Travel Diary. From here, you can add a quick note, which act like digital

Post-It Notes, for quick lists. Add a memo and the app allows you to write a longer note. Being able to access your Google Docs account also allows you to back up your notes to Google.

The most impressive function on Awesome Note is the ability to add documents from your Google Docs account. Simply sign into your Google account and select the documents you wish to import to Awesome Note. At present, this is limited to Word documents, although there's still space for Brid to add other docs too in later versions. Enter the All

Notes folder to view these docs on a notice board-style interface, with all notes organised in an easy to glance at format.

Balance

bit.ly/drSxGn
By **Connor Wakamo**
Price **Free**

The name of this application is an absolute giveaway to what it has to offer.

You first set an opening amount. Then, you just keep adding to your balance as you carry out your normal activities.

You can take an overall view of your income and expenditure, with the total figure at the bottom telling you whether you're in the red or black and you can also sort activities by earliest or most recent.

Transactions can also be exported to your computer by following the slightly complicated

instructions, or by emailing it to yourself then saving the received data as a .csv file.

Security is also ensured by letting users add either a numeric or alphanumeric password to prevent prying or unauthorised eyes from knowing about your financial ins and outs.

It's a bit like a budgeting spreadsheet but much simplified. And certainly more appealing for Excel-phobes than entering the spreadsheet world head on.

It's a nice app and really easy to use, but some people may still prefer to wait for the shock/

surprise of their bank statement landing on the doorstep each month and then working backwards from there.

Bejeweled 2 + Blitz

bit.ly/9t9N7S
By **PopCap Games Inc**
Price **£1.79**

It's a bit like Tetris, except with shiny gems rather than bricks. The aim of the game is to make as many sparkling matches as you can by lining the shapes up.

Each match has to result in a line of three gems of the same colour, but your intended swaps need to result in that match, otherwise they just ping back into their original position, leaving you back where you started.

If you clear two sets or more at the same time, you get extra points. The more matches, the bigger your score – it's as simple as that.

Bejeweled 2 offers users three different gaming modes (classic, action and endless) to vary the fun and keep you entertained. The game has an auto hint feature to help you and also works whether you want to use the iPhone in portrait or landscape mode too.

After playing this game for just a few moments, you'll become almost magpie-like at its shiny interface and become quite addicted to getting the highest score you can. Indeed, if you are a Tetris fan, or you're just very competitive, you'll fall madly

in love with this app. Be warned though, once you've started it's likely to leave very little time in your life for anything else.

Bento

bit.ly/aooGre
By **FileMaker**
Price **£2.99**

Bento is a portable database that can be used with the latest Mac version or on its own. If you don't have a Mac, you can build libraries from scratch or based on templates. They're displayed as lists like the menu structure found in Settings.

Entering a lot of information can be rather slow, as you have to jump back and forth to edit fields, rather than skipping through a form as in Safari, although Bento can store data that's more complex than simple text.

If you have the Mac version, too, calculations can be synced

with it and remain dynamic on the iPhone, but you can't edit their formulae or create new ones on the handset.

Records can be gathered into collections, but the iPhone version lacks Smart Collections, which limits what you can do with the app, making it harder to see all unpaid invoices, for instance. Compounding this is the lack of a spreadsheet-like table view, which we hoped would appear in landscape orientation.

At this price, though, it's worth considering Bento if there isn't a dedicated app that's tailored

to the task you have in mind. Even with some fiddly navigation and missing features, it comes at a great price.

Bible

bit.ly/9P8KP0
By **LifeChurch.tv**
Price *Free*

Like many religious documents, the Holy Bible is a mammoth text. This app brings that important document to the iPhone in a simple and easy-to-read format.

Once you've opened this app, you can choose from an array of language translations in which you want the text to appear, from English to Italian and Vietnamese and many more.

Within the English section, there are also sub-categories for the many and varied translations of the Bible, such as the popular King James edition and so on. You scroll through the text as you would do with any eBook and you can also search for particular words or phrases thanks to the in-built search tool, which has a neat functionality because you can track down the pages you're looking for just based on a single word or search term, rather than trying to remember exactly where the text would sit from memory, which is certainly a time-saver.

Content can be bookmarked for easy reference later and you can also drill down into specific books (such as Genesis, Ruth, Numbers and so on).

There's also a daily reading section, proving you with a few texts to read chosen by the app rather than the user.

 ## Bloomberg

bit.ly/dsdAFX
By **Bloomberg LP**
Price *Free*

Bloomberg is one of the world's most well-know financial news and share price websites.

And its iPhone app gives you access to much of its website content through this app.

Tabs along the bottom allow you to view the different content sections, including news, which is automatically updated from the website using your Internet connection. It displays almost like a Twitter feed, with the headline appearing next to when it was posted. Click on the headline to view the content on the app rather than on the website.

The next tab along is the Markets tab which enables you to view share prices across all of the major markets in the world. You can view a number of different markets including Equity Indices, Commodities, Bonds, Currencies and Equity Index Figures.

My Stocks allows you to add your favourite stocks so you can view progress in one place. To select a stock entry, you simply enter the company name and the position and price will be automatically updated for you.

The Bloomberg iPhone app is probably a lot easier to use than the website when viewed in the Safari browser. The sections are neatly arranged, and even the news stories are easier to read.

BMI Calculator

bit.ly/a5sl76
By **Data Supply**
Price *Free*

Although BMI calculators are scattered all over the Internet, this free app for the iPhone is accurate with results in line with the NHS website.

The interface is simple to use, with height (or length as it's described in the app) options in centimetre, inch and foot, and weight options in kilograms, pounds or stone. After you've entered your height and weight, you next enter your age and whether you're male or female.

Once you've done this, tap calculate BMI and a pop-up box will tell you your BMI and the normal weight range for your age and sex.

This is especially useful when working out the BMI for children because other BMI apps don't ask for the user's age and will calculate the normal BMI based upon an adult's safe weight.

You can view the results on a graph, which is perfect if you're trying to loose weight as it will identify you as being obese. It will also to track changes in your BMI so you can see your progression.

Although the app doesn't take into account other factors that may affect your BMI such as muscle tone, it's an accurate app that will save time compared to using the Internet.

Broadersheet

bit.ly/cwhNsh
By **Broadersheet**
Price **£2.99**

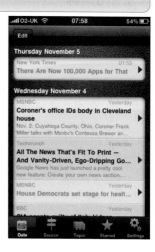

Do you want news from some of the world's most trusted sources in an app that's easy to set up? That's exactly what Broadersheet is for. It pulls articles from a list of respected publications and news agencies that includes CNN, Reuters, Forbes and the BBC.

Choose the sources you want from a fixed list and the topics you want to read about. New categories can be added if the ones you want aren't shown.

Once that's done, you can view stories by date, source or topic by tapping buttons at the bottom of the screen. There's also one that returns you to items that you've tagged with a star. Tap a story and it's displayed in the built-in web browser.

Tap the button at the top-right of a story and you get six links to coverage of the same story from elsewhere, including sources that aren't on the initial shortlist. That gives you a balanced view of events, and it saves you from wading through feeds in an RSS reader to get there. It just takes one tap, although you're at the app's mercy as to the sources it shows.

Broadersheet is clean, simple and a good way to absorb lots of news without the hassle of setting up an RSS reader.

Broken Sword: Director's Cut

bit.ly/bdUszR
By **Revolution**
Price **£2.99**

Broken Sword is a classic PC adventure game adapted for the iPhone with new scenes and puzzles. It sees French journalist Nico Collard and American George Stobbart globetrotting to discover the secrets of the Knights Templar.

Locations are examined by sliding your finger around to reveal small, pulsing circles. Tap them to direct Nico or George to interact with their surroundings and pick up objects and use them to progress deeper into the murder mystery. Revealing points of interest this way seems

like it should make the game too easy, but Broken Sword remains an excellent game for novice detectives and for taxing your grey matter with a mix of inventory-based riddles and puzzle-solving mini-games

Scenes and characters are beautifully rendered in a cartoon style that looks incredible

on the iPhone's screen, and it's worth playing with sound turned on to hear the expressive voice acting.

If it's brainteasing puzzles and an intriguing storyline that you're looking for in an iPhone game, this is most definitely the one for you.

 Brushes

bit.ly/dq1xO8
By **Steve Sprang**
Price **£2.99**

Aspire to be the next Pablo Picasso, or are you more a Vincent Van Gogh in disguise?

With Brushes, you can let your creative juices flow with a whole colour palette and brush selection at your fingertips.

Although Brushes is situated in the Entertainment section of the App Store, it's one of the many art productivity apps available for your iPhone, and is well worth £2.99 if you fancy producing some masterpieces.

The interface is simple; you can edit one of the four preinstalled artworks, add artistic

flair to a photo in your photo album or start with a blank canvas.

If you're starting from scratch, you can fill the background in a solid colour. To add detail, choose a colour from the vast colour palette, and then decide on the size of brush you require using the slider. The iPhone's top-class touchscreen makes it a lot easier to apply colour to your canvas, although you may need to find a stylus-like object to produce intricate details.

If you want to save your creations, you can do using Brushes' gallery feature. Simply

type in the IP address generated by Brushes and your images will be uploaded to your own personal virtual gallery space.

Camera Genius

bit.ly/dhdIBW
By **CodeGoo**
Price *£1.19*

★★★★★

Most people are aware that the camera on the iPhone is a far cry from a compact camera, but Camera Genius goes one step closer to improving the photos taken on your device.

A zoom tool adds a digital function to the iPhone. When you tap on the icon, a zoom bar appears at the bottom, simply drag your finger across it to zoom in and out. The app does sharpen up the image too, although results may look pixelated.

Anti-shake attempts to make your photos as sharp as possible by eliminating any hand tremors,

while big button turns the whole screen into a shutter button.

If you have issues ensuring the horizon is horizontal, tapping on the guides option will bring up a grid so you can line up your image, while the timer function adds a countdown before the shutter will go off.

The camera manual is a whole bank of knowledge, with tips to improve every aspect of your photos, including how to take better pictures.

Camera Genius really is a genius app when it comes to improving the quality of your

images. You can activate all options at the same time too, and coupled with its simple interface, this is a real winner.

 ## Car Driving Theory Test

bit.ly/aMMJGO
By **Eknath Kadam**
Price *£1.79*

★★★★★

Learning to drive a car can be a daunting experience, particularly as learners have to navigate their way around both a practical exam and a theory test.

This app serves up the official Driving Standards Agency theory questions – it contains more than 900 of them – and enables you to study different topics such as motorway rules, safety, hazard awareness and so on.

The questions generated appear randomly so you can't just memorise the order, you really do have understand what you're learning. You can also select just

how many questions you want to go through each time you study, so making it an ideal app to help squeeze in a bit of prep whether you have a spare two minutes or half an hour.

There's also a handy mock test mode so you can see just how well – or how badly – you would have done if you had taken the test for real. Rather than just giving a score at the end of the exam, the app will show you the right answers and an explanation of why that's the case.

This app was certainly an eye opener even for someone who

has been driving for some time. You can also chart your progress through these tests to see how you're improving.

Cha-ching

bit.ly/aBFhBl
By **Midnight Apps**
Price **£1.79**

Cha-Ching is a bank account monitoring tool, and differs slightly from expenditure monitoring apps like iXpenseit.

The app allows you to add a budget for every spend you make, then what you spend is set against these budgets.

Options in the Budget section are extensive. You can add everything from bank charges, credit card payments, a vacation and your mobile phone bill to iTunes spending, to groceries, insurance and utility bills. Once you've set up your budget, you can start adding scheduled payments for eventualities like rent/mortgage payments and loan repayments. Set the date that the payments are taken on, plus how often they're paid and which account they are taken from and you won't have to worry about doing this manually again.

If you have multiple accounts, you can add all of these to ensure you always keep on top of your incomings and outgoings.

One useful extra with Cha-Ching is the ability to sync your Cha-Ching iPhone account with Cha-Ching on your computer – this is handy if you keep accounts on your computer but need to add expenses while out and about on your iPhone.

 ## Children's Classics

bit.ly/9Enlqh
By **BeamItDown Software**
Price **59p**

If your children crave a particular book for bedtime reading then you need never be at a loss if they want their favourite book with this handy app.

The books menu is nicely presented and well laid out. We opted to view *Alice's Adventures in Wonderland* as it's a particular favourite from our childhood.

Once you've chosen your selected text, the app then launches straight into the book rather than a chapter listing. The default font is big and bold and very easy on the eye. You can, of course, change its size, font type, colour, and even the paper, in the settings menu. And, if reading from the beginning of a book to the end is not your style and you want to be able to delve into a specific chapter, you simply click on the chapter menu button from within the book and, hey presto, you have it.

If you tap on the screen, the app will also auto scroll the pages for you – as slow or as fast as you like – and you can double tap again to regain scrolling control. The way you control the scroll of the texts has been really nicely implemented and is an option many will probably use if they're having a lazy day. All in all, this app is an innovative new way to read the great children's classics.

Classics

bit.ly/ai94hl
By Andrew Kaz and Phill Ryu
Price £1.79

There's nothing better than getting lost in a good book to escape from the world around you. But some of the greatest books can be weighty tomes and not something you want to carry around with you.

This Classics app takes the best of the text world and puts it on the iPhone, so your favourite texts can be with you wherever you are. The interface is very cute – you're greeted with a bookshop-style shelf furnished with lots of titles and to get to the one you want, you simply scroll by using your finger.

We picked *The Time Machine* by H G Wells and were very pleased to find that the app's quirkiness is carried through to the texts themselves. To read the book, you flip through the pages with your finger like you would do if it were paper.

You can bookmark the text with a red ribbon that is also visible when the book is placed back on the bookcase. Should you select that book again, it'll open up on that page again.

If you don't want to flip through the pages with your finger there is a shortcut in the

form of a more basic chapter listing, but we felt being able to read a text more like an actual book adds to the experience.

 Coffee Finder

bit.ly/d027XH
By IntuApps
Price *Free*

Driving can be a very pleasurable experience. But it can also be monotonous and boring, particularly if you're stuck in traffic jam after traffic jam.

Coffee Finder is a driver's delight. In addition to helping perk you up, coffee in its many guises is also a treat. This app helps you track down your nearest Starbucks coffee house using GPS. You can also input a particular location if you're visiting somewhere new and want to check whether you can get your coffee fix there too. The ability to click on a map – the app

uses Google Maps for this – or call a store is quite handy and the user interface is very bright and inviting.

Unfortunately, you can't just click on the number like many iPhone apps allow you to do. Instead, there's a dedicated call button, alongside an Invite button, which creates an email with the subject 'Meet me for coffee' and includes your chosen location's address.

This app is likely to appeal to consumers and business users alike who want to meet up with friends or grab five minutes with

colleagues to brainstorm ideas outside the office environment.

And, if you're a coffee addict, it could become a life-saver.

Collins Pro Spanish-English Translation Dictionary

bit.ly/d1NJpM
By **Ultralingua**
Price *£14.99*

There are a whole load of Spanish translation and dictionary apps available for the iPhone, and although Collins Pro Spanish is one of the most expensive, it's also the most useful.

The app is an excellent teaching tool, and although you can search for individual words, you can also view every tense of that word, which is something we found to be essential when learning Spanish.

The app also features the widest selection of words we've seen on any language app. Every single obscure word we could think of was present when we typed it into the search engine.

If you want to translate a word from English to Spanish, you select English-Spanish mode and type the word in the search engine. Select it when the list of words appears and you'll be given the direct translation into Spanish.

To conjugate a verb, tap on the '–ir' icon at the bottom of the screen. Again, type in a verb and a whole list of the conjugated verbs will show up. Tap on tenses to see it in every single tense.

This is one of the most in-depth and easy-to-use apps for the iPhone and is a must for anyone learning Spanish

ColorSplash

bit.ly/ctRl3r
By **Pocket Pixels**
Price *£1.19*

ColorSplash gives you the ability to make mono images of your photos then re-introduces just a splash of colour to add a vibrant touch to the image.

Simply load up an image into the app and it will automatically be converted to black-and-white. Trace over those parts of the image that you want to return to colour with your finger and those hues will shine through.

Your finger effectively acts as a paintbrush, although those with larger digits may find this level of control a little tricky to use to at first, however, it is very intuitive to use. Thankfully, you can pan and zoom into your photos using the icon at the bottom of the screen.

If you make a mistake while you're creating your masterpiece, you can switch to the grey option situated at the bottom of the screen that will re-grey out areas of the photo.

You also have a range of different paintbrushes to use which allow differing degrees of colour to come through. There are two hard brushes, one that is lighter than the other, and two softer-edged, with one brush that lets stronger colour through.

An in-depth tutorial makes the app even easier to use, with videos illustrating exactly what you can do with the app.

CoPilot Live UK & Ireland

bit.ly/dab4Ds
By **ALK Technologies**
Price *£19.99*

CoPilot was one of the first serious SatNav apps to become available for the iPhone, and priced at £19.99, you would expect it to worth every penny.

Like all of CoPilot's mobile solutions, the interface is sleek and simple. Choose whether you want to find a destination, go to MyPlaces, change the settings or change the mode. CoPilot allows you to navigate for driving a car, motorcycle, bicycle or walking, so pick your option, and then head to the Destination menu.

Here you can find a destination by address (city or postcode),

point of interest, from an address in Contacts, choose a place on a map, find an intersection or enter the coordinates. Yes, this app is very in-depth.

Routes are calculated quickly after you've entered your destination, with the distance appearing at the bottom of the screen. You can scroll around the map (although not when driving), view the whole itinerary and view the map in either 2D or 3D, in landscape or portrait mode.

CoPilot works seamlessly with the iPhone hardware, making use of its loudspeaker,

large screen and fast-fixing GPS. We can't recommend it more if you're looking for an all-in-one phone and navigation option.

Copy2Contact Pro

bit.ly/bSuQl4
By **Anagram Technologies**
Price *£2.99*

The iPhone recognises certain information in text and lets you tap to view addresses on a map and create new contacts based on the detected details. However, it doesn't capture all of the adjacent information, such as website addresses and company names in email signatures. Copy2Contact Pro improves matters significantly.

Copy a block of text to the Clipboard, then open the app. It dissects the data and splits it between the various fields that make up a contact, which you can review before saving.

It successfully split our email signatures, even managing to pick out separate landline, mobile and fax number, and place them in the correct fields.

The app doesn't just discard information it's unsure about. It's placed in the comments field, so you can tidy up the loose ends.

However, the app doesn't deal well with numbers that include a country code and a zero in brackets. The brackets are discarded but the digit remains and has to be removed by hand. That's an irritating oversight but easy enough to work around.

Copy2Contact Pro is highly recommended if the iPhone plays a central role in managing your contacts and meetings.

Currency

bit.ly/cCIPFU
By **Jeffrey Grossman**
Price *Free*

Holidays are exciting. The build up, the packing, the airport and the change of scenery all add to and enhance the experience. But it's always a bit of an anti-climax to get the credit card statement through the post a few weeks after you've come back and your tan has faded.

It's often hard to keep track of just how much you're spending and how much of a bargain something is when you're in a different country and the price tags are completely foreign to you.

This app provides up-to-date exchange rates to help keep your spending in check. It's packed with data for more than 90 currencies and 100 countries, meaning unless you're traveling somewhere really obscure, it will most likely be of some value.

This app could be equally as useful to business people who have to travel a lot as part of their jobs – especially if they're charged with keeping a close eye on their expenses.

Whether you're a high-flying business executive who finds it hard to know what country you're in let alone its exchange rate or you're on your annual family holiday to Spain, this app will become a trusted part of your travel entourage, allowing you to know the cost of every purchase.

Currency.app

bit.ly/aFp5vg
By **Flux Forge**
Price *£1.19*

If you're a frequent traveller, or are even just heading out of the country for a short time, it's important to keep on top of the current currency rates.

Currency.app enables you to view multiple currency conversion in real time, so you can monitor exchange rates wherever you are, at any time of the day. The interface is a doddle, with the ability to add currencies to the app's homepage with just a couple of taps.

As default, Euros and US dollars are displayed, but to add new ones, you simply tap on the Add new box, where you're taken to an interface comprising two scroll wheels – the 'to' and 'from' currencies. Just swipe to find the currency you're after

One issue we had was working out the shortcodes for the currencies, but if you know these, you'll have no problem.

To perform a currency conversion, you simply need to enter a monetary amount in the box at the top of the app page. The conversion amount will then be displayed in the boxes below.

To track the changes in exchange rates, tap on the currency you're interested in, and you'll be presented with a graph of exchange rate changes over the past two months.

Day Bank

bit.ly/a6dxd3
By **Quantum Quinn**
Price **£1.19**

A frugal mind will carefully manage money, which normally means checking your records at home and planning your purchases. Day Bank lets you carry a record of transactions, regular payments and budgetary reports to put a view of your financial standing in the palm of your hand.

Transactions can be assigned to your own categories so that your view makes sense to you, rather than being shoehorned into awkward templates.

You can simply record the amount of each deposit or withdrawal, or attach memos, photographs of receipts and even your iPhone's GPS location, though that has to be done on the spot.

Avoid missing payments by tapping the filter, which shows what needs to be paid today, this week or this month.

Day Bank isn't good for tracking money spent abroad as it records in the currency based on your iPhone's settings, with no way to override them.

However, it's an inexpensive way to track your regular spending, and it syncs records to the free Day Bank Station app that's available for PCs and Macs, as well as exporting to Excel, Quicken and Microsoft Money.

 ## Daylight

bit.ly/9U4g8h
By **Philippe Casgrain**
Price **Free**

Getting up, going to work, coming home and sleeping, then doing the same thing all over again. It's a familiar story for the majority of us, so it's no wonder we're keen to maximise the amount of day we have between waking up and going to bed.

This Daylight app can help you do just that. The app displays sunrise and sunset times for your location as well as for any future date.

That means you'll know whether it will be dark or light when you get up or are heading home and can therefore plan accordingly. The app also claims to be handy for photographers, who might want to catch the golden halo during sunset and amateur astronomers, whose work tends to be heavily slanted towards the sun and moon. And it could prove a handy planning tool for both groups of hobbyists in helping them plan out their activities.

The Daylight app is very simple to use and the information displayed not too complicated or overwhelming.

It certainly stands out in a crowd of very samey apps in this space and is as useful for commuters as it is people trying to plan their journey home from a day out.

Delivery Status touch

bit.ly/dw3090
By **Junecloud**
Price **£2.99**

This app saves you the bother of logging into multiple websites to track packages by gathering them into an app on your iPhone. It's a great way to keep an eye on important business documents, gifts sent from Amazon, and items that you've sold on eBay.

It works with various couriers including FedEx, UPS and DHL. You'll find a complete list on Junecloud's website. Before you can track packages on your iPhone, you'll have to register at the website for an account.

After that, you can add new deliveries to the account using a web browser. You don't even have to copy and paste package details into Junecloud's website. Instead, you can use a shortcut bookmark that looks at the page you're viewing, extracts the details and automatically adds them to your Junecloud account for you. The account is free.

Open up the iPhone app and it grabs the latest information from the website. Its interface is clean as a whistle. Each package shows a countdown to the estimated delivery date in huge type, and it's easy to spot ones that have been delivered because they're shown in an unmistakable red. The enhancement we'd like to see is push notifications to be sure that people have received parcels.

Dictionary.com – Dictionary & Thesaurus

bit.ly/bGvJNG
By **Dictionary.com**
Price **Free**

Dictionary.com is more than just a dictionary for finding the meaning of a word, it also packs in a thesaurus as well.

When you begin to search for a word, options appear in a list. Even if you don't know how to spell the word, type in a couple of letters and scroll down the list to find the correct spelling.

When you've found your word, tap on it and you'll be presented with the word split up into sounds plus you can opt to listen to how the word is pronounced by tapping on the speaker icon.

Below the pronunciation, there's a description of the word meaning and examples of situations where you would expect to use that word.

The second tab along the bottom is a thesaurus where you can see similar words for the one you're searching for. All along the way, the words you've looked at are saved into your history, and remain there until you decide to delete your history.

If you're simply trying to expand your grammar, the word of the day section is highly recommended feature of this app. Every day a new word is chosen, again with the meaning and examples of how to use the word are listed below.

Documents

bit.ly/cTcMYv
By **Savy Soda**
Price **59p**

The ability to read and edit documents on the move is a key requirement for many of today's business people. Even those who don't want to necessarily keep in touch with their office when they're on the move are most likely to be writing a report or managing various budgets.

Documents is a small app that aims to take care of that need by enabling you to edit and manage text and spreadsheet files on the iPhone. The app comes bundled with several tools, which include:
● iSpreadsheet
● Text Editor
● File Browser
● Instant Email

There's also Google Sync, which enables you upload and download your files, and then view these mobile-born documents on your computer back at the office. A link to an online help page is also included in the app, just in case you want to do something that's not immediately obvious – although, in the main, the app is very simple to use.

The interface is a little bit garish with an odd shade of green, but that colour choice is more than overshadowed by the potential the app offers for a relatively low price tag.

 ## Documents To Go

bit.ly/9XhCO5
By **DataViz**
Price **£5.99**

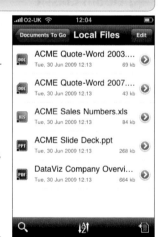

Documents To Go is one of the most-used apps for viewing, editing and creating documents on a smartphone, and it's popular for a reason.

The app gives you full functionality to use any of the main Microsoft Office apps in full, including Word, Excel and Powerpoint, plus it also has Adobe Reader for viewing PDFs.

In all, Documents To Go can read .doc, .xls, .ppt, .pdf, .htm, .txt, .jpg, .gif, .png, .tif and .bmp files, and it can also edit those files that are text-based. For .doc files it provides all the basic functionality you have in Microsoft Word, such as bold and italic options, underlining and bullet points.

Naturally, with the iPhone's landscape keyboard functionality, you can type your documents as though you're using a normal computer with the pop-up Qwerty keyboard.

Although you can't edit Excel spreadsheets, this is no bad thing, because the cells are simply too small to add text and formulae. You can view them as well as zoom in and out as you wish if you need a more detailed look.

You can download a desktop app for your computer to sync your docs with your PC or Mac over a wifi connection.

Done

bit.ly/aPm06n
By **Chilli X**
Price **£1.19**

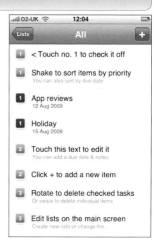

One of the biggest complaints of the iPhone is that it doesn't feature any kind of to do list app like some other smartphones.

However, there's a huge array of apps on the App Store to choose from, but we were most impressed by Done, probably the most simple out of all those available.

The interface is slick, while adding new tasks is speedy and simple. There's the option to create your own categories too, such as personal and work, each highlighted in a different colour to ensure you know what's what.

Handy additions, such as shaking the iPhone to reorganise the list by priority, and taking a snapshot of a task then saving it as your iPhone's wallpaper as a constant reminder of what needs to be done.

One minor complaint with Done is that there's no push notification functionality so if you fail to open the app, or don't look at your wallpaper often enough, you could miss an important task that desperately needs to be done.

This is just a small oversight by Chilli X though, the importance of having an app

where you can add events, jobs and tasks as you need them is paramount, and this is exactly what Done does.

 Doom Classic

bit.ly/1na3JW
By **id Software**
Price **£3.99**

This recreation of the 1993 game lets you punch, chainsaw and blast your way through the horrors of Mars across 36 levels. Being unable to crouch, jump and look up and down seems odd today, but Doom Classic's labyrinthine base has a real depth to its level design. Careful exploration will yield hidden arms caches, and some unpleasant surprises.

Enemies may look like cardboard cutouts, but coming face to face with a grotesque monster is still enough to set your pulse racing. Their grunts

and snarls are repetitive, and of similar calibre to the noise of Pac-Man guzzling down pills, adding atmosphere to the red planet.

However, the controls are a bit of a problem. Three variations are available, including one that lets you move, turn, strafe and fire. Our steps were more tentative than with a mouse and keyboard,

not out of fear of enemies, but of taking a wrong step and plummeting to our death in one of the game's pits of toxic waste.

Four-person cooperative and deathmatch modes over wifi add some longevity. Doom may look its age, but this is a fun if slightly dented walk down memory lane.

Drum Kit

bit.ly/bBwNDP
By **CrimsonJet**
Price **£1.19**

Like piano apps, there are also enough drumming apps on the App Store to keep Ringo Starr out of mischief, but Drum Kit is the one with all the hype at the moment, and rightly so.

Although when you first start the app, you're presented with an interface that comprises a full drum kit and, well, that's about it – the app will provide enough joy to keep you satisfied for hours.

Tap on the 'i' and you can change the type of drumkit, with options including Classic Kit, Rock Kit, Hip Hop Kit, Techno Kit and Dance Kit.

Each kit has its own particular sound, with the techno and dance kits allowing you to create some funky electro compositions, while the Hip Hop kit features more bassy sounds.

You can also record each jamming session, again by tapping on the 'i' icon in the bottom-right corner, so you can review your technique.

If you think you're a little out of time, turn the metronome on for guidance.

Although Drum Kit seems more of a fun app to pass the time, with extensive options and sound effects, it could prove an indispensable tool for more serious music makers too.

DSLR Camera Remote Pro Edition

bit.ly/cFfcu4
By **OnOne Software**
Price **£11.99**

DSLR Camera Remote lets you take pictures with certain Canon or Nikon digital SLRs, and immediately review the results on your iPhone. If you're unhappy with the results, you can adjust shutter speed, aperture width, ISO, white balance mode and exposure compensation right on your iPhone and retake the shot.

That lets you participate in group shots without darting back and forth, and experiment with camera positions that would otherwise be uncomfortable.

Your commands are passed over wifi to a small application

that runs on your PC or Mac. Your camera must be connected to the computer with a USB cable.

It captures images to a folder and sends a preview back to the iPhone app. Double-tapping gives you a closer look but you can't pinch to adjust or swipe around the photo. Cameras with live preview stream it to the app before you even shoot.

Advanced settings behind the cog button give you control over burst mode, automatic bracketing and shooting at intervals, and all of this is wrapped in an easy interface.

If you're a dab hand with your DSLR's shooting modes, you'll love the flexibility of this affordable remote control.

 eBay Mobile

bit.ly/aVa5U0
By **eBay Inc**
Price *Free*

★★★★☆

There's nothing worse than placing a bid on an eBay listing, popping out only to miss the end of the listing end and lose the auction, missing out on whatever it was you wanted.

eBay Mobile has been designed to be carried round wherever you go, on your iPhone so you can save the pain on a lost item and broken heart.

The app isn't as fully functional as the website, but you can bid on items and view My eBay, which are the most important aspects of being able to access eBay on the move.

You can't pay for items directly from the eBay app, however, you can with the PayPal app mentioned earlier, provided you have the seller's email address. Search is just as extensive as it is on the full site, with popular searches appearing at the bottom of the homescreen for quick access.

It's a simple task to ask sellers any questions you might have over their auction items, watch an item in My eBay and place a bid on an item using the large icons at the bottom of the item information screen.

Although extra features such as push notifications when you've won an auction are missing, this is an essential app for eBay users.

eBuddy Messenger

bit.ly/9G66yA
By **eBuddy**
Price *Free*

★★★★☆

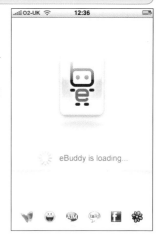

It's usually a bad idea to mix your different groups of friends together. They talk, compare notes on you, and in general perform character assassination by committee.

That's not the case with eBuddy though, which brings all your online friends together in a single place, so there's no need to go hunting through different apps to chat to them.

eBuddy is a simplified instant messaging app, supporting multiple accounts simultaneously. Feed it your MSN, Aim, Facebook, Yahoo! or Google

Talk details and it will sign you in. It even supports ICQ, for those old enough to still be using it.

Your contacts are lumped into a single list, regardless of where eBuddy found them. Some people might prefer to see whether they're talking to a Windows Live contact rather than Google Talk, but we thought it was easier to just view all contacts at once.

eBuddy also supports push notifications. Like other apps, you can choose how long you remain logged in to your networks after the iPhone app has been closed.

Although some organisation of eBuddy leaves a lot to be desired, it's great for uniting all of your friends in one place.

Echofon for Twitter

bit.ly/aAG8df
By **naan Studio Inc**
Price *Free*

It seems as though the world is on Twitter. Whether they're inane ramblings about breakfast and falling asleep on the last train home to breaking news stories this micro-blogging site has taken the Internet by storm.

And those that like to tweet often need to be able to do so wherever they are. Cue Echofon for Twitter. Once you've entered your Twitter account details, everything else is pretty much done for you.

The app pulls in your friends tweets and then gives you easy access to your @ mentions and messages by displaying a number next to the icon on the horizontal bottom menubar, much in the same way the iPhone notifies you of texts and missed calls.

Once you click on a tweet, you get a more info about the tweeter, such as number of followers and website. You can also reply to them, send a direct message (if they're following you) and retweet their message. You can also see their previous tweet timeline too.

Of course, the big draw is being able to update your own status, and this is quick and simple, with buttons if you want to add a picture or set your location.

Other Twitter apps are available, but this is our favourite.

Eight Glasses a Day

bit.ly/aaAFr1
By **Emblem Design Group**
Price *59p*

The human body is made up of at least 50% water and it's important to ensure we're replenished to enable our brain and organs to function correctly.

But remembering to drink the right amount of water each day can be quite an arduous task, or result in a mad scramble to drink a large quantity towards the end of the day – which just leaves you feeling bloated and needing the loo quite a lot.

The eight glasses app takes a serious health consideration and adds an element of fun to it. The premise is simple: every time you've drunk an 8oz glass of water, you just tap a glass on the screen and it empties. You continue doing this each time you have enough water until all the glasses on the screen are empty.

When you're not in the app itself, the icon will show how many glasses you have left to drink in a small red bubble in the top right-hand corner, in the same way missed calls or text message volumes are displayed.

The real beauty of this application is its simplicity. It's not over complicated or too fancy – in either design or function – it just does exactly what it claims to do and what you need it do to. Nothing more and nothing less.

Eponyms

bit.ly/dd6p9h
By **Pascal Pfiffner**
Price **£1.19**

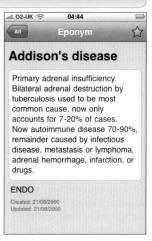

Once you've worked out what an eponym is (it's akin to eponymous and means a place/thing/era named after someone) you can then delve into the murky waters of medical eponyms.

This app plays home to short descriptions of more than 1,600 of the most common medical eponyms and displays them in an easy-to-navigate index, complemented by search engine functionality.

You can check for updates to the database at anytime and the app will pull in any new eponyms that have been added to the already quite substantial list. So if you're hungry from more knowledge in this area, this app is likely to please.

Once you've played around with it for a bit, you'll know – without looking – what Rovsing's sign and Virchow's node are and be able to share that niche knowledge with all your friends to show them you know something they don't. It's likely they'll either be very impressed or slap you across the face for boasting.

And for those whose business it is to know such things,

this app will serve as a helpful pocket guide that you can refer to when your little grey cells are on a go-slow.

Espgaluda II

bit.ly/ci9Aq0
By **Cave**
Price **£5.49**

Once you've beaten back the Space Invaders in Taito's excellent Infinity Gene, try your hand at Espgaluda II. We were surprised that the iPhone could pull off the more ambitious sub-genre known as bullet hell, where the screen is peppered with enough bullets to make you queasy. Espgaluda II blows away all doubts.

Our concern was that the iPhone's screen would make this sort of game unplayable, but it's not as inhibiting as you might expect. The protagonist is moved by dragging your thumb around

the screen. Forget the storyline, though: the focus here is fast-paced and frantic action, and it's pulled off with aplomb.

Focus on the bullets that swathe the screen and navigate the gaps between them. Like the best of bullet hell shooters, Espgaluda II keeps you on edge to the point that you dare not blink too often. Thankfully, the collision detection is forgiving and you can get very close to bullets without being injured. Espgaluda uses the free Open Feint to keep track of scores, bringing back memories of trying

to beat high scores in your local arcade. You'll need an iPhone 3GS, iPhone 4 or 3rd-generation iPod touch to play it.

ESPN ScoreCenter

bit.ly/aKYW12
By **ESPN**
Price *Free*

To many UK sports fans, ESPN has probably had little impact on their lives before the 2009 English Premier League season started. But along with the US sports broadcaster's entry into the big time in the UK comes their very handy ScoreCenter app.

ScoreCenter allows you to select the sports you wish to follow, including English Premier League football, rugby and tennis in addition to the US sports, golf, F1 and more. A simple slide of the page and you can view your next sport and click on the individual match or game, which leads to

in-depth reports, stats, scorers, league tables and so on.

Essentially ESPN has created a do-it-all app for the 10 or so most popular world sports, and it works well. ScoreCenter looks good and provides pretty much all the info you'll ever want. It also has ESPN Mobile Web built, meaning links can be clicked on without the app exiting and launching Safari separately.

Some apps for specific sports may offer slightly more functions, but there are going to be few competitors when it comes to a generic sports

app. ScoreCenter comes highly recommended, and provides all the most important information on your chosen sports.

Eurosport

bit.ly/a8DGii
By **Eurosport**
Price *Free*

The Eurosport app reproduces the content from Eurosport's website and TV programme onto the iPhone, in a specially optimised format.

The homepage is split into four different sections – headlines, in brief, live and results. Headlines give a more in-depth summary of the latest news, while in brief is presented in an easier to read format, without pictures.

The live section provides up-to-the-minute results for all major sports, while the results are equally as fast to come in, relying on a data connection to update.

Along the bottom, you can view the same sections, but for each sport. There are separate tabs for football, tennis, cricket, Formula 1, WTCC, IRC, Moto GP, rugby, snooker, cycling and athletics, enabling you to filter the headlines, in brief news stories and results for your favourite sports.

Once you're reading a story, you can skip to the next one without having to go back to the homescreen – just use the arrows in the top-right corner.

The share settings are a little sparse – you can share on Facebook or send stories by email,

but with few personalisation options, Eurosport is a little bland for the casual user but essential for a sport addict.

Evernote

bit.ly/aff3KJ
By **Evernote**
Price *Free*

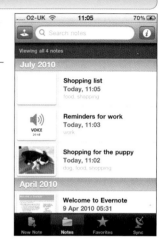

The latest version of iOS is able to sync notes with your Google account and MobileMe, but Evernote is an alternative that lets you add custom tags to your notes, and it searches through those tags and the contents of notes in a jiffy. You can organise notes into separate notebooks, too, so you can maintain one for all your home tasks, another for work and maybe yet another to use as your holiday planner.

You don't even have to pay for it, as a free account is provided. A premium option is also available for $5 (about

£3.29) per month, increasing the transfer limit to 500MB per month; free accounts are capped at 40MB. However, it can also record images and audio notes using the iPhone's camera and microphone, which may push you close to the limit.

Incoming calls, text messages, and unsynchronised notes are transferred to the web server, after which they're accessible through desktop apps on your PC or Mac, and through a web-based service.

It would be handy to be able to append to existing audio

recordings, but otherwise this is a great enhancement if Apple's built-in Notes don't live up to your needs.

F1 Insider 2010

bit.ly/dmJsVy
By **Greenius Mobile**
Price *£1.19*

Many of the sports apps on the App Store are news-based. However, F1 Insider 2010 adds a little more to the mix. Although it does feature a comprehensive news section, it's not the main focus of the app.

In addition to news, there's also an overview of every single race and qualifier in the F1 season, as well as each driver and team's standing.

When you launch the app, the next meet appears on the homescreen, accompanied by the county's flag. Here, you can view the time and date for each

practice, qualifier and race for that Grand Prix. Tap on the race and you'll see a countdown until the actual start.

If you select a race that has already taken place, you can view each driver's finishing position and their time. Tap on the feed tab and there's a minute-by-minute feed of the race as it happens.

Have a favourite driver or team? You can select them in the settings to follow their progress throughout the season.

Most sports apps are bland and provide little information

apart from news. However, F1 Insider has one of the sleekest interfaces we've seen and is a breeze to use.

Facebook

bit.ly/b9zwz2
By Facebook
Price *Free*

This official Facebook app means you never have to be without your trusty social networking companion as it can travel with you everywhere in your pocket.

Stuck on a train for four hours and already tweeted that fact? Time to update your Facebook status too.

This app provides a shrunken version of the full Facebook client, but it retains the familiar look and feel of its bigger brother. On opening the app you're greeted by a homescreen that details some of your friends'

feeds. On the main menubar, which is located at the top-right corner of the screen, you'll find access to most of the usual Facebook features. Here, you can access your Profile, see those of your Friends, check out your News Feed, emails in your Inbox, Chat and Photos.

It all works in much the same way as you'd expect and is a great way of keeping abreast with what your friends are up too – particularly as Facebook is now competing for attention in your life with other social networking sites such as Twitter.

Just remember not to post that hangover update when you're about to take a sickie from work.

 ## FeX for Facebook

bit.ly/9bfdLi
By CocoaMotion Inc
Price *£1.19*

The iPhone is all about convergence. Not only does it make phonecalls and send text messages, but it's capable of surfing the Internet, sending and receiving email, taking photos and planning a long road journey.

Friend Exchange (or FeX for short) for Facebook is one app that helps in this convergence universe; simply put, it communicates with the social networking site and retrieves valuable information that is then stored on your phone.

For example, when one of your friends calls you, their

Facebook profile image is displayed. This is because FeX for Facebook downloads these images from your Facebook friends list and adds them to your iPhone contacts automatically.

What's more, FeX for Facebook also makes a note of your friends' birthdays, so you need never endure the embarrassment of missing that big day again. You can consult a list that not only shows upcoming birthdays, but also displays your friends' current age.

It's even possible to add friends from Facebook to your

iPhone contacts, so if you know someone has provided their contact details on the site, you can instantly add them to your phone.

FingerPiano

bit.ly/apOKcz
By **Junpei Wada**
Price *£1.19*

There are a whole barrage of piano and music playing applications on the App Store, but FingerPiano is one of the better apps because it teaches you how to play the piano.

You can choose from a massive list of different songs to play, some well-known tunes to lesser known tracks, both for those right- and left-handed.

You're instructed how to play the songs by green and blue markers that appear above the correct keys. Blue marks the naturals (white keys), while green signifies the sharps (black keys).

Tap these in the order that they appear to produce music.

You can also play the songs in advance if you can't remember what they sound like. To fast forward through the track to see how a certain part is played, tap the fast forward key in the top-right corner. You can also rewind.

One small issue we had was more

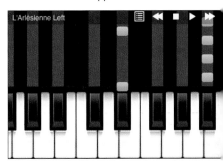

down to the iPhone's hardware than the app itself. Because you need to hold the iPhone in two hands, your palm may obscure the speaker, resulting in sever changes in volume. As a non-piano player, we managed to wow friends with our musical abilities. An app that's well worth £1.19.

Fitnessbuilder

bit.ly/bH20qo
By **PumpOne**
Price *£5.99*

Modern life leaves very little time or money for you to go to the gym for a workout with a personal trainer à la celebsville.

But you don't have to be an A-lister to get fit. You just need an iPhone. This application is a bit like having a personal trainer in your pocket, however, one that is less shouty and a more silent exercise partner.

It contains more than 400 different workouts so they should be something for everyone no matter what your level of fitness or how much time you can dedicate to the job. You can also

customise your own workouts, taking the bits you like from one workout and leaving the moves you don't behind.

In addition to guiding you through exercises, the app can help you chart your progress by logging and tracking your details before, during and after your longer term regime.

The real beauty of this app is it lets you workout at your own pace, wherever you want. It also costs about the same as most fitness DVDs and is a tiny price to pay compared to the ongoing costs of a charge-by-the-hour

personal trainer or monthly gym membership. And, if it keeps you happy and healthy, it's certainly money well spent.

Flight Control

bit.ly/dw6N2S
By **Firemint**
Price *59p*

Flight Control has the potential to become a mobile phone gaming classic to rival the likes of Snake. It's so simple, yet addictive.

Your job is to guide the incoming aircraft to a safe landing at your airport. On each level, there are the two runways and a helipad on to which you have to land a variety of planes and helicopters. The quicker planes land, the quicker new planes approach, coming from all directions and at different speeds.

It soon becomes tricky and while concentrating on landing one plane it is easy to miss two coming in the other side of the screen. Unless carefully guided, the planes will collide and when that happens it's game over.

Despite the relatively basic design, the game is aesthetically pleasing and is easy to control. There is a choice of three airports and the gameplay works nicely by simply dragging a finger from the plane to the end of the runway, with a dotted line showing the plotted flight path.

Ironically, the only downside is its simplicity. The game only has one level and unless further additions are made it's appeal may not last. Overall though, a good game that works well.

Folders – Private File Storage and Viewing

bit.ly/cE6Rfc
By **Ractor**
Price *£1.19*

With more and more business users opting to blur the lines between work and play with their iPhones, security of data is becoming even more paramount.

With this app, you can be safe in the knowledge that those files you've imported on to you iPhone can be hidden away – for use on the move – and password protected from prying eyes.

Transferring files from a computer to the device or vice versa is a very simple process that makes use of a wifi connection. This app also makes unzipping files an easy process as well as speeding up the transfer process. Locking folder access and folder management is very simple and the app also enables you to import files from the web as well. The app supports a variety of formats, including:

● Audio (.aac, .mp3)
● Images (.bmp, .gif, .jpg, .png)
● Office (.doc, .xls, .ppt)
● Text (.txt, .pdf)
● Video (.m4v, .mp4, .mov)

The app is incredibly easy to get to grips but comes with an in-built user guide just in case you have any problems. However, we found the buttons to be self-explanatory so it's unlikely you will need to consult this document unless they want to try something particularly tricky.

Free French Tutor

bit.ly/bzAv9J
By **24/7 Tutor**
Price *Free*

Bonjour! Ca va? If these words are just gobbledygook to you, this free iPhone app can help. Alternatively if your French skills are a little bit rusty because you haven't spoken a word of Français since you were at school, this app could help you brush up your linguistic skills.

This app isn't just another language learning program that barks words at you. Instead, it uses a mix of multiple-choice questions, puzzles standard 'write in' tests and flash cards to get the vocabulary to stick in your head. Audio is also used to great effect to find out how the word is pronounced rather than having to try and decipher precisely what all those accents mean.

The tutorials are broken down into categories so you can target your learning to the scenarios you're most likely to encounter, such as home and family, town and country and basic phrases.

The puzzles in particular are handy and not at all patronising – making them an ideal learning companion for adults and children alike. And the little red unhappy and green happy faces that appear when you input your answers make it an even more compelling way of learning a new language.

Free Grammar Up

bit.ly/cSu8l1
By **Eknath Kadam**
Price *Free*

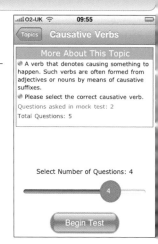

Free Grammar Up is pretty much self-explanatory – it's a free grammar education tool for non-native English speakers and children who are learning the intricacies and idiosyncrasies of the English language.

The first screen you're presented with is a list of the different aspects of the English language. The list includes adjectives word choice, adverbs word choice, causative verbs, conditionals and prepositions.

If you're not sure what any of these terms mean then you can tap on each of them for a detailed explanation. You also have the option to take a test for each of the categories.

At the bottom, you'll see a Mock Test tab. Click on this to take a test that combines all topics. Next to this, there's a progress meter that tracks your progress.

To native English speakers, Free Grammar Up will seem simple and not particularly necessary, however, if you're learning English then it's a useful tool to have on your iPhone.

Extra functionality such as shaking the iPhone to skip a question and deciding how many you want to answer in each test make this a handy tool for learners of the English language.

Free RSS Reader

bit.ly/9nzaxd
By **Simon Oualid**
Price *Free*

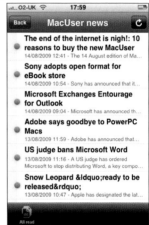

Everybody's talking about RSS feeds these days. RSS is a simple but effective concept that brings the information (whether news, sports or whatever) directly to you, rather than you having to go to it. Most websites have an RSS icon so that you can easily sign up to their feeds.

There's only one feed automatically entered into this app – unsurprisingly it's one about Apple. At a glance, you can quickly see all the latest news to come out of the iPhone's parent company. You can also easily add new RSS feeds to your reader.

You simply click the '+' button and enter the requested information about either the feed URL or by the site's main URL.

We entered *MacUser*'s feed details *www.macuser.co.uk/news/rss* and within a matter of seconds, we had added the feed to our reader's menu. You get a listing of the latest headlines and, with 'view website' button, you can summon more details about what that particular story.

The app also lets you import Google Reader, Bloglines and Newsgator too, provided you have accounts. However, it will

only import the first three feeds from these other apps.

All in all, RSS Reader makes keeping up to date easy.

 ## Free Translator

bit.ly/awzAfs
By **Codesign**
Price *Free*

Translators is one area where the App Store has become something of a specialist in. They're scattered all over the categories too – some are suites for Travel, others are geared towards Education, but Free Translator fits into reference.

The app is exactly what you'd expect from a translation tool. Simply decide on the language you want to translate from and to, type in the text you want to translate, tap on the Translate icon at the top of the app and it will transform your text into your chosen language.

You can choose to have the app auto-detect a language, which basically means it will pick English. When you've translated the text, you can email it to any address using the Mail.

The list of languages is extensive, ranging from French, German and Spanish, to Albanian, Filipino, Hindi and Vietnamese.

Sometimes the translations are a little off, directly translating the words rather than the expression, although natives should understand the gist of what you're saying if you choose to speak the text out loud.

However, this app is free while other apps charge for the same functionality, and the interface is easy to use.

Fring

bit.ly/c8GuHd
By **Fringland Ltd**
Price *Free*

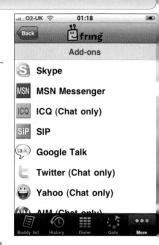

If you're an existing Fring customer, you simply add in your details. If not, you need to spend a few moments setting up an account and working out what user ID you want.

Our chosen moniker was already taken, so we had to settle for the same thing with a few numbers added on the end.

Fring is a little gem of an app that unites the myriad messaging tools out there, meaning you can send just one message to your friends, regardless of whether they're using MSN, Yahoo!, Google Talk,

Aim or something that hasn't even been invented yet.

You can also make free calls using the app, thanks to Sip, Skype and MSN. The app automatically made use of our phone book to call up contacts from within the app with the greatest of ease.

If you're a seasoned Fring user, you'll get to grips with this app easily and even if you're a complete novice, you'll be up and running in no time. Fring's little square icon is quite endearing and the cuteness continues with this app's interface.

It's a very easy-to-use app that unites you with the people you care about in a way they care about. And best of all, it's free.

 ## Golfshot: Golf GPS

bit.ly/ahfh7h
By **Shotzoom Software.**
Price *£17.99*

A serious golf app for serious golfers, Golfshot will definitely appeal to those who want to add another dimension to their game. In fact, it's so good, you could be accused of cheating.

Golfshot does all the things that you would expect from golf app, it works as a scorecard for you and up to three competitors. You can input handicaps, the players names and so on.

Nothing remarkable about this you may say, but Golfshot has a whole other dimension. Via the GPS function, it finds the course you are on, then the hole, then

the tee, all shown from an aerial photo of the course.

The app then shows you where to aim, and how far it is. Once it has sufficiently coached you as to where to hit the shot, you can then track the distance of each shot when you reach the ball and even set lay-up distances for different clubs.

The coaching and improvement doesn't end when you sink the last putt either, afterwards you can compare every shot and its outcome, view pie charts, stats and even compare your previous rounds at

that course. There is so much to this app it could easily cost a lot more, it will definitely help your game and it's fun to use too.

Gone Fishing

bit.ly/dt9nQk
By **Alex Hunt**
Price **£5.99**

Gone Fishing allows you to record in-depth details of every fish you catch. You can save the details of the fish, such as species and weight, the tackle set-up such as bait, line hook size and son. However, best of all you can photograph the fish and record the GPS location of each catch. This feature will make all the difference, especially when sea or lake fishing and you want to return to the best spots.

In practice, this app really does work well, although it hasn't been tested with frozen fingers yet. Being able to record all the details in your Fish log is an great way of both saving memories as well as improving your fishing.

The fish can be grouped by species for comparison. There's even a slideshow function to relive your greatest triumphs in all their glory.

Gone Fishing should be considered an essential for any avid angler with an iPhone.

There's no doubt that once you've started to build up your Fish log, you will become addicted, always trying to better your achievements (made much easier with the GPS function).

The only downside is, it will put a stop to the 'I caught a fish this big' stories – as now you may be asked to prove it.

Google Earth

bit.ly/ai6DXm
By **Google**
Price **Free**

Google Earth was hugely popular when it appeared on computers in 2004, and now Google has brought the app to the iPhone.

Google Earth allows you to view the whole earth via satellite imagery, and allows you to zoom in so you can even identify your own house.

The first screen is a revolving earth. Swipe your finger across it to move around and find the area of the globe that you want to zoom into. To zoom in, double tap on the land mass in which you're interested.

Alternatively, if you want to find your location on the map, tap the pinpoint icon, which is located in the bottom-right corner of the screen, and you will be quickly taken to your current position.

If you've gone a little out of kilter and have lost your bearings, you can use the compass tool in the top-right corner to re-centralise, so that north is at the top and south is at the bottom, as it should be.

Maps can sometimes be slow to load, but this is down to the huge amount of data required to render to constantly uploading maps. Your network connection will play a big part in how fast the map loads.

Google Mobile App

bit.ly/cPw3g2
By **Google**
Price *Free*

Many people consider Apple and Google to be the best of enemies, so it's quite interesting to see Google on the iPhone. But it's not necessarily Google as we know it. Indeed, the search concept is much the same, but it looks very different.

You're first greeted by the option enticing you to try out voice search on the app. It's a really innovative tool, but unfortunately it's not quite able to understand everyone's accent – our first few attempts to locate items about 'ponies' turned up 'chinese' and 'penny'. After a while

we got used to speaking a bit more slowly and the results did improve. If that's not your cup of tea, you can just opt for the good old typing. We entered *MacUser* and were greeted by a detailed list of terms. The search results displayed are very different to the traditional Google display, more of a list that might be relevant.

MacUser magazine wasn't too far down the original list and once clicked on, it takes you to the familiar Google search page.

This app does make simple search a little long winded, but if you're bored of the same old way

of finding what you want on the Internet, or having to go via the browser on the iPhone, this could be right up your street.

Grand Theft Auto: Chinatown Wars

bit.ly/aKwgoi
By **Rockstar Games**
Price **£5.99**

GTA: Chinatown Wars tells the story of Huang Lee, newly arrived in Liberty City and immediately pulled into the world of gangland warfare. It's broken down into bite-sized missions, perfect for playing on the move, and which see you taking on rival gangs, stealing cars and ramming police cars off the road.

Driving is easy, as the iPhone version steadily aligns your car to the road, and GPS helps you navigate the city, but on-foot segments are less appealing due to the lack of a good lock-on targeting system. Mini-games

vary the gameplay with tasks such as hot-wiring cars, but they work less well with a finger than the Nintendo DS version's stylus.

The impression of a bustling city is good thanks to the volume of traffic. Sadly pedestrians aren't very chatty. The story plays out in cutscenes that have a strong art style but desperately call out for movement

and spoken dialogue to bring them to life. Thankfully they aren't overly long so you're soon tearing up the streets again. In-game radio stations lack the humour of other GTA games, but Chinatown Wars is still one of the most polished iPhone games and a steal at this price.

Grimm's Fairy Tales

bit.ly/bSGzSS
By **BeamItDown**
Price *Free*

Grimm's Fairy Tales are stories that most people would associate with being read to at bedtime, and this iPhone app brings more than 200 of them to the iPhone so you can relive your childhood days.

The eReader was developed by BeamitDown and works differently to other eBook readers because it scrolls automatically depending on how much you tilt the screen.

If you tilt it backwards, it scrolls faster, tilt the phone towards you and the text will scroll much slower. You can also adjust the speed by tapping the screen and selecting the faster or slower option at the bottom.

Each of the books is presented as a chapter, and there's no search option if you want to read a particular book.

Also It can be a little hard to switch between reading the text and changing the book on Grimm's Fairy Tales compared to other eBook readers, which makes it feel quite cumbersome.

However, the app packs a lot of content compared to other eBooks and the way it works is intuitive. After some tweaking, Grimm's Fairy Tales could be a real

winner for those looking for some light hearted entertainment or if you want to read bedtime stories to children.

 ## Harbour Master

bit.ly/9mO40W
By **Imangi Studios**
Price *£1.19*

The App Store is full of fast- paced puzzle games, with Flight Control and Airport Mania included in this frenzied genre.

Harbour Master takes the same idea; you have to direct boats into their dock without crashing into any other boat in the harbour. Although it sounds simple, the further you progress, larger, slower moving cargo ships begin to creep into the port, and your organisation will have to take into account which ships will be able to dock, unload cargo and escape before a larger boat can be docked.

You'll have to think up your own organisation system, especially as you progress onto the harder levels where you'll have to look for (and shoot) pirate ships and multiple docks to land your boats in, all the time working out which boats to prioritise for docking.

You'll also have to ensure that you dock the boats with orange coloured

cargo into the orange docks and match purple with purple, otherwise they'll turn round out of the dock. There's no other way to describe Harbour Master other than thoroughly addictive; we found ourselves playing for three hours, non-stop without even noticing, and all for just £1.19.

Hipstamatic

bit.ly/bpIPep
By **SyntheticCorp**
Price **£1.19**

If you want to capture the feel of classic camera snaps, Hipstamatic has it covered. Its interface is even styled like an old-fashioned camera body to imitate the experience.

The app includes a selection of films, flashes and camera lenses that you can customise to capture the grain and colour appearance that you'd expect from old film cameras, rather than pin-sharp digital images.

The app comes with three lenses built in: John Smith, Jimmy and Kaimal Mark II. More lenses, films and flashes can be purchased inside the app. What you're getting are some top-notch photo filters that add an earthy sense of fun to iPhone photography, adding stylish black and white prints, extra grainy textures and warm tones to your photography.

Smartly, you can tap a previous photo to reuse the filters that were used to take it.

Our only disappointment is that you can't posthumously apply the effects to any existing photos you've already taken. Still, Hipstamatic is a heartwarming app, especially if you assign its retro shots of friends in the Contacts app, so you see them when that person calls.

 ## Huffington Post

bit.ly/aph7nd
By **Huffingtonpost.com**
Price **Free**

The Huffington Post is one of the web's leading satire and rumours site, so it's no surprise the makers have created an app for the iPhone.

The interface is simple to use, with tabs and clickable links.

Along the bottom, there are tabs split into categories, from news, video, entertainment and politics plus a More tab that includes blogs, media, business, style, green news, world, comedy, living, Chicago and settings.

At the top of the page, there's the headline story and, below it, a list of other headlines, each of which you can click on to view the content on-app, rather than having to head to a Safari page.

The app uses the same layout as the website, and although for many applications this isn't ideal, it works well on the Huffington Post app, with lots of pictures showing off the iPhone's top notch screen.

You won't be able to browse offline as it requires a wifi, 3G or Edge connection to reproduce the information from the web. Any stories that catch your eye can be posted to Facebook Connect, the social networking community site, or emailed, but there's no integration to post to Twitter as there is with some other news apps.

iBomber 2

bit.ly/aggjbU
By **Cobra Mobile**
Price **£1.79**

iBomber 2 puts you in the cockpit of a bomber sent on hazardous missions to wipe out specific enemy targets. There are 12 missions to choose from, ranging from destroying enemy bunkers to sinking a super battleship. You look through the bombsights as you fly over enemy territory, always in danger as the enemy tries to down you with an array of military hardware.

Tapping the red button releases your load. With the bombsight in the centre of the screen, you control your aircraft by tilting right and left. The aircraft's speed is decreased and increased by tilting back and forwards The controls are easy to get to grips with and you can set the sensitivity to suit your needs.

You're armed with an unlimited supply of bombs, and power-ups will endow you with specialist weaponry. iBomber 2 introduces

depth charges, torpedoes, artillery support, blanket bombs and fighter support from two spitfires, which you can hold off using until just the right moment.

iBomber 2's highly detailed graphics and addictive gameplay will soak up a considerable amount of your idle time.

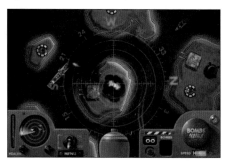

iColorBlind

bit.ly/9CxAzA
By **Tritap**
Price **59p**

Colourblindess affects up to 10 per cent of men, according to figures discovered by this application's creator, which means it's important for them to get diagnosed.

This app clearly states that it's not designed for a proper diagnosis, it's just for fun. But once you're clear about how this app is and isn't meant to be used, you can get down to using it.

iColorBlind guides you through a set of questions designed to test how well your eyes can differentiate between colours. When you get a question right, the text turns green. Get it wrong and it goes red and an explanatory message is displayed below the image in question.

That's all there is to it. The app doesn't have many layers – just the test and the legal blurb, but any more than that and it probably would confuse people as to its purpose more than it does now.

It's certainly an interesting app and quite novel too. Many people probably assume their colour detection skills are great, but it's not until you have to pick out numbers and paths in a test like this that you find out you're wrong. And being told you're wrong here could benefit your health in the long term.

 **iConcertCal**

bit.ly/dIEaxn
By **iConcertCal**
Price **£1.79**

You need never miss a concert by one of your favorite bands again with this app. iConcertCal looks at the music stored on your iPhone and shows you a list of upcoming concerts for those artists. Its search is based on your current location, though that can be overridden to see who is playing in New York City during an upcoming visit, for example.

You aren't limited to artists that you already like. You can browse all upcoming shows as well as by artist and venue.

If your iPhone doesn't contain your whole music collection, particularly if it's stored in iTunes on a Windows PC or Mac, be sure to check out the free iConcertCal visualizer. It syncs with your iPhone over a wifi network to give you a complete list of concerts that might interest you. Unlike that version, the iPhone app lacks automatic tracking of artists that aren't in your library. That

feature would be handy to alert you when a tour is announced. You can use the search feature to do this manually, but we would prefer to have automated alerts using push notifications. That's a small thing, though, and any discerning music fan should purchase this app.

 iEphemeris Pro

bit.ly/92JjOU
By **Marco Piccone**
Price **£1.19**

iEphemeris is a no-holds-barred astronomy app for the iPhone. Although the maker says that it's aimed at astronomers, it's also useful for those with an interest in moon, sun and earth phases.

The app features a sleek interface that constantly updates information. The first screen is used to select the location, which includes the coordinates of your location, date, time, Sideral Time, Julian Time and sunrise, transit and sunset times.

Swipe your finger across the screen to view information about the current moon stage.

When we were testing this app, we found that London was in the Waning Crescent phase. Here, you will find details about the moonset, moonrise, hour angle, moon age and distance. Below this, you can find out when the next major phases of the moon are due, including full moon and new moon.

Swipe again and the sun information will appear. This includes details about the length of the current day, earth's distance from the sun, angular diameter, ecliptic longitude and earth's axial tilt.

Like many apps, iEphemeris is packed full of information, but for those interested in astronomy, it's a must-have on your iPhone.

iFirstAid Lite

bit.ly/9xPOeP
By **Survival Emergency Products**
Price *Free*

It's horrible to feel helpless, particularly when the situation could potentially be a life or death scenario. While we all vow to go on first aid courses, we rarely turn words in actions. iFirstAid Lite can come to the rescue.

To ensure you're given the correct info in terms of emergency contact data, you first need to confirm which country you're in. You're also given the opportunity to add your name and email address so you can receive content updates.

The main menu is bright and vibrant, giving you the option to find out what to do for several first aid scenarios, such as CPR, bleeding, burns and choking.

The information given is clear and concise – exactly what you need in a seconds-matter first aid situation. Did you know, for example, that the way of giving CPR is quite different depending on whether the person in need is an adult, child or baby? You do now.

In the spirit of sharing your newfound first aid knowledge, you can also forward the app to friends via the Tell a friend button. If you fell ill, wouldn't it be nice to know someone else had it on their phone? It doesn't cost a penny but this app is invaluable. Both to the user and others.

iFitness

bit.ly/c1a3us
By **Medical Productions**
Price *£1.19*

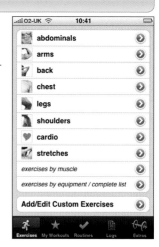

iFitness is a fully-featured fitness application that covers all aspects of your fitness regime.

When you start the application up, the first tab is highlighted, which lists all exercises by part of the body. You can view exercises for your abdominals, arms, back, chest, legs, shoulders as well as cardio exercises and stretches by clicking on one of the categories.

When you choose an exercise, you'll be presented with step-by-step images for each stage of the exercise. At the top of this screen tap on the text icon to view a text guide and the TV icon to view a video of your chosen exercise.

The third icon allows you to log yourself as you perform this exercise, so you can chart your progress. Enter how much of this particular exercise you did and it'll show up in your log section.

You can add personal workouts by tapping on the second tab at the bottom, or choose one of the pre-set routines and work out a certain part of your body, lose weight, or find a regime that fits your own type of lifestyle.

iFitness is a hugely in-depth workout app that suits any lifestyle thanks to its customisation options.

iFooty Plus

bit.ly/9PwUpw
By **Jeremy Debate**
Price **£1.79**

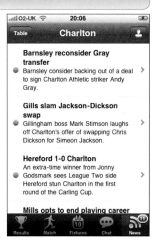

These days it seems as though the football season never ends, what with friendly games and transfer talk over the summer months, and there's no better way to track your team than with iFooty Plus.

iFooty itself is UK-centric featuring the top five divisions of English football along with the Scottish Premier League.

Head to the settings to make use of the push notifications, designed to alert you whenever there's news about your team. It will track all goals, so as soon as your team scores, you'll know about it with an icon appearing on the iFooty icon on your homescreen.

Other features include a chatroom, again with content that is specific to your team and fixtures that are drawn from the BBC Sport website. You can view fixtures either in the app or on the BBC website using Safari.

You can tap on any of the results to view a full commentary of the match. Tap on the people icon in the top-right corner and you can view the line-ups of both teams and the goal scorers. iFooty is a must-have app for any football fan. If you don't want to splash out £1.79 on the app, you can always opt for the free ad-funded version.

 ## iHandy Level Free

bit.ly/9Ahxyt
By **iHandySoft**
Price *Free*

One app that puts the iPhone's super-accurate accelerometer to good use is iHandy Level Free, which is a spirit-level app.

Although iHandy Level Free only has one function, it does that one function perfectly well and the app is free, while other identical apps charge you.

The interface features the spirit level in the centre of a circle with a measurement monitor in the top-left side. The aim is to get the measurement as close to 0° as possible.

A calibration button allows you to set the level to 0 using something that you know is perfectly flat as a guide.

There's a Hold button too, meaning you can set the level to 0 and draw a straight line on your wall, for example, so you can ensure that your shelf is level and your books won't slide down it.

In the settings menu, you can opt to remove both the calibration and hold buttons, plus adjust the bubble sensitivity for ultimate accuracy.

iHandy Level Free is the perfect app for anyone who needs to put up pictures, fix shelves or install anything along a straight line. It may not have any bells and whistles, but hey, it happens to be a very useful app.

iLaugh – Cool jokes and more

bit.ly/dbjwby
By **Azure Talon**
Price **£1.79**

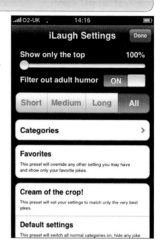

Everyone has the potential to be something of a comedian at times but often, when you really need a one-liner to fill that awkward silence or cheer up a chum, you search your comedy pockets only to come up with nothing but old boiled sweets and crumpled tissues.

iLaugh was born to make you – and your friends – happy. The app provides speedy access to a database of more than 50,000 funnies. These range from traditional jokes to spoof articles and stories that you can make your own.

And, unlike most of your relatives, the app serves up a new joke every time you start it up – or refresh by using the talent show judge-esque 'next button' – so there's no chance of you seeming repetitive, or people sussing that you're not actually that funny.

Of course, not all jokes will be to everyone's tastes and the next button certainly comes in handy here. In more extreme cases, you can flag the content as inappropriate. You can also adjust the settings to filter out adult humour and to select those

categories of jokes in which you're more interested. It's quite a basic act but comedy doesn't have to be complicated.

IM+ Push

bit.ly/9snRpj
By **Shape Services**
Price **£5.99**

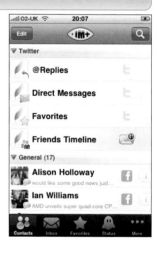

As you go through different stages of life, it's likely your taste in social networking will change. From MySpace to Facebook to Twitter and instant messaging, the ways we like to communicate with family and friends develops.

With all those different ways of connecting, it's hard to keep track of them all without opening up a multitude of different apps.

IM+ Push goes some way to fixing this issue by allowing you to sign in to multiple accounts at any one time, then sending push notifications to your iPhone when there's action on each account.

When you've signed in to all of your different accounts, you can view your different contacts, organised into a list.

Head to your inbox to view all of your messages, including direct messages, @ messages and chat from all of the sites you're signed up to. If you're having a conversation with someone, it appears in speech bubbles, just like the way text messages do in the Messages app.

Other handy additions include the ability to set a geo-location as your status to friends so they know where you are, a

built-in web browser for surfing the Internet, and a video function that enables you to send videos to your friends.

Instapaper

bit.ly/a8Ap5J
By **Marco Arment**
Price **£2.99**

Instapaper is a fantastic way to stash news stories and long articles that you come across during the day but which you don't have the time to stop and give due consideration.

The iPhone app installs a bookmark in Safari that takes whatever page you're viewing, strips away all of the unnecessary page furniture and leaves behind only the main article that you're interested in reading.

It stores the text on the server, so you can read it on your iPhone or on your computer when you have more time.

Better still, though, you can install an Instapaper bookmark in your computer's web browser. After all, it's likely that you'll be in front of that screen when time is precious. This bookmark lets you add to your Instapaper reading list with a single click, safe in the knowledge that when you fire up the iPhone app it will download all of the articles that you're interested in. It's when you see long articles reformatted by Instapaper that you begin to realise how much distraction and poor typography hinders your reading experience on the web.

For £2.99, Instapaper relieves those headaches and makes catching up with the latest news an absolute pleasure again.

iRetouch

bit.ly/9ZtaLV
By **Nick Drabovich**
Price **£1.19**

We're brought up to think that celebsville is filled with flawless individuals when, in reality, they're just lucky enough to have the power of airbrushing at their beck and call.

Indeed, most of us who have met a celeb will find they don't quite look like the way they do in the magazines as they do in the flesh. That's the beauty of photo retouching.

But you don't have to be a millionaire to tweak your images. iRetouch is an iPhone photo editor with advanced capabilities that enables users to crop, rotate,

invert and resize images among other things. You can also use the eraser and tweak the picture's hue, colour and brightness so the end result is just how you want it.

Got brown eyes but always wanted blue? Forget expensive and painful contact lenses and just change them using iRetouch instead. Similarly you can remove the pimples and spots that would normally spoil an otherwise perfect holiday snap.

Nobody's perfect but iRetouch allows you to at least give that impression. We certainly had fun playing around with our

snap of iPhone and Mac fan Stephen Fry, although we hasten to add he didn't really need any airbrushing.

iSeismometer

bit.ly/alzMFX
By **ObjectGraph LLC**
Price *Free*

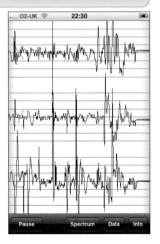

This is a novelty app but one that also helps you learn something new. The concept is very simple. You just leave your iPhone on a hard surface with the app fired up then tap somewhere nearby and watch what happens.

It looks like something you'd find in a hospital, but it's one of those things that is very captivating once you've looked at it once. In fact, we completely lost track of time when we played with this app as we tried out different tap-based compositions – *Top of the Pops* had nothing on us during this review.

You've got the ability to pause the 'recording' of movement around the iPhone, in addition to looking at a colourful spectrum graph of what occurred in the three seconds prior to requesting that data.

We didn't quite understand what the chart was showing us, but it looked pretty nonetheless and it'll make you look über intelligent to anyone looking over your shoulder.

The app will monitor movement for 10 seconds and report back on the last three seconds of activity. You can then upload that data in snazzy graph format to the web for all to see. Old friends will probably think you've changed career.

iSwap Faces

bit.ly/cZBgYC
By **Black Frog Industries**
Price *£1.19*

If you've ever fancied swapping faces with a friend, iSwap Faces is the place to see whether their face would suit yours.

It's a strictly fun app, where you take a photo of two of your friends, highlight their faces and then swap them. It sounds simple and it is with this app.

Some of the results may appear a little hideous, but this is mainly down to the app struggling to match the faces to different shapes.

To use the app, you simply load the app, and either pick one of your already snapped photos or take a new one using the iPhone's camera.

Highlight both faces using the grid, which you can stretch and rotate to try to get a best match for the faces. There's a choice of three different templates to suit different face shapes, although your victims will have to use the same shape.

Once the faces are fully in the templates, tap on the arrow icon and the faces will be swapped instantly. To get rid of the template, click on the eye icon.

It will take a while to perfect your matching, but iSwap Faces is a simple application with amusing results.

ITN News

bit.ly/avQ7MB
By **ITN**
Price *Free*

★★★★

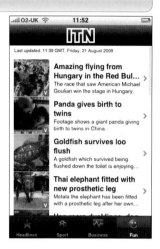

The ITN News app claimed to be the first video-focused news app to be launched on the iPhone.

This is not immediately obvious until you tap on the fun tab at the bottom of the screen that brings up a list of funny and less high-brow news stories in full moving picture quality.

When you click on any of the video stories, you can opt to watch it in video by tapping the video button in the top-right corner, then the full-screen player will open, streaming the video.

In addition to these more light-hearted headlines, you can also view the latest news headlines, sport and business stories. A small blue 'v' in the bottom-left corner of the picture identifies the video stories.

Share options are pretty limited, with only email being available if you want to share a story that's caught your eye. Tap this option and you can share it using the iPhone's in-built Mail app, choosing to send the email from any one of the email accounts set up on your device.

One notable point about the ITN application is that there aren't any ads plastered over the content as there are on other free news apps, plus you can cache the stories, allowing you to view them when you're offline too.

iTrans London Tube

bit.ly/dn1PFp
By **iTrans**
Price **59p**

★★★★

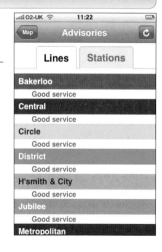

The UK App Store is filled to the brim with London Underground applications, most trying to make sense of the complicated network of coloured lines.

iTrans is one of the many available, but this is more than just an app to show you where the tubes run. You can search for tube stops on the map, or find directions using the Tube network.

If you choose the latter option, simply enter your start point and end point when prompted. After calculating your route, the app explains to you each change you need to undertake, with an illustration on the map.

A handy extra feature is a locate tool, that shows you where you are on the tube map. Although it won't tell you how to get to the nearest stop, it will illustrate which are the nearest.

The final function is to provide you with information about any problems on the Tube network. Tap on the warning triangle and you can check the status of all underground lines.

It's a shame extra modes of transport are missing, such as the DLR and the overground rail network, but this app is clearly designed to get you from A to B using the London Underground.

iTranslate

bit.ly/9Tc4Ms
By **Sonic GmbH**
Price *Free*

If you're planning a trip abroad whether for a holiday or for business, iTranslate is a free translation app that can help you along the way when trying to speak the native lingo.

The only screen on the app is the translation screen. There are two boxes – one for text entry, and another for the translation to appear in. You operate the app by simply typing the text you want translated in the top box and it will be transformed into your desired language.

The variety of languages on iTranslate is extensive. The alphabetical list includes idioms from every continent, including the basics such as Spanish, French and German, to more unusual lingos such as Galician, Tagalog and two different Chinese dialects. If you want to find out what a foreign sentence means in English, simply tap the squiggle, and the interpretation will be reversed.

The app is ad-funded, so the odd advert will pop up at the bottom, but this doesn't get in the way. iTranslate is a simple application, with none of the complications you find on so many other translation applications. You can even email the translation if you need to help out a friend in need.

 ## iWiki

bit.ly/bqweav
By **Comoki Software**
Price *£1.19*

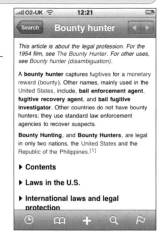

iWiki is one of the many Wikipedia apps that have sprung up for the iPhone. Type in Wiki in the iTunes Store search engine and you are inundated with a multitude of apps covering both general and specific topics.

This app, iWiki, aims to provide you with basic access to the wealth of information contained on Wikipedia and Wiktionary websites. It formats articles perfectly for the iPhone and retains all the rich multimedia content you need.

On longer articles, the ability to jump straight to section headings is a great time-saver and likewise it's great to be able to quickly pull up a list of all the other articles that are contained within similar categories.

While tapping normally on a link whisks you away to the relevant item, holding a moment longer will add the article to your queue until you've finished reading the current page, which we thought was a nice touch. Once in the queue, a quick click initiates the download with most pages arriving in seconds.

Alternatively, you can select the option to auto-download anything added to the list so that it's ready and waiting for you to read, even if you don't have access to wifi or the network.

iXpenseit

bit.ly/dwuL5n
By **FYI Mobileware**
Price **£2.99**

iXpenseit is one of the most in-depth finance tracking tools on the App Store.

Although buying it will set you back £2.99, it features a huge amount of categories, including Auto, Electronics, Entertainment, Food, Home and even an iTunes category.

You can divide your expenses into Personal and business and even take photos of your receipts by tapping on the camera icon next to the transaction amount.

After you've added transactions, you can return to the application homescreen where there's an illustration of your bank account. If you're overdrawn, the scale will appear in red. If you're in the black, it will be green. Next to this level, your average daily spend, income and expenses are all displayed.

Below this, there's a calendar-style function that displays your expenses day by day, plus the ability to view your expenditure in the form of a bar or pie chart, then email the graph to yourself.

iXpenseit is an essential app if you need to monitor your expenses and have the willpower or memory to add a transaction.

It does give you a sense of how much you spend, which can be a bit of a shock, but helpful if you're trying to rein in your finances.

Jirbo Match

bit.ly/cjOuOh
By **Jirbo Inc**
Price **Free**

Remember how much fun you had playing Snap! as a child? You may not have known it at the time but you were actually learning and helping your brain to remember things that were the same. Memory Match takes that concept and plonks it onto the iPhone.

In addition to providing adults with a way of keeping their little grey cells alive and kicking, this app also delivers a great way of keeping children busy and, hopefully, quiet.

The app looks really simple but the game is actually quite difficult as each time you press an icon to reveal the character underneath you have to memorise the image and its position, unless you've successfully matched a pair, so that next time you find its partner you know which icon matches it.

Although be warned, when you flip the icons around to reveal the animal characters, it does have an associated tone, which can be annoying so we'd advise turning the sound off using the settings option.

There's a competitive element too as you have to try and get the highest score in the shortest amount of time possible. And most people love a challenge.

Last.fm

bit.ly/aRqBrS
By **Last.fm**
Price *Free*

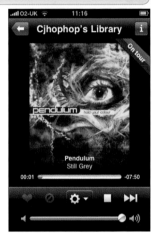

Last.FM was certainly the nation's favourite streaming music player, until Spotify came along and stole the limelight.

However, it's still a great website, with the ability to build your own radio station according to the music you like, and recommendations from its community.

The Last.fm app on iPhone gives you the same functionality as you'll find on the website, including the ability to listen to your favourite artists' radio stations and bolstering your music collection.

The interface is less cluttered than the website, making it more favourable in our eyes. When a track is playing, you can view information about it, favourite a track, share it to other users, tag it, add it to your playlist and even buy it on iTunes.

You can stream music over wifi or 3G, which is another bonus, meaning you can listen wherever you have signal.

Simply log into your account and you're presented with the Radio screen, which includes your radio station, and recommendations from the app.

If you're already a Last.fm user, the app is a must-download. If you don't use Last.fm, just try it – you'll love its simplicity.

 Learn Chess

bit.ly/ap7fxB
By **Tom Kerrigan**
Price *Free*

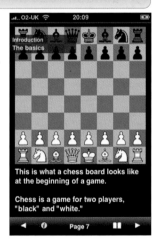

This is what a chess board looks like at the beginning of a game.

Chess is a game for two players, "black" and "white."

Before you've even got a chance to see what this application is like, you're greeted by a screen asking you to support the cause by purchasing either Chess Lite or Chess Pro. We thought the assumption was a bit premature, but we carried on regardless and were very glad that we did.

The app guides you through the basics of how to play chess, using text and instructions on the chessboard diagram. There's 118 pages of information included in this app, so you more than get you money's worth for a free app.

If you don't want to scroll through the whole guide, you can click the book icon to see the chapter breakdown. Then, it's just a case of clicking on that shortcut to by-pass the pages you're not interested in.

The info page also lets you email either Learn Chess' support, tell your friends about the app, or directs you to the App Store to write a review.

If you want to know your checkmate from your pawns, this is the app for you. Although it is unlikely to get you to the level where you'll leave modern-day

champs quaking in their boots. You might need to at least get near a real chess board before that happens.

London JamCams

bit.ly/cWFB5w
By **Sendmetospace**
Price *Free*

London is a great city. It's a vibrant place full of different people from different cultures and the hustle and bustle of its fast-moving pace is one of the reasons people love living in and visiting London. But its busy nature often causes congestion, particularly if you're traveling by road rather than public transport.

London JamCams has the answer. The app syndicates a Transport for London feed of its vast network of cameras around the capital so you can see, at a glance, just how busy your chosen route home may be.

It's very easy to select a camera to view the state of play thanks to an A-Z searchable index and you can then save that place for quick access at a later date. Indeed, you can create and your own 'routes' of cameras, perhaps for journeys you conduct the most, so you can find out what is happening at the touch of a button in future.

And if you're feeling a touch *CSI*, you can also zoom in on the camera image. Although, unlike on TV it can't tell you what the driver sitting in the first car in the queue had for breakfast. All

in all, this is a really innovative and useful app that will benefit regular and occasional London road users alike.

London Tube Deluxe

bit.ly/a0Ds2p
By **Malcolm Barclay**
Price *59p*

London Tube Deluxe is just one of the Tube mapping and planner apps available to down load from the App Store. However, this app includes a lot more than just a map of the London Underground network.

Unlike its competitors, Tube Deluxe also displays each station's departure boards, meaning you can narrow down your plans to the exact minute.

Useful for those that keep more irregular hours, there are also separate updates on the first and last trains running. You can even see which station your train

is currently at, and how many minutes it will take for it to reach your station.

This feature requires a data connection as it downloads information from Transport for London's own website, so you won't be able to check this information while you're on the Tube. However, the planning and map features don't need an Internet connection. You can plan your route too, although this isn't as in-depth as you will find on the Transport for London's website.

London Tube Deluxe also makes great use of the iPhone's

push notifications feature. You can get updates pushed to your phone if the status of a Tube line changes.

London2Go

bit.ly/aokIcS
By **Ulman Solutions**
Price **59p**

London2Go allows you to dump your tour guides in place of a simple-to-use, information-filled app on your iPhone.

Upon loading, you're presented with a list of categories of points of interest around London – Entertainment, Historical, Transport and Top Places among others.

Using either GPS or your Internet signal, London2Go automatically tries to find your location, which feeds into one of the app's most useful categories, nearby attractions. Tapping on one of these will either bring you a list of more sub-sections or the actual list of points of interest.

The map displays the locations of any attractions from whatever list you navigated from. They show up very clearly as red markers, while tapping on one brings up the name of the attraction and a link to its Wikipedia page.

London2Go's strongest feature is that none of this information has to be pulled off the Internet; it's all included in the initial 80MB-plus download. This makes the maps very quick to update and scroll through when you're out in the streets, far faster than if you were accessing them online, even with a 3G connection.

Lotto UK

bit.ly/ctO5uy
By **WeesWares**
Price *Free*

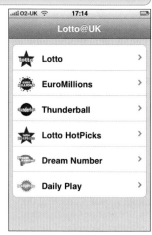

This app does exactly what its name suggests – it checks the UK lottery draws for you. It could, effectively, hold the key to your future fortune – fingers crossed.

Of course, what this app won't do is tell you the winning numbers in advance, only after the event. Ho hum.

On the homescreen, all the different types (and there are lots of them now) of lottery games are listed, such as the main game itself, EuroMillions, Thunderball, Dream Number and so on.

To get information about the winning numbers for each game, you click on the menu listing. Clicking on Lotto, for example, brings up the latest draw results in the shape of lottery balls, while the previous six games' results are listed underneath in simple text format. That's what you get without scrolling. If you scroll, you get an even longer history of winning numbers that goes back several months.

This app is very simple but also very effective and does what budding millionaires want it to do without any unnecessary fuss or frills. And it saves you having to traipse to the local newsagent, surfing the web or asking a friend whether their chosen numbers have changed their life or not.

Love Art: National Gallery, London

bit.ly/aK4TcS
By **Antenna Audio Inc**
Price **£1.79**

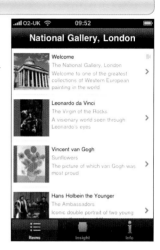

If you live a little too far away from London to head to one of the many art galleries, Love Art provides a comprehensive insight into the great masters including Van Gogh, Da Vinci, Rembrandt and Renoir.

There are 11 artists profiled, each with a selection of paintings that you can get up close and personal with using the pinch to zoom feature. Curators also talk you through some of the masterpieces. At present, there are more than 250 works of art for you to enjoy, including some lesser known pieces for you to discover should you ever take a trip to the gallery.

You'll also find an overview video about the National Portrait Gallery, which is streamed from the app and not the Internet. However, be warned this is a huge app for the iPhone, at more than 210MB it takes up a fair amount of space as well time to download, but we think it's worth it just to have access to this much artwork on a portable device.

And because Love Art is an application that's fully loaded onto the iPhone and not streamed from the Internet, it makes for great reading whether you're on the train, plane or discussing art down the pub and you don't have a decent 3G signal.

 ## MacUser

bit.ly/cYUpEr
By **PixelMags**
Price **59p, includes latest issue**

Save yourself a trip to a newsagent and get the latest news, reviews and advice from the Mac experts at *MacUser*, the same team behind this guide, right on your iPhone.

Having the UK's longest-running magazine dedicated to all things Apple in digital form means you can search all of the issues that you own in seconds, and without any of the clutter of printed issues.

Hold your iPhone in portrait or landscape to show one or two pages. Double-tapping zooms into a page, which you can move around by dragging with one finger to soak up a huge amount of Apple know-how. Links to major sections are always on hand, or tap once to scan previews of each page and bookmark ones to read later.

Share your issues without worrying that you'll never see them again. After four days, they're returned to your library without having to hassle the other person. You can read your issues on an iPad, too, without having to buy them again. Back issues from July 2009 onwards are available, and neither they nor new issues will break the bank at only £1.79 each, while a six-month subscription will save you even more at just £17.99

mBox Mail

bit.ly/9rxL3J
By **mFluent**
Price **£5.99**

Hotmail on the iPhone?
Whatever next. There are still millions of people using Hotmail as at least one of their email accounts.

Historically, those who have pledged allegiance to the iPhone have had to make do with accessing their emails using Safari when on the move. But now mBox Mail has rewritten the rulebook.

mBox Mail is a fully featured client that enables you to experience all the benefits of Hotmail, such as folder management and Windows

Live Contacts, from within the app itself. It can handle multiple accounts and offers password protection to make sure that if you lose your iPhone then you don't loose control of your email account too. Trust us, it's not a pleasant experience.

It may not seem like a hassle to have to fire up Safari each time you want to check your Hotmail account, but until you've tried this app you won't really know what you're missing.

At £5.99, it is quite expensive, but if you're tied to Hotmail then it's worth the investment.

Considering you can't buy many things with change from £6 these days, this app is both nice to use and useful to boot.

 ## Meal Diary

bit.ly/ahnczL
By **Minimalistech**
Price **Free**

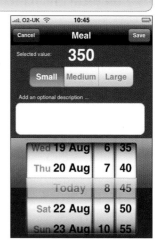

It's always hard to keep on
track when you're trying to lose weight or even track the amount of food you eat each day, but when you have an application on the iPhone to record every time any morsel passes your lips then the process is a whole lot easier.

Enter Meal Diary. It's a straightforward app, but this means it's quick to enter any food you've eaten during the day, plus it keeps an eye on those calories consumed and burnt off.

You can't enter specific calorie values, but you can get an approximate value by adding

up snacks, main meals and breakfasts to get a reasonably accurate amount in any meal.

When entering your weight, there aren't any units, but this serves as an advantage because you can choose your own units without having to convert anything. Your weight, along with calories consumed and number of daily meals can all be tracked in a series of graphs.

One aspect we like most about Meal Diary is that it's so simple and quick to add entries into any section – whether that's exercise, calories or weight. So

many people fail in tracking their meals because the apps they're using are just too complicated and time consuming.

MedCalc

bit.ly/d44qZV
By **Tschopp and Pfiffner**
Price *Free*

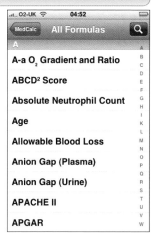

This is another great app that feeds those – with plenty of time on their hands – who have a thirst for knowledge.

If your job or studies involve medical formulae and calculations, MedCalc is most likely to be the iPhone app of choice for you.

The app provides its information in four languages (English, French, German and Spanish) with detailed data and bibliographic references served up with each formula. Equations can be searched for using their name or associated keywords

and you can also customise a list of your favourite (and most used) equations.

MedCalc is an open source project and relies on user feedback to add additional formulae and scores to the database, so it is likely to evolve as time goes on – and, of course, you can be part of that evolution too by having your say.

If you have no idea what an Absolute Neutrophil Count is, you'll probably find this app completely baffling and want to hide somewhere until it goes away or you might be intrigued

and keep on reading. If, however, you know exactly what that is and need more information, this handy calculator will be of use.

 ## Medical Encyclopedia

bit.ly/awwB6m
By **UMMC**
Price *Free*

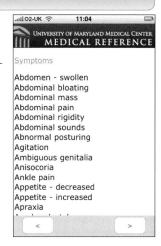

Having a medical encyclopedia to hand is always useful, especially if you have children.

The University of Maryland Medical System's encyclopedia is in-depth and accessible to anyone, whatever your medical knowledge. The app is broken down into a number of sections, including symptoms, that relate to illness, injury, disease, surgery, nutrition, special topics and poison and tests.

Both symptoms and injury can be used as diagnosis techniques to help you decide whether you, or anyone you

are diagnosing, needs medical attention. You're presented with a list of symptoms or accident situations in alphabetical order. Pick a symptom and the app will provide you with information including a definition, considerations and common causes. You can also view any treatments too.

Disease and surgery both outline different medical terms and illnesses, while nutrition is handy at giving advice about how to stay healthy.

Medical Encyclopedia is packed with information – most

of it you won't use, but for those moments when you need some quick medical advice, this app is well worth a free download.

Mediquations

bit.ly/cPPjle
By **Mediquations**
Price *£2.99*

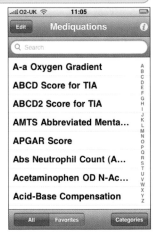

The iPhone isn't just a place to hold fun applications, it can be an important tool for serious use too.

One industry that the iPhone has really revolutionised is the medical profession, and it's apps like Mediquations that are helping hospital staff to perform their duties every day.

This is a medical calculator that can calculate everything from an individual's Body Mass Index to a dosage of medication.

Although the app can't be relied on completely, it can really help medical professionals quickly calculate anything, including the severity of a stroke, the risk of breast cancer in an individual, even down to the conversion of gas units.

You have the choice of finding the calculation you need to work out from the extensive alphabetical list by scrolling or using the search box at the top of the homescreen.

The interface is simple, making it ultra quick to use in urgent situations. Simply enter the answers to each of the questions asked and the results will appear at the bottom of the screen.

Although Mediquations isn't an app everyone will need on their iPhone, it's essential if you're a medical professional or a carer.

MegaWeather

bit.ly/aPS0NU
By **DeluxeWare**
Price *£1.79*

Weather reports that tell you what the outlook is in your current location or country are all well and good, but some people crave a slightly more far-reaching tool that can show how the wind is blowing on foreign shores too.

If you're called away on business quite a lot, with overnight stays here and there, it helps you to keep your luggage light if you know what to pack and what to leave behind. And for holidaymakers, the fewer unnecessary clothes that are packed, the more room for the souvenirs on your return journey.

MegaWeather contains weather data from more than 40,000 cities around the world, detailing local time as well as high and low day temperatures, wind direction and speed and other key data.

The homescreen is managed by the app's city manager menu and the spinning globe on the right-hand side of the screen is a really quirky touch.

You can also press on any of the smaller icons on the left in the forecast to bring up a tab with even more details if you're hungry for more data still.

MegaWeather is a really nice app to use, which has been well-designed and is a must-have for the avid traveler.

Mocha VNC

bit.ly/d3Kg0x
By **Mochasoft**
Price **£3.49**

Mocha VNC is one of the many remote access clients available to buy from the App Store. The app allows you to access your computer from your iPhone.

It's compatible with both Macs and PCs, and is simple to set up, especially on a Mac, which is the platform we tested it on. Mocha VNC features both landscape and portrait modes, which you switch between by simply changing the orientation of your iPhone. We would recommend landscape mode because your computer screen is most likely to be landscape rather than portrait.

Mocha VNC is simple to use, with the ability to zoom in and out of the screen as if you're using a web page. You can also move around the screen by dragging the cursor.

Although the app doesn't display your computer screen in full resolution, it's clear enough for you to perform many simple tasks. Be aware though that Mocha VNC

will struggle to work on a high-resolution screen.

We used Mocha VNC on a 4.5Mbits/sec wifi connection, and although there was a distinct time delay, it was nothing major. The only thing that took longer than we almost had patience for was the initial screen drawing.

 ## Movie Genie

bit.ly/9KskTf
By **Taylan Pince**
Price **59p**

If you love movies but need help choosing one, Movie Genie is an ideal app for you. It takes information from the IMDB website and reformats it for the iPhone's screen, even splitting off the cast and crew information into a separate tab, which cuts down on the amount of scrolling you have to do to reach the important sections such as parental guidance and trivia.

The app keeps track of the movies in a history list, and you can be sure of not forgetting the ones that interest you most by adding them to the list of

favorites, so that it's easy to find if you're researching before you even get to a rental store.

Movie Genie helps when picking a movie to round off a dinner date or that's suitable for the family because it retrieves guidance information from IMDB, too. That helps you avoid risqué nudity that might spoil the evening, never mind unsuitable language and violence that might concern you as a parent.

At 59p, Movie Genie is a bargain. Being able to browse IMDB so quickly while you're at a rental store is a real help,

especially when you've got impatient kids in tow that just want to get home and settle down in front of the TV.

Movies

bit.ly/9YGbu2
By **Flixster**
Price *Free*

There's nothing worse than turning up at the cinema only to find that the film you've chosen to see started 20 minutes ago.

Cue Flixster. You have a variety of options for finding a movie for you and your friends to go and watch. The first is that you can search for a particular film and then see which cinemas it's playing at and the showing times, or you allow Flixster to tap into the iPhone's GPS function and locate the nearest cinema to you. Here, you're given a list of that cinema's films and their showing times. You can even select a

cinema as your favourite, so it appears at the top of the list.

When you first fire up the app you get the chance to watch a trailer at random. If you don't want to watch the trailer, you can just skip it. The trailer option is great as you get the chance to find out if the film is for you.

Each menu follows pretty much the same format, with the film listed, a snippet of detail about the stars, rating and length and then a popcorn symbol with a percentage rating of how good the film is according to the Flixster community. Select a

film and you'll get a synopsis, the ability to rate the film and play the trailer and a roundup of what other Flixster users think.

myBatteryLife

bit.ly/cAp8ol
By **KVapps**
Price *59p*

There's nothing worse than heading off on a long journey only to find your battery has started to die and you're, unsurprisingly, without a charger.

Clearly, the battery monitor bar on the top right of the iPhone has its place. And it does a good job of telling you just how much, or how little, juice you have left. But, it doesn't go into any detail, so you're never quite sure whether that little section on the bar means half an hour or a couple of hours. And often, you only find out your guestimate was wrong far too late.

myBatteryLife claims to be the 'first and most accurate battery monitoring application'. This app is made up of just one page that brings all the detail about battery life together in a really nice diagram format.

The display is large and provides the information that matters most for users – whether they use their iPhone for work, play, watching films or just making calls and texting.

myBatteryLife is a basic, but very clever, little app that takes the guesswork out of battery power management.

It leaves you free to enjoy the benefits of your iPhone without the worry of wondering whether you have enough charge left.

MyBus

bit.ly/bWEvzi
By **Kizoom**
Price **59p**

MyBus hooks into a list of routes and timetables from all around the UK to help you get around. It grabs your location over GPS and shows your location on a street map. Nearby stops are flagged up with an arrow indicating the direction of travel.

The search bar lets you find stops by postcode, place name or a landmark that might be in a stop's name, such as a church. Tapping a stop shows the routes that serve it and when they're due, and there's also a link to a list of nearby taxi firms. The developer claims these are

carefully chosen, which may explain why nearby firms in our area weren't listed. Stops can be saved as favourites under names you choose, and they can be arranged across several pages, much like the iPhone's Home screen. That's a good way to divide them up if you regularly visit other cities.

There's a missed opportunity to plug in to Google's Street View and jump along the street until you find the stop you recognise, though. That would help if you have difficulty interpreting 2D maps.

MyBus's main flaw is that it lacks a way to find the stop nearest to you that will get you to your intended destination.

 ## myDreams

bit.ly/av1OcN
By **WebGate (part of Melon Inc)**
Price **59p**

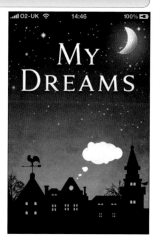

Have you ever woken up and wondered what the hell all that stuff that happened in your dream meant?

Many pass dreams off as completely meaningless – as though your brain has been emptying its bin while you sleep. Others believe some of what you come up with while in the land of nod is actually representative of something.

Cue myDream. It's a dream analysis tool at your fingertips. So, if you're on the train en route to work and suddenly recall that thing you were doing while at a

party (in your dream), you can find out what it all means quickly thanks to an alphabetical listing and useful search tool.

The app contains more than 4,000 real-life dreams in addition to 6,500 interpretations to help you work out what your mind is trying to tell you, making use of keywords and descriptive analysis to do so.

We found this app really useful for helping us understand a bit more about what goes on when we're switched off in bed. And, if nothing else it will certainly help you pass the time

while you're trying to wake up from your very active slumber, whether at your desk or on your daily commute.

National Rail Enquiries

bit.ly/cdzCeF
By **Agant**
Price **£4.99**

If you rely on trains to get you from A to B, it's very handy to have a train planner and information service at you fingertips. National Rail Enquiries is exactly this.

The first part of the app is the departures and arrivals boards. Frequently-used stations can be saved to the app's homescreen for quick access. Tapping on the station's name shows a list of all the trains leaving that station, which platform the train will be departing from and even where that train is now if it hasn't already arrived at the station.

The second part of the app is the journey planner that lets you organise future trips. You can specify the date of your future trip and what time you want your train to arrive or depart, or choose to see times for the first or last trains of the day.

Usefully, the 10 most recent journeys are automatically saved so you can view trip itineraries without an Internet connection.

You can specify a home station in the app's settings so you can find details for the next train home from your current location by tapping the Next

Train Home button. You can also specify your departure station manually or let the app find the nearest station using GPS.

 ## Nearest (free)

bit.ly/d6VJcJ
By **The Really Nifty Group**
Price **Free**

When you start a new job, move to a new area or just find yourself in a new place when on a business trip it can be easy to feel a bit lost, particularly when you don't know where anything is.

This iPhone app aims to bring a wealth of information to your fingertips to help you find practically anything – whether it's a business, restaurant, pub or other establishment. By telling the app what you're looking for, it responds with listings, how far those services and businesses are from where you are and it includes a useful mini-map.

For the times when you're most in need of such information and can't spend the time typing, the app comes pre-loaded with 1,000 of the most commonly used search terms.

The app is easy to use, with maps and information loading very quickly. The menus are clean with nice icons and the drilled down data that comes up when you click on an entry is nicely presented, with one-click access to telephone numbers where available, in addition to directions (via Google Maps) as to how to get to your chosen location.

If you need a help finding a business for work or play, it's likely that you will find a friend here with this app.

Nearest Subway series

bit.ly/bmuVk0
By **acrossair**
Price **£1.19 each**

This collection of apps from acrossair guides you to nearest station in major cities around the world, including New York, London and Tokyo. Each app covers just one city's transit system so you have to buy multiple maps if you want two or more cities. The apps are an example of augmented reality, which shows what the iPhone's camera sees and superimposes data on top of it.

In the case of these apps, that information is about nearby stations on a transit system. As well as the lines that run through each one, the iPhone's

compass and GPS module are used to show the direction to those places.

Hold the phone flat and you see stations through 360° as arrows that point in the right directions. Hold it upright and the information appears as signposts, though in that orientation you'll have to turn your body to find stations that are behind you.

The series of apps lives up to its name, but it would benefit from route planning features to expand its meaning. You might want to ask it which station is the nearest to get to Madison Square

Garden. That's not possible. You will need to combine it with a subway map to work out how to get to places farther afield.

New York Subway

bit.ly/aWsVA3
By **Presselite**
Price **59p**

The New York subway system can be quite a shock to the system, especially if you're used to travelling on London's wonderfully colour-coded Tube.

It's not just the lines that may confuse, but also the stop names. After all, how are you to know whether you need to alight at 103rd Street/Broadway, 103rd Street/Central Park or 103rd Street/Lexington?

New York Subway will hold your hand throughout your trip, with an in depth map of the subway, including a simplified map of the city.

You can also get directions from one street to another using the subway, and there is a map of each individual line, from start to finish in an easy-to-read format.

You can even find which subway stop is the closest using GPS, to prevent you asking the locals where the subway is (not that you wouldn't want to, just that you may want to save face if you're standing directly next to your specified stop).

Although the full subway map can be a little complicated, as the London Tube can be to tourists, the New York Subway

app is a real winner. It will guide you around the transport system seamlessly, and ensure you never get lost underground again.

Night Stand

bit.ly/c1sAaZ
By **SpoonJuice**
Price *59p*

Many people use their mobile phones as alarm clocks rather than opting to purchase a separate, dedicated machine as well as. After all, your mobile goes wherever you go, so if you find yourself staying somewhere at short notice or travel a lot for business, the alarm functionality of your iPhone could help ensure you don't miss that plane or important meeting.

Five different clock variations are available, ranging from a binary clock to an analog glow clock and everything in between. A smart alarm is also featured as

is a customise snooze feature and the ability to choose from the bundled tunes or one from your music library.

The app's creator reckons that more than 3 million users have thus far downloaded Night Stand, giving some indication of just how popular this app is. If you don't see the point in buying a separate alarm clock or forget to set them, this app could help.

After all, most people sleep with their phones close by and check them just before bed so why not set the alarm at the same time?

For just 59p, this app could mean the difference between getting a seat on the train or missing it altogether.

NYTimes

bit.ly/biRQ0k
By **The New York Times**
Price *Free*

***The New York Times* is one of** the most popular newspapers in the US, so for all those interested in what's going on in the Land of the Free, the newspaper has launched its own news app.

NYTimes is also the most in-depth news app if you're looking for breaking news. The first tab is a list of the latest stories that you can refresh as and when you like. The second tab is the most popular stories.

Open up each story and you can adjust the text size and email the stories. You can save any news you want to view later, which is

extremely handy if your commute to work includes travelling without signal.

At the top of each story, there are previous and next icons in the top right, so you can scroll through the stories to get up to date whenever you wish.

Tap on More and you're taken to an extensive list of categories, including arts, health, NY/region (local New York news), obituaries, opinion, politics, T Magazine content and technology.

The only foible we have with the NYTimes app is the ads that

pop up along the bottom of the screen. Other free news apps don't feature ads, so it's slightly disappointing to see them here.

Ocado

bit.ly/cu7QaF
By **Ocado**
Price **Free**

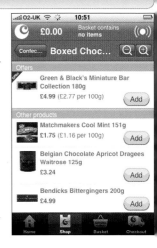

Online shopping has revolutionised the way you can shop for groceries, making it easier for people who don't live near a supermarket or don't have the means to visit one.

Ocado is the online shopping arm of Waitrose, and the company has introduced an app for the iPhone that makes shopping online even easier.

When you first start the application, you'll have to log in or register using the website. The catalogue will then be downloaded to your phone, allowing you to add items to your order when offline too, so you can add items on the move.

Once you're in, Ocado will show you the next available delivery that you can select according to when you're available to receive it.

To start putting together your order, you can search for a product, browse categories, choose from the products you buy the most or view recommended products, based on what you've ordered previously. As you add items, you can keep tabs on how much your order will cost with a running total in the top-left hand corner, and when you're finished, you can head to the checkout, book your delivery and pay for your order.

Occasions

bit.ly/9q3S6r
By **Hand Carved Code**
Price **59p**

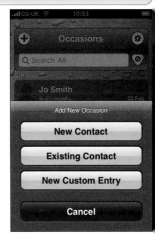

Push notification is one feature welcomed with open arms when iPhone OS 3.0 was released. It means you can now get notifications even when you're not in an application.

Occasions puts this to great use as an app that will remind you about every special occasion, from birthdays to anniversaries and any other reminder you may need. If you've input birthdays for your iPhone contacts, these can be imported from your Contacts. If you have other special dates to add, you can add these manually using the scroll-wheel interface.

At all times, you can view how long it is until each occasion, and as the special day approaches, the date will change colour and an icon will appear next to the person's name.

Tap on any contact entry and you can view the their phone number and make a call to them if you wish, or send them an email. The contact's star sign and birthstone will also be displayed, although we're not sure how many people will be interested in these features.

The most impressive point of the Occasions app is the push notifications. When the occasion has arrived, an icon will appear on the Occasions widget, alerting you of the special day.

Pac-man Championship Edition

bit.ly/aursWv
By **Namco**
Price **£1.79**

One of gaming's oldest icons hits the iPhone with added pizazz in this souped-up sequel. The graphics are still decidedly retro, but with a glorious neon ambiance.

The gameplay is also significantly tweaked from the original. Once you clear all of the pellets on one side of the map, a special bonus appears on the other. Grab it and the empty side of the map regenerates in a new configuration that gets ever more complex as the game progresses.

Swipe towards a wall that Pac-man is moving along and

he'll coast around the next corner, gaining a bit of extra speed.

The game comes with five maps and 20 challenges in mission mode, and you can purchase an additional 25 maps and 100 extra missions from inside the game. Championship mode has you trying to survive for up to five minutes while trying to rack up

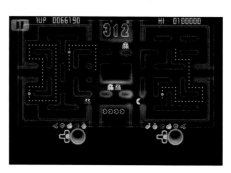

a high score. Online tournaments set challenges on a specific map every week, and you can check your global ranking on Facebook.

Pac-man's core gameplay is as addictive today as it was 30 years ago. The additional gloss and varied playing modes are simply the cherry on top.

PayPal

bit.ly/cDGn0s
By **PayPal**
Price **Free**

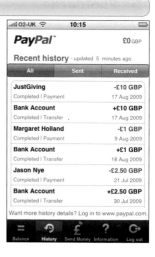

PayPal is the easiest way to move money around on the Internet, especially for those who are a little security conscious.

This iPhone app allows you to make payments just as if you are using the website on your computer. You can check you account balance simply by logging in using your username and password and your account balance will be displayed. Click on the next tab to see your history, including payments that have been sent and received.

To make a payment, click on the third tab at the bottom

of the screen and you'll simply need to enter the email address of the payee, the amount of the transaction and a note, normally an order number or other payment reference.

You can change the currency by clicking on the GBP icon when entering the amount of money. The app will then ask you whether you want the funding to come from your PayPal balance or your bank account. Click on send and the payment will be made.

There's not much to sending payments through PayPal, and the iPhone app ensures the

experience of sending payments from your mobile is as simple from your phone as it is from your computer.

Perfect Photo

bit.ly/9P6Fbt
By **MacPhun LLC**
Price **59p**

There are those of us that absolutely love having our picture taking, even going so far as striking the perfect pose and being able to snap into that position at the mere glimpse of a camera lens.

But some of us are not so graced with the ability to make the camera love us. In fact, often the camera clearly has a vendetta against us if what the camera has done to our image is anything to go by.

Rather than being at the mercy of the lens, you can now fight back by editing your photo post snap to how it would have looked in an ideal world, this is where Perfect Photos comes in.

This app takes bite-sized pieces of some professional photo-editing tools and brings them to your fingertips, such as:
● Denoise
● Cropping
● Rotating
● Flipping
● Gamma
● Contrast
● Balancing

Tweaking an image to get it the way you want it is easy – most results are just a few taps away.

If you're incredibly vain or just always caught by the camera at the wrong moment, this app is likely to become a firm favourite.

Photogene

bit.ly/b53D6J
By **Omer Shoor**
Price **£1.19**

There are so many photo editing apps to choose from on the iPhone, most with just a couple of filters and tools to improve the photos snapped with the iPhone's camera.

Photogene is just one of these applications, but the range of filters and functions is more than most similarly priced tools.

Basic functions include crop and rotate, but the more useful tools are further down the list. Filters are pretty limited, with only sharpen, pencil and three photo effects onboard. However, the icon that resembles a colour wheel is the handiest for improving photos. Tap on it, and you can adjust the levels using a histogram-like graph. If you've ever used any photo-editing program on your computer, you'll find this a breeze.

There's also the option to change the exposure and contrast with a slider and alter the colour saturation and temperature, or RGB colour balance, again using sliders.

As you would expect from a small app, the options offered by Photogene aren't as advanced as a computer-based editing program, however, it does incorporate some really useful functions, which is unusual for an on-phone editing app.

Picturesafe

bit.ly/b0Qoc5
By **collect3**
Price **£1.19**

One area that the iPhone falls short on is its photo management abilities. Although your photos are set out beautifully in the Photos folder, there are not many ways that you can organise them.

Picture Safe attempts to improve this by allowing you to organise your photos into separate folders that can all be locked and then synced with your computer.

When you first start Picture Safe, it asks you to enter your password. Once you're in to the app, you can view different folders in a list. Tap on the folder

you require and you can add photos from your photo library.

To add photos from your computer, enter your iPhone's IP address as found in the Start web access menu from the Settings. Enter this into your computer's web browser and you can begin to add photos to your iPhone.

Picture Safe duplicates any images you want to hide from snoopers, so to completely remove them from prying eyes, you have to delete them from the original source as well as.

Other additions include a slideshow feature and a

'quickhide' function that brings up a picture of a random graph if you need to hide your photo library in a hurry.

Planets

bit.ly/anHvjf
By **Q Continuum**
Price *Free*

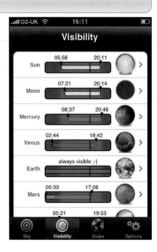

If you've ever walked along on your way home from a night out, looked up at the sky and wondered just what is going on up there then this app could quench your thirst for knowledge. Or if you've always been interested in astronomy and have a fondness for Mars or Venus and want to know exactly when the prime time is to spot your favourite planet then this app could be a great help.

Planets provides details of location, maps of stars and constellations, sunrise and sunset, key time information of planet

and moon activity, phases and much more.

There's a 3D globe view of all of the planets for you to focus your senses on with this nicely designed and easy-to-use app, in addition to planetary factsheets and more detail than you could shake a stick at.

It's unlikely that you'll become an expert overnight by using this app, but over time you'll certainly build up a good knowledge base on the subject.

If you want to look up and smile with knowledge rather than ignorance, or are helping children

to learn the different between a comet and a star, this app will prove very useful. Particularly as it's completely free.

Pocket God

bit.ly/c8mTK8
By **Bolt Creative**
Price **59p**

Pocket God could almost be described as a game, although there's no ending and no real objective as there is in a game. You play at being god and can decide whether you want to play good guy or bad guy with a group of Pygmies living on a remote island.

There are several different weather conditions to inflict, threat from sharks, fire, a volcano and dinosaurs, and it is you who decides whether the little critters live or die. It took us a while to get the hang of the app, and work out how to carry out certain actions, but when we understood how to catch fish, make a fire, escape from shark attacks and change the weather, we were engrossed. There's a toolbar at the top that allows you to add or take away tools and threats. You can use it to decide whether the Pygmies have access to a toilet, have the facilities to produce a fire and change

the weather to less favourable conditions. You do get points for either being good or bad and there's been a lot of controversy surrounding the app, but it certainly is addictive, in the same way that you'll struggle to resist the temptation of simple games such as Harbour Master.

PocketGuitar

bit.ly/cxQqcv
By **Shinya Kasatani**
Price **59p**

It's all the fun of air guitar but with an iPhone. The best of both worlds surely?

This app turns your shiny device into a mini guitar, allowing you to pluck and strum to you heart's content. You also have a choice of six different types of guitar from acoustic to the ukelele, so you can choose a different sound to suit what type of mood you're in.

Unless you're a guitar-playing pro, you're likely to spend quite a bit of time moving your fingers around pointlessly and not hearing any sound. Or hearing something that sounds like a cat being strangled. That's because you're strumming where you should be pressing and vice versa, but once you've worked that bit out, you'll have lots and lots of fun.

With many different types of guitar and effects to choose from, it'll be a while before you get bored from with this app. In fact, you'll probably never want to close this app once you've started strumming. But this new found music enthusiasm may also cause problems as well as bringing you joy. It might make friends and

loved ones want to kill you as it is quite noisy, and you will be playing it all the time. You have been warned.

PocketWeather

bit.ly/bJ5dBy
By **SBSH Mobile**
Price *Free*

The Weather app that comes with the iPhone is very basic and leaves out a lot of detailed information that's helpful for planning weekend activities. PocketWeather gives you much greater detail than just whether it's going to rain or shine in your local area. When you move to another major location, PocketWeather adds it to the list of cities that appear in the Summary tab.

Swiping left and right takes you to the next city, so you can keep an eye on areas where you're going to be traveling for

work. Even where it duplicates features of Apple's app, it presents information about high and low temperature forecasts in a better, more graphical way that clearly pictures how things will change over the next few days.

Forecasts can be shown as a broad overview, or in finer detail that shows the chance of showers on upcoming days. There's even an hourly forecast that's a great help for planning outdoor activities, such as a picnic.

The Maps tab provides a range of graphical readouts of clouds, temperatures and other

phenomena, and if you dig into the settings, you can set how frequently forecasts, images and other data is updated.

Podcaster

bit.ly/df5hR8
By **Alex Sokirynsky**
Price *59p*

We're all familiar with desktop RSS readers and now they've made the jump to the iPhone (for example, Free RSS Reader, which we explore on page 39), but what if you want that little bit more than just text to feed your appetite for information on the move?

This iPhone app was designed with that in mind.

With a cool and quirky, colourful interface, this app is multimedia chic personified. You add feeds by pressing the top-right '+' button, can flag your favourites by pressing the heart, create a playlist-like agenda and

queue download items without much effort at all.

Once you've got a podcast open, the media control buttons continue the funky theme, offering you the usual play/ pause/forward/rewind button options in addition to letting you add the podcast to the Player or download the file.

If you're an indecisive type, you can get the app to suggest a podcast for you.

And you don't need to worry if the podcast that you want to listen to is particularly large because there are no limits to

download if you're using the app over 3G or Edge – just keep one eye on your phone bill, should you exceed your daily bandwidth.

Postman

bit.ly/auYt8B
By **Freeverse**
Price **£1.79**

It's always a rush to find, write and send postcards when you're on holiday, particularly when the postal service in remote areas can take so long to operate. Most of the time, you'll find that you arrive home before your friends receive their postcards.

Freeverse has developed an app to eliminate the hassle of buying, writing and sending postcards when you're on holiday.

The app allows you to produce your own postcards using preloaded photos, photos already taken and stored in your photo library, a map of where you are or you can take a new photo especially for the occasion.

Once you have your background, you can work on the text, both on the front and back of the virtual postcard.

There are a whole host of different themes and effects you can add, from a classic white border, to making it look like a discarded message in a bottle, a Victorian postcard or a billboard. When you've produced your masterpiece, write a message on the back and it's ready to send. The options are extensive to say the least. You can Tweet it, send it to Facebook, post on Tumblr, email it, or upload it to postmanapp.com.

Puzzle Bobble

bit.ly/bSmQXM
By **Taito**
Price **£2.99**

Puzzle Bobble is Taito's classic match-three puzzle game redesigned for the iPhone. You're given a continuous supply of random coloured bubbles and have to fire them towards the clump of bubbles already hanging from the top of the screen, using your best judgment of angles to squeeze and bounce them into place.

Form a chain of three or more of the same colour and those bubbles burst. Any others that become detached from the main cluster fall off the bottom of the screen. Each round is complete when you've cleared all of the bubbles from the screen.

The challenge comes from the bubbles being pushed down a row every few seconds. If the lowest bubbles pass the line at the bottom of the screen, it's game over.

Puzzle Bobble features a story mode with dozens of levels, a two-player versus mode that works with another iPhone over Bluetooth, and if you're not exhausted after all of that, you can test your mettle with the continuous Challenge Mode. An online leaderboard shows your worldwide ranking, or you can post to Facebook and Twitter just to show off to your friends.

Quickoffice Mobile Office Suite

bit.ly/9cZXpA
By **QuickOffice Inc**
Price *£5.99*

Quickoffice claims to offer 'fast and responsive app performance' and we have to agree with its developers on that point.

This app isn't going to make you wan to ditch your laptop or netbook so that you can travel even lighter with just your iPhone when you're away from the office. That said, it does offer a happy medium for those who still want to look at and touch their vital documents when you're on the move and using a laptop isn't convenient.

Quickoffice includes Quickword and Quicksheet that enables you to edit Word documents and Excel files on your iPhone – you can even create documents from scratch if you suddenly find that your boss needs an urgent report. For this you can format and style text, set its alignment and several other useful layout functions.

An innovative 'quicksave' tool also ensures you don't lose valuable data if someone calls you – as soon as you finish the phonecall, the app will reload and present you with the document as you last saw it before you were interrupted.

The app looks quite bland but it more than does the job if you need to edit text and spreadsheet files when on the move.

 ## QuickVoice Recorder

bit.ly/91efy4
By **nFinity**
Price *Free*

QuickVoice is an essential tool for anyone who uses a Dictaphone or takes a lot of notes in meetings or lectures. The app is essentially a Dictaphone, although the full version of the app (there's a lite version too) adds in voice-to-text functionality thanks to SpinVox.

There's little to QuickVoice. The main screen comprises a list of previous recordings as well as record and play buttons. At the bottom are the options to add a title, send the recording by email as a sound byte or as text, translated by SpinVox.

There's no functionality to view the text created from a recording, and SpinVox can sometimes struggle to accurately turn the sound into text.

We tried recording a sample from the TV, and the sound quality was poor – SpinVox failed to turn a news bulletin into text, but live speech provided much better results, and SpinVox did manage to translate it, but with a couple of mistakes, which were acceptable given this app's usefulness.

Emailing the sound wasn't instant, but this will depend a lot on your ISP. Emailing the text will of course take longer as it has to go via SpinVox, but in our tests it still arrived within 10 minutes.

Radio Times

bit.ly/dhGkEW
By **tvCompass**
Price **£2.99**

As the name suggest, Radio
Times is the TV planner
magazine's application for the
iPhone. At £2.99, it may seem a
little steep, however, the app is
incredibly detailed.

After you've selected your
country and which service you
have (such as Freeview, Sky, Virgin
and so on), you're taken to a list
of programmes that are currently
showing. Swipe horizontally and
the app will show what's on next,
and you can view the day's lineup
in 30-minute increments.

Along the bottom of the
app, there are a range of options

including Radio Times Choices,
Films, and your Favourites that
you can add when viewing
listings by pressing the star icon
next to each programme.

More options include Sports
to see which sport programmes
are on at what time across all
channels, and Search which
allows you to find a listing.

If you want to change the
date, you can do so by tapping
the time at the top of the screen.
This takes you to a rotary date
option screen where you can
change the date up to a week
in advance.

Radio Times is an in-depth
application with *Radio Times*-style
descriptions of each programme
– a must for TV addicts.

Real Racing

bit.ly/bgsDEf
By **Firemint**
Price **£2.99**

If you're a fan of racing games,
Real Racing certainly sits at the
top of the pile. Real Racing uses
every gaming feature of the
iPhone, from the faster processor
of the 3GS and the accelerometer
to using the touchscreen to
apply the brakes.

If you're a newbie to racing
games on the iPhone, Firemint
has attempted to help you
break in by starting you off in a
hatchback, with semi-automatic
options such as braking enabled
from the off.

As you build up confidence,
you can opt to tone down the

braking and rip your way around
the various tracks.

To control the car, you can
use the accelerometer and tilt the
iPhone to turn left or right, or tap
different parts
of the screen
to control the
steering. As you
become more
confident, you'll
move up the
car ranks, and
drive a whole
host of different
cars, including
touring cars,

that have a lot less control and
are much faster. Real Racing is
possibly the closest you'll ever
come to driving a car on a track
using your iPhone. It beats other
racing games hands down, in
both graphics and gameplay and
is well worth the top rating and
the high price point.

RedLaser

bit.ly/bUTiso
By **Occipital**
Price *Free*

Selling unwanted possessions becomes much easier with this amazing barcode scanning application. Point your iPhone's camera at a barcode to scan it. The app then looks up prices for that item online to give you an idea of the going rate to help you decide on reserve prices for your eBay auctions.

One of the most impressive features is that you don't have to tap a button to take a picture of the barcode. You only have to line it up with the on-screen guides and hold the iPhone as still as you can.

Once the app recognises the barcode, it is decoded and used to look up prices on a variety of sites through Google.

The app isn't just good for eBay sellers, though. It also links to review sites, making it a super fast way to check on scores for items such as videogames while you're out and about, rather than visiting a site such as metacritic. com and typing in titles.

Even so, it's eBayers for whom this is a must-have app. It has the potential to save you hours sitting in front of your computer because it records all of the products you've scanned and lets you email the whole product list to save you writing down each of the results it finds.

Relax with Andrew Johnson – Deep Relaxation

bit.ly/ceXqSt
By **Michael Schneider**
Price *£1.79*

If you suffer from insomnia, or struggle to get to sleep sometimes, Relax with Andrew Johnson – Deep Relaxation is an app that could make your life a lot more bearable.

However, the app isn't just designed to help you get to sleep – it also includes tips on de-stressing, pain relief and ME.

The training starts with physical relaxation, starting from your toes to your head. For deeper relaxation, the app will set a relaxing scenario. Andrew Johnson has a very soothing voice and is always

accompanied by relaxing music in the background.

Using the app is simple. There aren't many options, only four stages of relaxation (starting with the instructions) that you can fast forward through if you wish. In the settings menu, you can choose the short introduction if time is scarce.

If it's late at night, you can set the app not to wake you up when it ends, apparently resulting in a deeper sleep for you.

We found Relax with Andrew Johnson to be a soothing experience. It's best not to listen

to the app while doing any activities where concentration is needed, as it does relax you more than you can imagine.

Remote

bit.ly/darjaA
By **Apple Inc**
Price *Free*

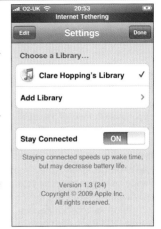

Remote was the first app to become available for the iPhone and it's still going strong with version 1.3 now available.

The app essentially allows you to control iTunes on Apple TV, PC and Mac using your wireless network.

Remote's interface is identical to the iPod function found on your iPhone, so you can view all of your music on your computer or Apple TV by Playlist, Artist or Album. You can also search for a particular track as well as control movies and podcasts through your iPhone too.

If your music collection on one computer is looking a little drab, Remote allows you to connect more than one computer to your iPhone, creating a whole music network in your home.

iTunes DJ means you can use an iPhone or iPod touch running Remote to give guests the chance to add to a playlist at a party.

Remote version 1.3 adds extra functionality to the original application, introducing gesture controls for Apple TV, but not on Mac and PC.

This is a much easier way to navigate around your music

collection, but it's a real shame Apple has neglected computer users, because after all, not everyone owns an Apple TV.

 ## Rolando 2: Quest for the Golden Orchid

bit.ly/bvPTqm
By **ngmoco:)**
Price *£2.99*

The lovably rotund Rolandos are on their way to a distant island in search of a fabled flower that will cure a disease that afflicts the royal family. The simple scenario is appealing to kids, while adults will enjoy the whimsical stylings and a superb soundtrack from British DJ, Mr Scruff.

Tilting the iPhone rolls the Rolandos around the landscape. To advance to the exit, you'll need to get them to push objects, depress switches, use explosive fruit to clear blocked paths, and use spring-loaded plungers and even vehicles to pull off

some amazing stunts. Larger Rolandos sink in water and can reach underwater areas that are inaccessible to their more buoyant friends. Rolando's life is extended by the compulsion to beat your previous score by finishing levels quickly, collecting every crystal and getting every Rolando to the exit. This is taken further with

Xbox Live-style achievements and the free Plus+ network's online scoreboards.

Rolando 2 does what all sequels should do: it builds upon all that was good about the original to deliver a genuine gem of a game. One of the iPhone's best, in fact.

RunKeeper Pro

bit.ly/95BqR8
By **Fitness Keeper**
Price **£5.99**

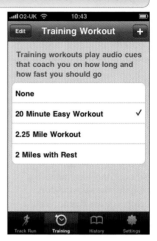

If you're a runner, RunKeeper Pro is an application that should be on your iPhone.

It's the most feature-packed running application available for the iPhone and although it may be on the pricier side, we found it to be more accurate than Nike+ for iPhone.

The app will first try to find your current location using the iPhone's GPS feature. As you run, it will track all vital stats including your speed and distance.

If you'd like prompts on your progress, you can choose a pre-loaded training workout or add your own, including warm up/cool down and pace (slow, steady or fast), varying the speed according to your preference throughout the workout.

When you're on a run, you can still listen to music and answer phone calls at will. If your phone rings, the app will pause, allowing you to take the call without affecting your workout.

You can also change the activity, and although there is a selection of activity types already on the app, you can select other if you find that your sport isn't on the comprehensive list.

When you've finished, you can track your route and your speed at each point of the run using your online account.

 # ShakeItPhoto

bit.ly/d9o1tz
By **Nick Campbell**
Price **59p**

Digital photography has been with us for long, it's hard to remember what life was like when you had to send film off to be processed and the only way to have instant images was with Polaroid. Yet part of Polaroid's fun was watching those photos develop in front of your eyes, wondering how it will turn out.

ShakeItPhoto allows you to relive those days with its fun way of producing a photo from a shot taken on your iPhone.

The interface for taking a photo is exactly the same as it is when using the camera in normal mode, so there's nothing complicated about the app.

Once you've taken the snap using the photo icon at the bottom of the screen, ShakeItPhoto will ask if you would like to use the photo. Tap on 'use' and the photo will appear as an undeveloped Polaroid.

Shake the iPhone to develop the photo, and see your image appear before your eyes. The slower you shake, the longer it will take for the image to appear fully developed.

ShakeItPhoto may not improve pictures, add filters or do anything fancy, but it does add a whole lot of fun to taking photos, and gives them a certain grainy Polaroid quality.

Shakespeare

bit.ly/b0RwMH
By **Readdle**
Price *Free*

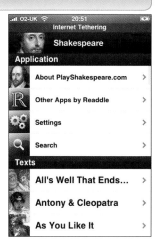

If you're a little rusty on the plays of William Shakespeare, you can catch up with the Shakespeare app for the iPhone.

It's a comprehensive collection of all the great bard's plays, poems and sonnets, although there are numerous plugs for the app's creators before you are able to reach your chosen text.

The plays are split up into Acts, making it easy for you to skip to the text you want to read or resume at the same point if you terminated the app mid-way through reading a script.

Text flows down, meaning instead of turning a page as you would in a book or other eBook reader, you have to continually scroll down to read more text.

You can change the settings to move the page down by tapping the screen, but using an iPhone, you'll probably feel more accustomed to scrolling. You can also change the size of text and colours to make it easier to read.

Using the iPhone's built in accelerometer, Shakespeare works in both portrait and landscape mode to enable it to fit more text on its screen.

It's a shame the app is so basic for an eReader, although it does the job well and makes reading Shakespeare as easy as possible.

 ## Shazam

bit.ly/c4Pkq0
By **Shazam Entertainment**
Price *Free*

Shazam is everyone's secret music quiz weapon. In fact, if you regularly attend pub quiz, you may be one of the people who ensures that your team are the closest to the speaker so you can secretly cheat using this music recognition app.

Shazam is faster and more intuitive to use than dialling the shortcode, which is also offered by the company, and the app is a free download unlike the phone service which costs a few pence.

When you are ready to find out what that tune is, just tap on the 'tag now' icon in the top-right

corner. A circle will appear as the app is listening to the music, and seconds later, the music will be analysed and if successful, the album art, song, artist, album name, label, genre and your location will all appear.

Under the tagged music, you can choose to preview the song and buy on iTunes if you wish. And if you prefer to see your favourite artists in action, you can opt to watch a video on YouTube.

When you return to the homescreen, you can view all of your previously tagged tunes. Shazam is the most-rounded,

but simple app on the App Store. It's already become a classic but makes tagging music on the go easier than ever. And, it's free.

Sky+

bit.ly/9IwcOA
By BSkyB
Price *Free*

Sky+ is a remote recording tool and Electronic Programme Guide (EPG) for your iPhone.

To use it, you'll need to have a Sky+ account with remote recording set up, which you can do through Sky interactive on your TV. It's a simple process and you'll only have to set it up once.

When you launch the app, you're presented with different TV categories such as Entertainment, Sport and Movies. Tap one and an EPG will pop up, showing you all the programmes that are on for the following week with their relative times.

When you tap on an entry, a description of the programme and the option to record will appear. Tap record, and your request will be sent to Sky to authorise and pass onto your Sky+ box.

We tested with two different programmes on two different channels. One was starting in the next half an hour, and this failed. The other we set to record in two hours, and this was successful.

The interface is seamless, but in this case, it's the unreliability that may let you down. You should allow an hour before

sending the request through, otherwise you may return home to be very disappointed by a missed recording.

Sky News

bit.ly/9gggVx
By BSkyB
Price *Free*

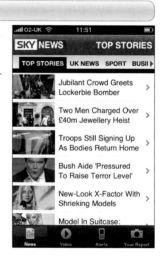

Sky News is just one of the major news players that has thrown its hat into the mobile ring with the launch its iPhone app. It's free, which is always a bonus, and features a sleek, easy-to-use tabbed interface.

When you start the app, the news headlines are the first thing you'll see in a list format. Click on any one of them and you're taken to the full news story on a page optimised for the iPhone's screen.

If the story includes a video (as most of the stories do on this particular app), the video will appear at the top with a red play

icon overlaid on the image. Click this and the video will stream in a full-page window. Click Done to read the story. A video tab is split into categories such as top stories, showbiz and weather. Again, tap on any of these options and you can watch the full bulletin in video.

One handy feature to the Sky News app is that you can set up SMS alerts. Although this does cost up to 25p per text, you'll only receive a maximum of two messages per day.

The final tab is Your Report. Here, you can report a news story

you think that Sky News would be interested in. This is probably the least used feature on the app, but a nice touch.

Sky Sports Live Cricket Score Centre

bit.ly/bccKf1
By **BSkyB**
Price *Free*

★★★☆☆

There's nothing quite like the sound of leather hitting willow in the summer, but if your schedule doesn't allow for you to watch every cricket match, you can download the Sky Sports Live Cricket Score Centre app to keep you up to date with scores wherever you are.

You can track international Test, One Day Internationals and Twenty20 matches. The tabs along the bottom enable you to view league tables, fixtures and scores for the season.

To view more information about a fixture, simply tap it from the homescreen and you can view a match summary.

To track a particular match, enter the fixtures list and tap on the '+' icon next to any of the fixtures. This will then be added to the My Scores section. Not only can you view match results, but also there's a scrolling ticker along the bottom of the screen that displays all the latest cricket news as it breaks, whatever screen you happen to be on.

There aren't any push notifications on this app, which is a little disappointing considering that most other sports results app now include them as standard with their latest updates, but still for cricket fans it will be one of their first app purchases.

Sky Sports Live Football Score Centre

bit.ly/bUQAB8
By **BSkyB**
Price *Free*

★★★★☆

Mobile Internet brought a vast improvement to people's lives. But not as it was intended by bringing mobile banking, emails from the office or tracking stocks and shares to your phone, but for something far more important; football scores.

The iPhone needed an app for that, and BSkyB has done it with aplomb. Its Sky Sports Live Football Score Centre app provides all the information for all the games being played that day across Europe, from the English Premier League to the Unibond Division and from La Liga to the Champions League and beyond. The layout works exceptionally well and gives access to live scores, tables, news, team line-ups and formations, and minute-by-minute match commentary.

The app is also aesthetically pleasing – it even has a vidiprinter for all scores as they happen and a My Scores section that enables you to add different games from across the divisions, cups or countries in a similar fashion to a playlist, allowing quick access to your chosen matches.

Essentially Sky has created a very good handheld *Sky Sports Soccer Saturday* on your iPhone. And, for those who are fans, it even has a picture of Jeff Stelling on the title screen.

Skype

bit.ly/9SJTBl
By **Skype Software**
Price *Free*

If you don't know what Skype is, there's a chance you've been hiding in a dark room with your fingers stuck in your ears for the past few years.

For those who do know what it is and have an account, they'll be pleased to hear the free phone calls and messages are now available on the iPhone.

Once you've got a Skype account set up, logging into the app on the iPhone is easy. If you haven't got a Skype account, you can quickly and easily set one up, but good luck trying to find a nice username that's not already taken.

After you've signed in for the first time you can conduct a test call with an automated voice to check everything is working as it should be. The rest, such as adding contacts and making calls is self-explanatory and easy to work out thanks to the interface. Although you do need to buy a Skype number from a link on the info screen.

It's common sense that you need the app running if you want to make any calls, but you also need it to be alive to receive calls too, which makes the app more suited for intensive Skype

users rather than occasional fan dabbler who may forget that they need to click on the icon to get it going.

 # Skyscape Medical Resources

bit.ly/cKOYra
By **Skyscape**
Price *Free*

This is not really an app for the layman or laywomen. In fact, it's probably more targeted at medical professionals, or medical students who need access to clinical data while on the move.

Skyscape's free app contains a database with a wealth of free resources – too many to count or list here – including drug brand data, dosing calculators, clinical trial results and MedAlert summaries.

The content spans many areas of medicine and is a result of a partnership between Skyscape and more than 50

leading healthcare publishers.

But before you can get access to any of this you have to first create a Skyscape account, which requires name, postcode, email address, job title and specialism to set up. Some people don't like handing out data such as these, but it's a small sacrifice if you want what the app has to offer. You then have to download the free resources outlined above, which can take several minutes to complete.

In terms of navigation and layout, the app is easy to use (provided you know what

all the various medical terms actually mean) and clearly has a valid role in the healthcare professional industry.

Sonic the Hedgehog

bit.ly/9oH1qr
By **Sega**
Price **£3.49**

Sonic's debut adventure from all the way back in 1991 has sped onto the iPhone and, quite remarkably, the design still holds up well. That's thanks to its distinctive visuals and great level layouts packed with hidden areas and multiple routes.

Green Hill Zone introduces the core mechanic of building up enough speed to carry Sonic through 360° loops and up short vertical surfaces and, when curled into a ball, straight through rock walls. The Marble and Labyrinth Zones are a tad too slow and rely on genre clichés of lava and water,

but it's the pinball-inspired Spring Yard Zone and the blisteringly fast Star Light Zone that are the game's highlights. To conquer the game, you'll need to beat the special stages, where Sonic tumbles through a constantly revolving maze to find the Chaos Emeralds he needs to defeat Dr Robotnik. These areas are perhaps the game's most

challenging, as you have fairly limited control to bounce Sonic off walls and towards his goal. Sonic plays well on the iPhone 3GS and iPhone 4. Avoid it on older phones, though, as the slowdown is painful. Otherwise, take the spikey blue hero for a spin in this enjoyable blast from the past.

Space Invaders Infinity Gene

bit.ly/aGwpeL
By **Taito**
Price **£2.99**

Never before has Space Invaders spawned a sequel like Infinity Gene. Its first stage fools you into thinking that it's a sedate affair by pitting you against the original invasion fleet for a few seconds. Then the garden-variety invaders are blown away, and Earth's last line of defence turns into a starfighter to strike back at the aliens.

The original invaders are merely the front line of a more powerful fleet. Destroy flying saucers and they drop alien DNA that increases your ship's power. The theme here is evolution –

collect samples to unlock new weapons and levels.

The only control to master is sliding your finger to move the ship, which fires automatically. The vector graphics don't look great in stills, but they're fantastic in motion. Massive carriers launch fighters at you, gunships swarm the screen, and massive end-of-level bosses threaten to overwhelm you with their tremendous firepower.

The action is backed with a pulsating soundtrack, and the game creates new levels based on the tracks in your iPod library.

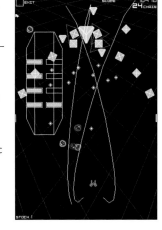

Infinity Gene compacts the scrolling shooter genre into a frenetic shooter that's the best of its kind for the iPhone.

Speed Bones MD

bit.ly/caSyYv
By **Benoit Essiambre**
Price **59p**

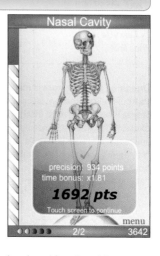

Speed Bones MD is a quiz-style app that teaches you where the different bones in your body are.

The object of the game is to match the bone name that appears at the top of the screen with the part of the body where the bone is situated.

There are both practice modes and the actual game, where points count. The practice mode includes all bones, so you can practice with even the trickiest of bone names.

The app starts off relatively easily, with obvious bones such as skull, clavicle and shoulder blade all making an appearance, in addition to tibia, fibula and patella.

When the bone name appears at the top of the app, you have to tap the skeleton in the correct place to identify that bone. The closer you are in accuracy, the more points you get. The test is also against the clock, so trying to recall those biology lessons as quickly as possible is a distinct advantage.

As you move up levels, the bones get trickier – after all, there are 206 bones in the human body, most of which are in the hands and feet. Speed Bones MD is a great educational game for children that can become addictive after a while.

Spell Check

bit.ly/9G8yhP
By **Achoom**
Price **59p**

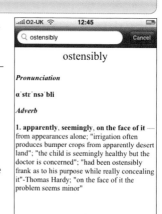

Spell Check is a complete dictionary and pronunciation tool for the iPhone. Type in a word and Spell Check provides you with the correct spelling (if you've typed in it wrong) and the correct pronunciation as well as highly detailed descriptions as to what the word means.

If a word has more than one usage (for example, it might be used as a noun and a verb) then it also gives information and appropriate examples.

As well as providing this indispensable data, Spell Check also suggests alternative words that are close to the one you entered. For example, typing in 'machine' will give you 'marching', 'chine' and 'mashing' as possible substitutes.

Granted, sometimes these can be a little on the random side but they're useful if you're trying to find a word and you're unsure about how it's actually spelt.

Spell Check also stores all of your searches so you can consult them again at a later date. This is especially handy if you have a few words that you always struggle to spell correctly. Then using the iPhone's copy-and-

paste function, it's possible to locate these correct spellings and drop them into other apps – such as email or text messaging.

Stanza

bit.ly/ahTPey
By **Lexcycle**
Price *Free*

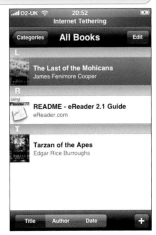

One thing the App store is not short of is eBook readers, but Stanza is one of the most intuitive to use. When you fire Stanza up, you're taken to your library. At first, there's not much to choose from, but enter the Online Catalog and you're taken to the biggest book store in the world.

You can decide where you buy your eBooks from, although unfortunately, most sites are American, so you're charged in dollars. However, all is not lost as there is a huge selection of free books on offer. We opted for *The Iliad* by Homer, which

took a matter of seconds to download. Locating the book was easy as it had been added to the Titles section.

To turn pages using Stanza, you tap the right-hand side of the screen. Tap on the left side to go back a page. Tap in the centre and you can view the controls and see how far through the book you are. You can use a slider at the bottom if you want to skip to a specific section and you have the option to search the text too.

There are several handy options including night mode, which changes the background

to black and the text to white, plus you can change the size of text, font and background colour to your own preference.

Star*burst

bit.ly/coeSsX
By **Super Happy Fun Fun**
Price *£1.19*

Star*Burst is a match-three puzzle game with its own unique spin on the genre. Tiles fall down the five alleys of a ramp towards your waiting paddle. You fire them upwards to assemble horizontal, vertical and diagonal lines of three or more of the same colour. If it looks and sounds familiar, that's because it's essentially Atari's classic Klax.

Things start off slowly enough to absorb the mechanics of the game, but anxiety goes through the roof as the speed increases and an increasing number of tiles fall down the

ramp. Matters are made worse by the paddle only holding five tiles. If too many fall uncaught or you fill the 25-tile space at the top of the screen then it's game over.

Strategic moves require fast thinking to assemble four or five-strong chains. Form a giant X to get the best rewards, including warp zones to leap through the game's 100 levels.

Star*Burst's controls are slightly oversensitive, but that's part of what makes it such a challenge. It doesn't rival Bejeweled in the longevity stakes, but there's plenty of fun for quick

bursts of gameplay, aided by the instant pause feature so you can pick up where you left off after taking a call.

Starmap Pro

bit.ly/aEd78v
By **Fredd**
Price **£11.49**

Who didn't love visiting planetariums or listening intently to Sir Patrick Moore's in-depth talks about what's in the sky at night when they were children?

This app does cost a bit more than the majority of apps for the iPhone, but in our opinion it's worth every penny because it gives so much fun.

The menu lists planets, constellations, stars and what is happening in the sky on that particular night. Each planet can be looked at in a card-like fashion with information like distance and magnitude.

This app is a perfect companion for a telescope and it is a great aid if you want to keep a log of your night-time activities and set alarms so you don't miss certain sky occurrences.

The menu is very extensive with many settings and options on offer to you. It's actually a little overwhelming at first and you need to take a step back and decide what you want to do first rather than just acting on the temptation to press everything.

If you don't know your Arrow from your Cepheus, or even if you do, this app is likely to have

something that appeals. It's a very innovative app and is fun for adults as well as a good learning tool for children.

Strategery

bit.ly/cFvRUX
By **Affogato**
Price **£1.19**

Strategery presents you with a map that's divided up into many smaller pieces of territory. The more of it you claim for yourself, the stronger your military might becomes and the greater your chances of dominating the world.

But you're not the only one with an eye on conquest. Play against the computer and you'll be up against four other nations, each one with its own unique colour. Or you can play against a single friend online.

It's best to start out on small maps and, once you're confident you understand the best way to

defeat your opponents, step up to the larger sizes.

Eventually, the battles will reach epic proportions, and you'll need to have mastered an understanding of when it's appropriate to shore up your defences and when to expand your territory. Get it wrong and your opponent will cut straight through the middle of your nation, reducing your ability to rebuild and strike back, as that is directly related to the longest chain of areas that you control.

Once you've worked out the tactics, or rather the maths, of the

gameplay, Strategery becomes a little too easy. But by that point, you'll have enjoyed many hours of fun battling friends.

Street Fighter IV

bit.ly/avqjQM
By **Capcom**
Price **£5.99**

Capcom's latest brawler will make your eyes bulge as much as your muscles when you see its graphics, although concerns that the lack of tactile feedback might deal a crippling blow to the game are only natural.

Street Fighter puts you in a series of one-on-one fights. This version has a roster of ten characters, including favourites such as the formidable M. Bison and the marvellous Chun Li.

Newcomers can step into the dojo to learn and perfect a strategy against a training opponent. The real challenge

comes in three forms: free sparring lets you pick an opponent and arena, tournament is a series of matches, or you can fight it out with a human opponent over Bluetooth.

The game records stats but there's no online leaderboard.

Capcom has wisely allowed you to reposition the joystick and buttons exactly where

you want them. The joystick is tricky to master and initially led to us jumping up instead of backwards to safety.

There's also no vibration when you land punches and kicks, but none of these niggles detract from this being a lean, mean fighting machine.

Sunrise Sunset

bit.ly/9IGiQ9
By **Kekoa Vincent**
Price **59p**

Sunrise Sunset is a fully- featured iPhone app for calculating what time the sun will rise and set around the world.

By default, the app is set to calculate the sunrise and sunset in your GPS location. These defaults can be changed using the tabs along the bottom.

Tap on date to change it – the calendar goes on forever because sunrise and sunset can be calculated using the phase of the moon. Tap on location to change the location. This section is first split up into country, then area, then town.

Tap back onto display to be presented with the information. You can scroll through previous or future days to see how the times change. You're also provided with information about the destination including the time difference from your GPS location and the coordinates of the location. In addition to the sunrise and sunset, the app also displays the time at which civil twilight begins, ends and transit, or solar moon.

Although Sunrise Sunset won't be of use to everyone, it's perfect for photographers who

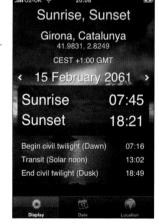

want to capture magic moment before sunset or after sunrise, as well as anyone who relies on daylight hours.

Super Monkey Ball 2

bit.ly/88pbsT
By **Sega**
Price **£3.49**

Super Monkey Ball 2's premise is simple: tilt platforms to roll your monkey in a ball towards the finish line. Bananas that litter each course provide points and extra lives, although many are deviously placed on narrow ledges and near pinball-style bumpers. One slip will send your simian careening dizzily.

The iPhone's accelerometer makes it an ideal controller – tilt the phone and the in-game world leans with it. The game features an on-screen tilt meter to help you judge the angle that will bring the ball to a dead stop. However, there's no way to calibrate that centre position.

This version packs in 115 new levels, but the best additions are multiplayer and three mini-games: bowling, target and golf.

Multiplayer works over local wifi and shows other players as ghosts on your screen. As if single-player mode

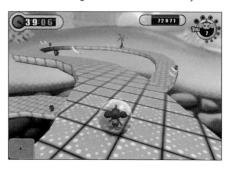

didn't provide enough tension with moving platforms, sloping surfaces and the desperation of getting your monkey's momentum just right, seeing other players rush ahead will heighten that, but competitive laughs will abound when they get themselves into a sticky mess.

Surf Report

bit.ly/aShwgA
By **Oakley Inc**
Price **Free**

There aren't many places that surf dudes can congregate and do their thang in Blighty. Mother Nature has seen to that. But what surfers can do is go somewhere else for the perfect swell.

This handy iPhone app brought to us by Oakley, doesn't look that much based on the first menu you come across, but it is pretty cool nonetheless.

You just choose your worldwide location, then drill down into more specific locations, for example, we looked at beaches in the northeast of England. The app will then furnish you with details as to what the weather is like there that day, as well as provide further details regarding the tide and so forth.

There's also the familiar Google Maps pin, so you can get a bit more data to help guide your surfing plans, including directions from your non-surfing hell to your surfer's paradise, just by clicking a button.

You can adapt the way information is displayed (temperature can be Fahrenheit or Celsius, for example) in the settings panel. There's also a little community button where

budding – or more seasoned – surfers can keep abreast of the latest surfing news as well as looking at surfy pics and videos.

Tax Calculator

bit.ly/9fg6xE
By **LePetit**
Price **£2.39**

Knowing exactly how much you'll pay at the checkout requires that you know all about local taxes. Tax Calculator helps you calculate exactly what you'll pay in Australia, New Zealand, Canada, Japan, Singapore, the UK as well as the various states of the US. The app shows a list of countries in a list and also lets you refine the choice by region in the US, or by the reduced or standard tax in the UK.

Once set, just tap in one of the three fields above and enter the price with or without tax or the monetary amount

of tax you're paying. The app calculates the other two values for you. There's little to fault in the interface except the font size used in the fields.

Although it's labeled a calculator, the app could go further with advice for travellers. There's no link to the Wikipedia page on US sales tax, which would help you look up items that are subject to higher or lower taxes, such as pharmaceuticals That would be especially helpful for long periods spent travelling, especially when you're taking in more than one state or country.

Even so, with a bit of preparation, this app will save on mental mathematics when you're totalling the cost of your trolley.

 ## Tetris

bit.ly/cy3wOa
By **Electronic Arts**
Price **£1.79**

Tetris needs no introduction. Having been around for more than two decades, it proves the old adage of if it ain't broke, don't fix it. However, like everything, even Tetris needed a bit of a makeover to keep it up-to-date with both the competition and the iPhone platform.

The game has been given a complete aesthetics overhaul, with some brightly coloured, very nice graphics making for a more modern, funky look. Obviously the biggest difference though, is its touchscreen format. The app also offers two versions of the

game. Marathon, which is the old Classic game with a full 15 levels, or Magic which gives you a target number of lines to clear to complete each level, and has varying different special items such as the Minimizer, which you can use to squish the blocks to fit in to a space.

Tetris definitely hasn't lost any of its appeal over the years and can still provide enough entertainment to be worth the money. However, the touchscreen is its biggest downfall. Once you reach the faster levels, tapping the blocks to turn them

and sliding them into position is virtually impossible. Still an excellent game, even if slightly flawed in this format.

The AA Theory Test for Car Drivers

bit.ly/dBfVi9
By **Abel Learning**
Price **£1.79**

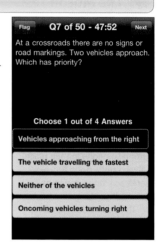

Used diligently, this app could really help you pass your test. The Theory Test is essentially a bank of questions to help you revise for the theory exam element of your driving test.

As an educational tool, it doesn't really teach you anything as it uses multiple choice questions. However, it is handy as a way of practising for the exam or if you are one of those fortunate people whose brain is like a sponge and able to soak up information very quickly.

The test takes the form of three modes – theory test,

practice theory test and revise all questions. The first provides you with 50 questions and gives you 50 minutes in which to answer them. There's no option to backtrack if you want to check your answers and when the test is over, you'll only get brief explanations as to why the incorrect answers are wrong.

Practice test lets you answer a specified number of questions in a particular section, which is handy if you're weak in one area. If you get an answer wrong here, you can try again or opt to be shown the answer.

Revise all questions takes you through every possible question on the theory test, again split up into sections, again in test format.

 ## The Curious Case of Benjamin Button, by Francis Scott Fitzgerald

bit.ly/9IR6QC
By **Your Mobile Apps Inc**
Price *Free*

When we first opened this app, it displayed a page entitled 'Tales of the Jazz Age' then quickly changed into a menu display called Books with just one listed: *The Curious Case of Benjamin Button* by F Scott Fitzgerald.

This start had us a little confused, but as soon as we clicked on the book icon, we were back to familiar eBook territory with chapters listed in sequential order. Once you've opened a chapter, you can scroll through the text at your own pace, just using your fingers. The default font is a good size, but you can

also adjust this by visiting the settings menu if you find it too large or small.

Alas, it doesn't have automatic scrolling like some eBook readers, but those who like to be in complete control of the speed at which they move through the book might actually find this preferable. A neat tool we liked was the ability to bookmark an area of the text so that you can easily find your place later on.

Anyone who has previously read this book or indeed seen the recent movie will know that it's quite hard going on the brain

– in a good way. But, this eBook app makes light work of a heavy text, adding positively to the literary experience.

The Moron Test

bit.ly/csnXfm
By **DistinctDev**
Price **59p**

Do you know someone who thinks they're the brain of Britain? Why not catch them out and make them feel stupid?

It may sound quite petty, but putting someone in their place is always quite good fun. Now there's an iPhone app to help speed things along.

The app loads in landscape mode, and you're greeted with four coloured buttons. Despite it saying you need to press the red button to start, you can't help but be distracted by the other colours and inevitably end up pressing anything but red – instant fail.

Sometimes the app asks you not to do something that actually looks like something you should do. For example, a big red button in the middle of the screen that says continue on it is contradicted by the instruction telling you not to press the button.

The cheeky messages the app serves up when you fail are also smile worthy. Our

favourite was: 'Everything with a brain makes it this far. You are now an average mammal.'

And so the game continues. It's looks so easy, but it's not. The Moron Test is utterly addictive and we were playing it for what felt like two minutes only to find out we'd been playing it for half an hour.

The Secret of Monkey Island: Special Edition

bit.ly/bcFxJH
By **LucasArts**
Price **£4.99**

There have been a whole host of retro games released on the App Store, and The Secret of Monkey Island is just the latest one of these. Originally launched in the 1990s, The Secret of Monkey Island follows the adventures of Guybrush Threepwood, a rather scatty pirate wannabe.

The remastered game is controlled via a cursor that you drag around the touchscreen to select places that Guybrush can go, objects he can interact with and characters he can talk to on his travels. To activate an action,

you simply double tap when the cursor icon changes, or bring up the action menu to select what you'd like to do with an object or person.

This does take a little getting used to, but quite often you're prompted along the way, as options pop up now and again giving you advice.

If you wish to revert to the

original 1990s game, you can swipe across the screen to see the pixelated graphics edition.

As a story game, there doesn't seem to be a rush to complete any tasks that are set. You can stroll through the game, chatting away to pirates to your heart's content. It's a perfect game if you're on a long journey.

The Sims 3

bit.ly/d1c4QB
By **Electronic Arts**
Price **£3.99**

The Sims 3 is one of the most eagerly awaited games on the iPhone, and it certainly doesn't disappoint. The iPhone Sims experience is almost as extensive as it is on computer, although some aspects have been canned to keep the file size small and the speed as fast as possible.

For starters, you can't change your Sim as much as you can on the computer version, neither is gameplay consistent; you'll have to wait while you move from your home to the town.

You'll go through ups and downs with your Sim, including the hardships of finding a job, making friends and earning money. You'll also have to satisfy your Sim's wishes, such as kicking over a bin and making a friend jealous. Once all of these wishes are satisfied, you can unlock a new career and gain the option to buy a car.

Throughout the game, you'll have the option of completing mini-games, such as fishing if you head to the pond. To complete these, you'll need the equipment, and to buy that, you'll need money.

At the start, the game feels a little slow, while you find a job to buy things and meet people. After an hour's play, you'll find that Sims is a satisfying experience.

The Telegraph

bit.ly/9yFE79
By **The Telegraph**
Price **Free**

Once you've got through the quite lengthy terms and conditions then clicked to agree to them, you're free to enjoy the delights of the Telegraph's iPhone app. The menu is certainly pretty funky, with its blue on a black background and a cool choice of display font.

All the usual Telegraph suspects are present on the menu, from news and sport to travel and technology. We opted to browse the latter section and were greeted with a nicely spaced sub-menu detailing story headlines and summaries. You just hit a button to get the story in full and you can scroll down to view more article snippets too.

The Telegraph's videos are also displayed in the same menu format, with the full video just a click away. This is just fine for viewing short videos, but you may prefer to wait until you're at a desktop if they want to view a longer piece of content.

The spinning Telegraph logo is present against a cool blue background each time it's loading up your chosen menu item. And, while content doesn't take long to load at all, it gives the user something nice to look at, rather than a blank screen, while it does.

A broadsheet favourite in the palm of your hands.

Things

bit.ly/bMVgUN
By **Cultured Code**
Price **£5.99**

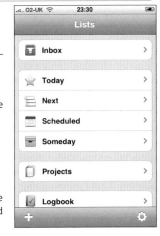

Things isn't just another to do list app. It's a task manager that blends all the features you need to make the most out of your time. Rather than providing a basic interface that doesn't really do anything more than a paper-based to do list or create something with so many bells and whistles users are overwhelmed, Things gets the balance just right.

In addition to helping you manage basic day-to-day tasks, this app can also help users keep a handle on project progress, due dates and notes. All brought

together in an interface that makes you want to use it again and again. There's also a cute little 'someday' menu listing which is presumably a repository for all those items that get written down each day, left undone and then added to the next day's list.

Outstanding items are flagged when the app's not in use in the same way as you're notified of unread texts or missed calls, which is handy for busy people who won't necessarily remember to open the app frequently.

At just under £6, this app isn't the cheapest out, however,

with the amount of time it could save you it could easily pay for itself many times over during the course of its use.

 ## Thomson Reuters News Pro

bit.ly/aeEXMh
By **Thomson Reuters**
Price *Free*

This app offers you breaking news, pictures and stock market data in one place. If you see a headline that interests you, you simply click and it brings up the full story from within the app.

There's a market data ticker that's constantly changing to show different information. At first the eye is drawn to this movement in the top-right corner of the app but you soon get used to it.

When it comes to pictures, you can click on an image from the main picture menu and then scroll through the others by

swiping your finger in the same way as you'd view an album on the iPhone.

Market data is in-depth, with information abut that stock market's previous day's movements as well as the current performance clearly shown. The data is similar in detail when it comes to viewing individual stocks and shares.

Video is not as good an experience however. The video automatically plays in landscape mode, meaning you have to tilt the device and the quality, to our eye, is a little grainy.

But, this downside is more than outshone by the rest of the goodies it has to offer. It's certainly a handy pocket companion.

Tip and Split

bit.ly/cz6dQm
By **Infobank Corp**
Price *Free*

We've all been out for dinner with friends and then had to rely on rusty maths lessons learnt at school to work out who owes what and how much to tip.

This handy application does all the hard work for you. It features a really nice little interface with calculator and the data you need hovering over a cafe-style table cloth and some tomato-shaped ketchup bottles

You simply enter the total bill, then use the slot-machine style scrolling menu to select how many people have indulged and how much tip you want to leave.

Then, in a matter of seconds, a bill appears on the screen with exactly how much each person needs to pay.

Another nice touch is the fact that, next to each tip percentage, is a smiley icon that depicts a sad or happy face depending on how much of a generous tipper you are.

It's a great app and we can

see it being of particular use to teenagers where every penny really does matter, whereas adults may be a bit embarrassed to tot up who owes what in minute detail in such a public fashion.

If you're always the one who ends up paying more than everyone else, this app is for you.

Tips & Tricks – iPhone Secrets

bit.ly/bhyV6n
By **Intelligenti Publishing**
Price *£0.59*

If you don't think you're making the full use of the iPhone, Intelligenti's Tips & Tricks application will talk you through how to use every one of the device's features.

The app covers everything from using shortcuts and to solving problems as well as how to use the range of preinstalled applications such as Safari.

The interface isn't the most intuitive to use, however, as there's no index at the start of the app, although you can access the index by tapping on the screen to bring the controls up or by

tapping on the icon located in the centre of the bottom strip.

If you want to quickly navigate through Tips & Tricks, you can use the scrollbar at the top of the screen to turn page by page, or you can click on the right side of the screen to get onto the next page while clicking on the left-hand side will take you back a page.

We found Tips & Tricks to be slightly cumbersome when navigating through the application, but the content is useful if you want to speed up using every aspect of the

Tip 62   A *Scientific* Calculator

The usual calculator provides large, easy to use buttons for basic arithmetic. If you tip the phone sideways, you'll see a scientific calculator. You can now perform more complex calculations. OS3.0 adds *Copy & Paste*.

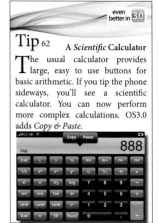

iPhone. Version 3.0 includes tips and tricks for the iPhone 3GS, which is very useful if you've just purchased a new iPhone.

To Do's

bit.ly/bRB4oP
By **AustinBull Software**
Price *Free*

In this world, there are to do lists and *to do lists*. This app unashamedly self-proclaims to be in the latter camp – the camp that is actually worth having. Its makers claim it's a 'convenient and easy way to manage your to do list'.

The app offers three different priority levels for tasks: low, normal and high, that you can assign to items on your list. This is useful as many people tend to create a to do list as a stream of consciousness with no thought of the urgency of the jobs until they get to the bottom then it just

becomes a bit of a mess – one that often makes you not want to do any of the tasks on it at all.

The different priority levels are also colour-coded for added emphasis, with red, orange and black for high, normal and low levels respectively.

You can also initiate the icon badge to show at a glance just how many tasks you have left to do. This will appear like text message volumes in a red bubble when you're not actually in the app itself. There's nothing like a big number to shock you into action or spur you on to get it

down to zero as soon as possible. In summary, downloading this free app should be high up on your to do list.

 ## TonePad

bit.ly/b0ETAI
By **LoftLab**
Price *Free*

Imagine the fun you have with bubble wrap. It's a seemingly endless supply of amusement. Now add music to the mix and you have a whole lot of fun.

TonePad is essentially a pad full of tones – you simply press them in a random fashion (or in a stick dog shape as we did, right) and it creates a synthesised tune based on your pattern.

You can change the colours of the bubbles and save your chosen composition. You can also upload it to a central base of tunes to share it with others – when you do so you'll be given a

unique code, which your friends can use to access your tunes.

Similarly you can download the work of others to see how they've fared with the musical tool. If you want to use either your own creations or those you've listened to as ringtones on your iPhone, you'll need to spend a whopping 59p to upgrade to the Pro version of the app to do so.

It's a great way to while away the time waiting for something to happen, whether it be a train arriving or a friend turning up at the pub.

Before you know it, you'll look up at the clock and find you've been playing for hours and hours.

Trails

bit.ly/dtHoxO
By **Felix Lamouroux**
Price **£2.39**

Trails is a journey-tracking app that uses Locate to track your position and speed.

When you first start the app, you're invited to add a new trail or import trails already tracked from a number of sites including Bikely and Mapmyrun or add your own GPX file. If you decide to add a new trail, you're taken to the main interface where you can start tracking your journey.

In the centre of the screen, the app will load up a map, marking your current location. The timer will begin to time your trail, while the journey is tracked on the map. You can label points you pass and even take photos of landmarks along the way.

You can move around the map with your finger, just like on Google Maps and the graphics will render as you move, meaning you will need a network connection all the time.

Trails isn't just limited to tracking one type of transport. You can set it to view roads on the map as well as view pedestrian or cycle routes.

The idea behind Trails is simple, as is the interface. With the option of uploading the data from the app onto the EveryTrail website, it's a top app for tracking where you've been and how you got there.

Trip Journal

bit.ly/9izvhX
By **iQapps**
Price **59p**

Social networks have already changed the way we share holiday snaps and memories with friends. Trip Journal wraps the tools for doing that in wonderful faux notebook graphics and typefaces.

The app automatically tracks your location and lets you add waypoints for places that catch your eye. You can attach photos and (on an iPhone 3GS or iPhone 4) video clips, and record details for later reference, so as to give your friends an idea of what you thought was special. That's done through integration with Facebook and Twitter, and you can also plot the journey on Google Earth and post to Flickr and Picasa galleries as well. Your friends might want to see these places for themselves, so if you're concerned about accuracy, locations can be pinned down manually or you can rely on the values that the iPhone's GPS automatically provides. The app tells you a little about signal strength and accuracy there, too.

Trip Journal is remarkably well presented and simple to work with. Even if you're taking better photos with a digital SLR, it's worth having this to hand to record your travelogue on the spot, rather than struggling to recall finer details later on.

Tube Exits

bit.ly/bk853p
By **Wavana**
Price **59p**

★★★★★

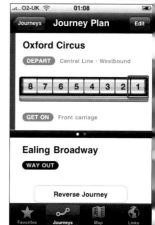

Time is everything. A second saved here, a minute saved there, it all adds up.

So what if you could make sure you got on at the right end of a train or the right carriage, rather than having to walk the entire length of the platform stuck behind a group of tourists to get out once you've reached your destination, causing you to miss your connection.

Now you can, thanks to the Tube Exits app.

This information-based gem holds the key to which carriage you need to get on in order to get off right opposite your desired exit or interchange, which is good for everyone but particularly commuters where every second counts in their stressful quest not to arrive at work late and in a crumpled heap before turning around a few hours later to do it all again.

The app's makers reckon that travellers can shave about 10 minutes off the average journey during peak travel time.

The app is a joy to use, mixing text with great visuals of exactly which carriage is the one for you. And, the real beauty is you don't need to be online to use this app, making it perfect for overground and underground travel alike.

Tube Map

bit.ly/aRK06L
By **mxData**
Price **Free**

★★★★★

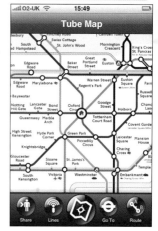

The London Underground network is an amazing creation, but it's also a complex beast, made tamer thanks to this app.

The first screen asks you to provide some details about yourself (gender, age and home station) but you don't have to give this if you don't want to and it's easy to skip that part of the app and move on.

Our default station was set to Oxford Circus and, on skipping the request for info screen, we were taken straight to a colourful Tube map with a vibrant menu underneath. Changing the default home station is easy from within the settings menu.

You simply move around the Tube map using your finger – it really is that easy. This app is great for tourists, but equally as useful for people who live in or near London just trying to find their easiest route home, thanks to the in-built route planner.

You can also click on the lines icon to get real-time status updates about whether the Central Line has delays or the District line has engineering works and so on. This app saves you the hassle of having to look at the always-crowded Tube maps at stations, meaning you can be much more discreet about not knowing where you are.

TuneIn Radio

bit.ly/dtP5Q5
By Synsion Radio Technologies
Price **£1.19**

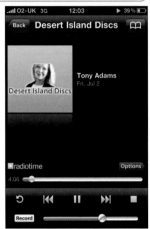

The iPhone doesn't have an FM tuner like the iPod nano, but it doesn't matter as TuneIn Radio lets you listen to over 30,000 online radio stations from the RadioTime directory, and you can also enter an unlisted stream's address. It supports a good range of audio formats, too: MP3, AAC, WMA, Real, Ogg Vorbis and FLV.

The directory can be browsed by music genre, talk radio stations, language and location down to region level, where you can filter out unwanted listings using the genre option – just one of several

smart design decisions. TuneIn can also find local stations using GPS and wifi. Up to 30 minutes of radio is buffered, so you can rewind if you're momentarily distracted. Even better, you can record the current stream or set a schedule.

While listening, you can inspect the station's schedule, get suggestions of others you might like, and pick from a list of alternative streams at different bitrates, in case your connection is proving a little slow. It also sports an alarm clock and the ability to schedule recordings.

Also, TuneIn plays in the background if you jump to another app, so long as your iPhone is running iOS 4.

TweetMic Pro

bit.ly/adcwlO
By Voicetal
Price **£1.19**

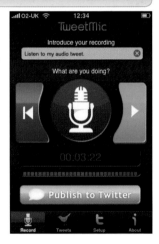

TweetMic is an app designed to get your audio clips onto Twitter in the most straightforward and intuitive way possible.

It has no limit to the amount you can record and the clips can be published directly into your Twitter stream with a short text introduction once you've provided your username and password.

Recordings can be previewed before you publish them and once uploaded they are securely hosted on creator Voicetal's servers, where the company promises they will never be removed unless you delete them.

A large red mic button starts and stops recordings, a large green play button plays back the clip, a blue rewind/restart button does just that and a Publish to Twitter button will send them straight to your Twitter feed.

Tapping the text box brings up the virtual keyboard so you can introduce your recording while a soundbar tracks the volume and a timer shows how long you have been recording. Along the bottom are four basic categories: Record, Tweets, Setup and About – as obvious as they sound.

TweetMic is a straightforward app. There aren't any frills, but it doesn't matter when an app works as well as this one does.

Twitterrific for Twitter

bit.ly/bZPXfb
By **The Iconfactory**
Price *Free*

Although the interface of the web-based Twitter site is seamless to use on Safari's browser, nothing beats a dedicated Twitter app, with tabbed sections allowing you to access your feed, direct and @ messages in an easy-to-read format. Twitterrific for Twitter is just one of the apps that make Tweeting away from your computer a joyful experience.

Choose to access your feed and you're presented with all posted Tweets from the people you're following. Any @ messages aimed at you appear in brown, and any Tweets from you are coloured green. Even if you send or receive a direct message, these too will appear in your feed in the same colours.

There's no need to use a picture uploading app with Twitterrific either because a built-in function can be found in the Tweet screen, identified by its speech bubble icon.

Just like on Twitter, you can view all of the information on someone you're following by tapping on the star icon when one of their posts is highlighted. This screen also allows you to view their Tweet history too.

This is one of the most fully-featured Twitter apps available. As it is a free version, you'll have to put up with ads.

 ## uHear

bit.ly/dbaFcL
By **Unitron Hearing**
Price *Free*

If you're concerned about your hearing, and let's face it, you should be, uHear is a handy tool to test your hearing ability for frequencies and speech in noise.

When you first start the app, you're encouraged to carry out some tests to measure your hearing ability. The first is to test how well you can hear high and low sounds as they get quieter.

To get the best results, it's recommended to use earphones, find yourself a quiet spot and listen as hard as you can. When you hear a sound, tap the I hear it icon. The test will take you through a range of pitches, which will always get quieter. The app will first test your right ear, then your left.

The next measure is how well you can hear speech with background noise. Here, you have to crank up the volume of the noise in the foreground, tap on the lock icon, and then adjust the background noise to the highest you can listen to it while still hearing the main speech. The third test is a questionnaire that asks you a series of questions about your hearing. You can view all of your results in colourful graphs on a scale of hearing loss to normal hearing. It also provides advice to prevent your hearing from getting worse.

UK Postage Calc

bit.ly/dfuvIZ
By **John ZL**
Price **£1.19**

We've all been there. Standing at the end of a very long line in the Post Office is not a fun experience. It eats up your entire lunch break leaving you with very little time to eat your lunch. But what if you knew exactly how many stamps your parcel or letter for special delivery needed before you even got to the Post Office?

Enter this app: all you have to do is enter the weight of the item you want to post (so you'll need scales handy) and the app will do the rest for you.

Now that Royal Mail bases its prices on size of package as well as weight, sending mail isn't quite as straightforward as it used to be. But this app also includes a handy weight and size guide to help you work out what's what.

The app will show you prices for the UK, Europe and the rest of the world, as well as giving you more in-depth postage options such as insuring your item. The latter can help you decide whether that extra few pence is really worth it or not, rather than lamenting after you've posted the item and it hasn't arrived.

And it takes literally seconds to work out how much that package will set you back. We can certainly see this app coming in handy for eBayers as well as those who just hate queuing.

vTie

bit.ly/99jTPs
By **Lab48**
Price **Free**

If you're the sort of person who likes to secure your tie in a quirky, but sturdy way, you're likely to enjoy this novel app, even if you already know how to tie a four-in-hand knot or the footballers' favourite, the half Windsor.

The menu is a little basic, but the app makes good use of animation to show the various stages involved to get to the finished knot. Underneath each diagram, text details exactly what needs to happen and in what order. The images lack colour save for the green instructional arrows.

If you press the 'i' button at the top of the main menu, you can adjust the step speed so the instructions can run as quickly as three seconds or as slow as eight before you move on to the next step. You press the play button to begin the instructional process and you can also use the back, forward and pause buttons in case you miss anything.

While the app comes with instructions as to how to tie five different types of knot, the end result looked the same in each case as far as we're concerned. But then again, we rarely have the opportunity to wear a tie to work. A bit of a novelty but unlikely to be something you'd need to use again and again.

Wallet

bit.ly/dk4Y9J
By **Acrylic Software**
Price **£2.99**

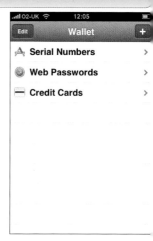

People enjoyed this app on the Mac desktop and now they can do the same in their pocket. And, as your wallet is often in your pocket or handbag next to your iPhone, the union seems quite apt.

If you're forgetful and can just about remember what your name is and where you live let alone the vast array of different passwords and phone numbers you need to get by, this app has your name on it.

Once you've gone through the set-up process, the interface is clean and easy to navigate. What's more, searching for the vital bit of information that you need when you need it most is a quick and painless process.

If you're a bit forgetful or just overloaded by information, this app is likely to appeal to you, although clearly you have to remember to open it when you need it as.

It is worth noting that many security experts advise you not to keep all your password-related eggs in one basket, but to try to alleviate any concerns you might have, the app features 256-bit AES data encryption. This app won't be for everyone but for those who are overloaded with passwords it will prove an invaluable resource and create some brain space for other things

 ## Wattpad 100,000+ books

bit.ly/d6CGdM
By **Wattpad**
Price *Free*

Everyone's talking about eBooks these days, to the extent that the high street book shops are more than a little bit worried. But shelling out a couple of hundred pounds on an eBook reader is not to everybody's taste or budget. Enter Wattpad.

The My Library section of the app is already pre-populated with six titles, which you can easily replace with other titles. Within the main menu you search for the books that are popular, new or recommended.

We opted to look at old favourite *Frankenstein*. The text is self-scrolling, the pace of which can be determined by the reader based on the slow-fast bar. You can also override this speed by using your finger to slide the text up, which is handy as it does take a while to work out what speed is just right for you. You can change the size, colour and type of font, in addition to the background colour.

There's also a neat 'social' button that lets you share your new-found eBook joy via email, Twitter and Facebook. This button also lets you provide feedback on the app as well as rating the book in question. The only thing that really lets this app down is the ads running along the bottom, which proved a bit of a distraction.

Weather Pro

bit.ly/ay7ycg
By **MeteoGroup**
Price **£2.39**

★★★★☆

The UK's weather is completely unpredictable, and most of the time it changes so quickly that the morning's forecast on TV is out of date by lunchtime. Weather Pro ensures that you're always up to date with the weather wherever you are.

The homepage shows information the temperature, wind speed and direction, dewpoint, humidity, pressure precipitation and cloud cover. Tap on the graph icon at the top and you can see how the temperature and precipitation levels have changed over the past week.

Under this, you can view basic information about the next week. Tap on each of these forecasts to view a more in-depth forecast for that day.

In addition to viewing the information in this form, you can also take a look at a radar image of the surrounding area and a satellite image of the cloud cover. At the bottom of these two aerial images you can see how the conditions have changed over the past couple of hours.

You can either find your location using the search tab or you can use the Locate function

to collect information about your current position. For what it offers Weather Pro is a superb weather app, even at the price of £2.39.

Wikipanion

bit.ly/9M7Eic
By **Robert Chin**
Price **Free**

★★★★★

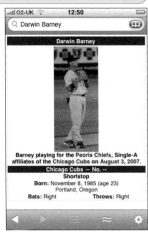

Since there are so many Wiki apps available for the iPhone, we've included a second in our list. This is the Wikipanion, which enables you to access the wealth of trivia contained on the Wikipedia site.

The premise is quite familiar. You search for things and Wikipanion retrieves them from the Wikipedia database. In addition to surfacing a main page overview and a dedicated search for a particular term or reference, you can also opt to be served up a random page – our first was about Baseball player Darwin

Barney and the second about the Coalition for an Emerging Benin. Fascinating stuff.

Of course, you can also search within a page, adjust the font size of the content on that page, bookmark it, email the link to your friends or colleagues and much more. You even have the option of opening the page in Safari, searching the Wiktionary and even locking the orientation so that the phone doesn't flip that page from portrait to landscape or vice versa if you're being particularly animated while showing it to someone.

Wikipanion harnesses the power of Wikipedia and is a true companion for the knowledge hungry all in your pocket.

Wind Meter

bit.ly/boU3mc
By **Going Apps**
Price **59p**

The UK is probably known more for its miserable weather with its wind and rain than anything else. However, for some the wind can be a blessing, step forward wind and kite surfers, as well as those into sailing, as they all need certain conditions to make the most of their chosen activity. For these people, working out how the wind will behave that day is key.

This app turns your iPhone into a Wind Meter so that you can quickly and easily measure wind speed. It does this in a clever way by making use of the handset's in-built microphone.

Getting a reading is simple, you just need to launch the app, hold the iPhone in the air, turn it upside down (as the meter will be upside down otherwise) wait for a moment or two then press Get Wind button. The meter on the front of the phone will move around like a traditional meter and then come back with a reading, which can be converted into a range of measurement formats depending on your personal preference.

For those with sporting interests that are reliant on the weather being just so, this app

will prove very appealing. And for those who aren't into wind surfing and the like, it could become their new favourite toy.

Words with Friends

bit.ly/afdDJ3
By **Newtoy**
Price **£1.79**

Words with Friends is a variation on Scrabble, with the points values of many tiles altered. Multipliers on the board are arranged differently, too, but the rules are essentially the same.

A clever vocabulary isn't the only thing that will help you beat your friends. You'll also need a keen eye for strategic moves that will reap the best rewards from the tiles in your rack.

What makes this better than the official Scrabble game for iPhone is simple: online play. Where Scrabble forces you to play with others on the same wifi

network, Words with Friends lets you play with friends at any time, wherever they are in the world.

You can have several games on the go at once, and each one has its own chatroom. The major disappointment is that only two people can play in each game.

You can play with someone in the same room by passing the iPhone back and forth, but Words with Friends doesn't let you play solo against the computer. You'll need to pick up the official Scrabble app for that, but we think it's much more satisfying to play against a real

person, even if that's a stranger somewhere else in the world that you've been paired up with by the game.

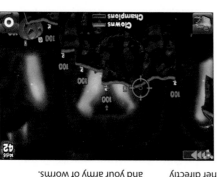

World Factbook 2010

bit.ly/cXc2f0
By JDictionary Mobile
Price 59p

World Factbook is an in-depth
reference tool that provides you
with information and statistics
for almost every country in the
world. The number of facts on
offer, even for the most obscure
countries, is mind-blowing.
At the tap of a button
you can pull up a wide
range of statistics from
population demographics and
communication networks to
transport infrastructures and
economics, as well as many more.
Each country has its flag
clearly displayed, alongside a
brief but fascinating synopsis of

its history and foundation. Areas
that are not defined as countries
in their own right, such as oceans
or deserts, can still be searched
for, and have their own sets of
statistics. The ownership of such
areas is also explained.
Although World Factbook is
pretty basic, the sheer number of
countries included is staggering.
The information updates
automatically over the Internet
when you open it, so you don't
even need updates the app from
the App Store. Every element of
World Factbook is impressive,
and although there's not a huge

amount of information about
each country outside of statistics
and history, it's worth a download
at the princely sum of 59p.

Worms

bit.ly/blq6s8
By Team17 Software
Price £2.99

Worms is a classic turn-based
combat game, where your role
is to blow up opposition worms
using a range of weapons.
If you're a fan of the
game, originally released in
1995 for Amiga, you won't be
disappointed. The concept of
Worms hasn't changed in this
iPhone variant; you control a
team of worms and have to take it
in turns to try to blow each other
up, ensuring your own worms are
out of the way and hard to reach
for the other team.
You have the choice of a
range of different weapons, with

aim tactics at the forefront of
success. You must determine the
best weapon to use at any given
time, and the best way to launch
that weapon, whether directly
at the worms or
in the air so it
detonates at the
precise moment
it needs to.
The main
problem with
the iPhone
version of this
classic game
is the controls,
specifically the

zoom and pan functions. To pan,
you must use two fingers to
scroll across the screen, which
feels unnatural.
However, once you have got
used to the way these functions
operate, you'll find that you
become addicted to the game
and your army of worms.